DOING BUSINESS WITH THE NAZIS

DOING BUSINESS WITH THE NAZIS

Britain's Economic and Financial Relations with Germany 1931–1939

NEIL FORBES

Coventry University

With a Foreword by
RICHARD OVERY

FRANK CASS
LONDON • PORTLAND, OR

First published in 2000 in Great Britain by
FRANK CASS PUBLISHERS
Newbury House, 900 Eastern Avenue
London IG2 7HH

and in the United States of America by
FRANK CASS PUBLISHERS
c/o ISBS, 5824 N. E. Hassalo Street
Portland, Oregon 97213-3644

Website www.frankcass.com

British Library Cataloguing in Publication Data:
Forbes, Neil
    Doing business with the Nazis: Britain's economic and
    financial relations with Germany, 1931–1939
    1. Great Britain – Foreign economic relations –Germany
    2. Great Britain – Foreign relations – Germany 3. Great
    Britain – Foreign relations – 1936–1945 4. Germany –
    Foreign relations – Great Britain 5. Germany – Foreign
    relations – 1933–1945 6. Great Britain – Economic
    policy – 1918–1945 7. Great Britain – Commerce –
    Germany – History – 20th century 8. Germany –
    Commerce – Great Britain – History – 20th century
    I. Title
    337.4′1′043′09043

ISBN 0-7146-5082-X (cloth)
ISBN 0-7146-8168-7 (paper)

Library of Congress Cataloging-in-Publication Data:
Forbes, Neil
    Doing business with the Nazis: Britain's economic and
    financial relations with Germany, 1931–1939 / Neil Forbes.
        p. cm.
    Includes bibliographical references and index.
    ISBN 0-7146-5082-X (cloth)
        1. Great Britain – Foreign economic relations – Germany.
    2. Germany – Foreign economic relations – Great Britain.
    3. Great Britain – Commercial policy. 4. Nazis.
    I. Title.

HF1533.Z4 G34 2001
337.41043′09′043–dc21   00-057004

Printed in Great Britain by
MPG Books Ltd, Bodmin, Cornwall

Contents

List of Illustrations

List of Tables

Foreword

One day in July 1945, the former German Economics Minister, Hjalmar Schacht, found himself under interrogation in an internment camp about why he had thrown in his lot with the Hitler government in 1933. The elderly, thoroughly bourgeois banker was distraught at being treated like a common criminal. At one point Schacht broke down when he thought about his friend Montagu Norman, the governor of the Bank of England. What if he appeared in court and said 'Schacht, you have become a scoundrel'? Schacht, the interrogators recorded, 'cried bitterly'.[1]

The relationship between Schacht and Norman dated back to the 1920s; Norman was godfather to one of Schacht's children. The personal bond became strained during the late 1930s as the political antagonism between the two states, Britain and Germany, became more marked. But Schacht still saw himself as a member of that special club of international financiers whose work he supposed could transcend the grubby world of popular politics. His place among the war criminals of the Third Reich he hotly contested, and the tribunal at Nuremberg finally acquitted him on all counts. His historical reputation has revived. The German economic recovery in the 1930s has come to be seen as his brainchild, before it was hijacked by the Party radicals to boost Germany's preparations for war.

The link with Norman was symptomatic of the deeper ties between the business communities of the two countries. These ties survived the shift to a Hitler regime in 1933. In most respects Britain was an important economic partner up until 1939 and the outbreak of war. The nature of that relationship has never before been properly explored. Neil Forbes has succeeded with scrupulous scholarship in reconstructing the complicated story of British-German economic relations, together with the motives and objectives that lay behind them. Britain was a major trader and lender to Germany, and did not want to lose that position at a critical time for the British economy. The Germans needed credit lines abroad and access to the raw materials and foodstuffs from Britain's Empire. Economic expediency, then as now, could always bridge the most incompatible political divide.

The temptation half a century later is to argue that Britain deliberately aided and abetted German Fascism; British businessmen and politicians can be portrayed as fellow-travellers, more hostile to communism than to national socialism. Economic appeasement seems to confirm the conventional Marxist view that capitalism in crisis gravitated towards right-wing authoritarianism. Norman can be seen to be as guilty as Schacht in underestimating Nazi radicalism and facilitating the establishment of a criminal regime bent on war and genocide. The great merit of *Doing Business with the Nazis* is the recognition that British policy towards Germany in the 1930s had a practical economic core to it, and was not the product of pro-fascist sympathies, any more than the current vast trade with Communist China suggests that western liberal governments endorse one-party dictatorships and the suppression of human rights. Britain traded with a great many unpleasant regimes in the 1930s. This was not yet an age of political correctness.

Forbes demonstrates convincingly that British business reacted to the Hitler regime in ways principally designed to improve their own economic interests. German government control over currency transfers, trade flows and debt repayment created an entirely new context for German relations with the external economy. British bankers and manufacturers needed the assistance of the government in navigating the new system, and protecting established claims. Schacht's presence helped to assure the British that the new government would not embark on a radical economic course. Policy was always more concerned with safeguarding British capitalism than with offering succour to dictatorship. When the political relationship soured in 1939, Forbes shows that British business did not try collectively to sustain appeasement and sell Poland short. Businessmen on both sides would have preferred peace, but their power to influence the political and military establishment was negligible in both states. Though it is sometimes recalled that Allied soldiers were shot at with shells containing copper bought from British Empire sources, it is also the case by the late 1930s that German machine tools helped to build British weapons. Trade has its own rationality. It was Norman who said with regret in 1938 that international economic relations were now characterised by 'politics and not ethics'.[2]

In this sense *Doing Business with the Nazis* highlights a central issue of our age. Why has it not proved possible to trade and loan abroad on entirely personal grounds? The explanations presented here for the survival of British-German economic links in the Hitler period show that there are no easy answers to what appears a deceptively straightforward question. For those currently debating the morality of trading with dictatorships, this admirable history should be required reading.

Richard Overy
King's College, London
September 2000

NOTES

1. Imperial War Museum, Speer Collection, Box S366, interrogation of Hjalmar Schacht, 31 July 1945, p.8.
2. Bank of England, German central bank papers, file S.89 (1), letter from Montagu Norman to Thomas Lamont, 24 August 1938, p.1.

Acknowledgements

In traversing the frontiers between disciplines I have depended on the advice and wise counsel freely offered by a number of scholars, colleagues and friends. It was a great privilege, and my good fortune, to be guided by Leslie Pressnell at an early stage of this study. I would also like to thank the following for their helpful comments: Robert Boyce, Mike Dorrington, Michael Gasson, Lesley Gordon, Edwin Green, Henry Gillet, John Keyworth, Frank Magee and Clemens Wurm. I would like to extend my thanks to Rosemary Lazenby for helping to make my visit to New York a fruitful and pleasant experience. For advice on how to arrange parts of the manuscript, I am indebted to Ian Talbot. In particular, I would like to thank Mike Strutt for generously devoting a considerable amount of time to read draft chapters; many improvements were made to the text under his expert guidance. I am especially grateful to Richard Overy for supporting the project over a lengthy period, for his incisive observations and for ideas on how to structure the book. In all respects, of course, I am entirely responsible for any remaining errors and inconsistencies.

For permission to reproduce copyright and other material I gratefully acknowledge the following: The Bank of England; University of Birmingham; Department of Special Collections and Western Manuscripts, Bodleian Library, University of Oxford; Archives Division, British Library of Political and Economic Science; BP Amoco Archive; Churchill Archives Centre, Churchill College, Cambridge (Phipps Papers); Confederation of British Industry; the Editors of the *Economic History Review*; Federal Reserve Bank of New York Archives; Group Archives, HSBC Holdings plc, Midland Bank Archives; The Robinson Library, University of Newcastle upon Tyne (Runciman Papers); and the Vickers Archives, Cambridge University Library.

Most of all, I have depended on the support and encouragement given to me by Pamela, Cassie and Ellen.

North Oxfordshire
Christmas 1999

Glossary and Abbreviations

Bank for International Settlements (BIS): owned by the major central banks, the BIS was set up at Basle, Switzerland, in 1930, to manage German reparations transfers.

Clearing agreement: a method of settling international trade and financial claims by avoiding the foreign exchange market. As Germany enjoyed a favourable balance of trade with Britain, the latter could have imposed a unilateral agreement. This would have required British importers of German goods to have paid their debts, in sterling, to a clearing office. British creditors would then have had their claims against Germany settled by payments from this office.

Committee of Imperial Defence (CID): comprising leading members of the British Cabinet and Chiefs of Staff of the three services; the Committee sought to create a unified approach to defence policy.

Federation of British Industries (FBI): predecessor organization of the Confederation of British Industry.

Golddiskontbank: a central banking body set up in the Weimar Republic in 1924 to facilitate the flow of credits from abroad and alleviate Germany's shortage of capital. Under the Nazis the bank bought blocked marks, at a large discount, for free currency.

Import Duties Advisory Committee (IDAC): set up in 1932 to advise on the level of duties imposed on imports entering Britain.

Industrial Intelligence Centre (IIC): set up in secret by the CID in 1930 to analyse the industrial and economic condition of potential enemy powers and consider how Britain might conduct economic warfare.

International Standstill Agreement (Standstill): the agreement, signed in 1931 and renewed until 1939, under which Germany's international short-term debts were frozen.

Joint Committee of British Short-Term Creditors (Joint Committee): formed in 1932 to act on behalf of British creditors involved in the Standstill; the Joint Committee comprised representatives from banks and acceptance houses.

Konversionskasse: an office set up in 1933 to collect the interest and sinking fund (amortization) payments on Germany's foreign debts and convert a proportion of the amount into scrip (blocked mark certificates).

Reichsmark (Rm): the official German currency, which remained linked to gold. As the Nazis refused to devalue, the Reichsmark became, in practice, a domestic currency. International transactions frequently used one of the many types of blocked marks.

Reichswirtschaftministerium (RWM): German Economics Ministry.

1 billion: 1,000 million

Abbreviations in Notes and Bibliography

BoE	Bank of England Archive
BP	BP Amoco Archive
Cmd	Command Papers
Parl. Deb.	Parliamentary Debates (Commons)
DBFP	Documents on British Foreign Policy
DGFP	Documents on German Foreign Policy
EcHR	*Economic History Review*
EHR	*English Historical Review*
FBI	Federation of British Industries Archives
FRBNY	Federal Reserve Bank of New York Archive
JCH	*Journal of Contemporary History*
JEEH	*Journal of European Economic History*
JMH	*Journal of Modern History*
MB	Midland Bank Archive
NA	National Archives, Washington, DC, USA
NC	Neville Chamberlain papers

At the Public Record Office:

CAB	Cabinet minutes, memoranda and papers
BT	Board of Trade files
FO	Foreign Office files
PREM	Prime Minister's office
T	Treasury files

The place of publication of sources cited in the notes and the bibliography is London unless otherwise stated.

1

Britain and the world economy

The Great Depression which began in 1929 was one of the pivots on which the twentieth-century world turned. International affairs in the inter-war years were mired in the related problems of reparations and war debts. In this sense, an economic dimension became a permanent, almost unchangeable, feature of the making of foreign policy. These developments had been predicted. In his famous philippic on the folly of the post-war peace settlement, Keynes had accused Sir Eric Geddes[1] of providing the 'grossest spectacle' in demanding that the German lemon should be squeezed until the pips squeaked. International trade, of which Anglo-German trade was of such importance, had worked with almost perfect simplicity until 1914 and it was trade-generated prosperity, Keynes argued, which would enable international co-operation to be restored and Britain to recover.[2] With the implementation of the Young Plan in 1929, hopes were raised that a line could be drawn under the problems of the post-war world: reparations were modified and a Bank for International Settlements (BIS) was established at Basle to receive and distribute the receipts.

But the arrival of the Great Depression made a mockery of plans to ensure financial stability: international investors first lost confidence and then panicked. When, in June 1931, Germany's credit crisis threatened to engulf the American banking system, President Hoover decided that a one-year moratorium on all intergovernmental debts was essential in order to avoid a global collapse. In the desperate search to find a solution to the problem of war debts and reparations before the expiry of the Hoover Year on 1 July 1932, British diplomacy was successful in persuading the Young Plan countries to paper over their differences.[3] When reparations were effectively annulled at the Lausanne Conference in 1932 internationalism appeared to be reborn. The question was whether Lausanne had come too late to enable the Weimar Republic to avoid political extremism; the resentful reaction of the German public to the settlement indicated that success would be fleeting. At this crucial juncture, Britain turned to consider the impending Ottawa Conference. But how could the policy on Empire be reconciled with the policy to save Europe?

The rise of Hitler made the question all the more poignant. Britain was turning away from Europe and embracing economic nationalism at the same time as the Weimar Republic faced collapse. Many in public and private life began to suspect that there was nothing coincidental about this synchronism. By abandoning the gold standard in 1931 and adopting Imperial Preference the following year, a great swath was cut across traditional economic relationships, particularly those between Britain and her important European trading partners. At the very least it was not difficult to imagine how change on such a scale would help to make Europe less rather than more politically stable. If Britain was doubtful about the extent of her power in the world, few doubted that it was wrong to exclude the issue of European stability from any list of responsibilities. One of the purposes of this book, therefore, is to show how the disorientating and disturbing effects of Britain's economic volte-face cast a deep shadow over the 1930s as a whole.

As the effects of the international economic and financial crisis dragged on, voices in the democracies calling for stabilization were drowned by the nationalist trumpeting of extremist ideologies. With the development of international markets for all kinds of goods, liberal democracies have been forced to contend with the dilemma of how to conduct peacetime trade with authoritarian and oppressive states which threaten to make war. When Hitler achieved power in 1933 Europe was confronted with a problem of unknown proportions. As the nature and significance of National Socialism became clearer in the course of the 1930s, Britain struggled to maintain commercial and financial relations with the Third Reich. But, with the international political climate deteriorating, Britain's dilemma became acute. International trade was in the nation's economic interest. But what kind of trade should be carried on with a state which was powerfully rearming? More to the point, by doing business with the Nazis was Britain helping to ensure the survival of the nation in the event of war?

Issues concerning the Great Depression, economic recovery, the managed economy and rearmament in the 1930s continue to demand the attention of economic historians. Yet, surprisingly, the study of Britain's commercial and financial relations with Nazi Germany has been neglected. Economic considerations figure in political and social histories, but largely as evidence of the policy of appeasement. In the continuing and emotive debate on the origins of the Second World War, the National Government of the 1930s has been more frequently condemned, especially by the political left, than exonerated. Typical of the genre is a work by Noreen Branson and Margot Heinemann in which Chamberlain is castigated for behaving as if Birmingham business ethics and municipal accounting would deal with the crisis and with Hitler. Worse than this, they accuse Chamberlain of looking to strike a profitable business deal between his own industrial supporters and Hitler's, which would allow German industry to find outlets in eastern Europe and Britain to continue in her old way.[4] Parker's recent and succinct survey, *Chamberlain and Appeasement*, is rather more authoritative in pointing out that economic approaches to the Nazi government were political in aim; economic advantages would follow later.[5] Paul Einzig, the journalist and author, was a contemporary critic of government policy. He was the first to attempt to show a consistency of purpose running through apparently isolated and individual acts of what he termed 'economic appeasement'. Einzig held the City of London responsible for pursuing a disastrous economic policy towards Germany and especially blamed Montagu Norman, the Governor of the Bank of England.[6]

Within the extensive literature on appeasement there are frequent allusions to the importance which should be attached to economic issues. In a landmark work, *The Roots of Appeasement*, the historian Martin Gilbert claims that the most serious efforts at appeasement, unbeknown to the general public, took place in the world of economics and trade. But while Gilbert points to various plans embraced by British officials in the 1930s, he does not explain what economic appeasement amounted to in practice.[7] One of the criticisms levelled at Gilbert's study concerned his analysis of the British Foreign Office. In emphasizing the desire of the Foreign Office to regain the initiative in foreign economic policy-making and, in the mid-1930s, to reach an agreement with Germany, W.N. Medlicott has pointed out that it was a question of how approaches were to be made. With the problems of economics and defence making up the substance of Anglo-German discussions after 1931,

Medlicott showed how the Foreign Office, or at least its Permanent Under-Secretary Robert Vansittart, was particularly disapproving of the activities of the Bank of England and the Treasury in negotiations with Germany.[8] The frustration felt by the Foreign Office is not difficult to identify. In a memorandum written for the Cabinet in 1934, Vansittart characteristically sounded the alarm. He feared that Germany was rearming by means of fraudulent bankruptcy and that autarky, or the drive to self-sufficiency, would make Germany less vulnerable in the next war. It was of the greatest significance, Vansittart suggested, that 'The City – whose policy in respect of Germany has been a mill-stone round the neck of this country – believes the Foreign Office is anti-German'.[9]

The use of the word 'appeasement' is, of course, one of the best examples of the elasticity of the English language. In the inter-war years it was understood to indicate international negotiation to relieve tension. With the coming of war the term suffered a degradation of meaning: appeasement represented a policy of simple piecemeal surrender to the dictators Hitler and Mussolini, in a futile attempt to ensure peace. In the early 1970s Bernd Jürgen Wendt, the German historian, set himself the task of releasing the term from a narrow political meaning. In *Economic Appeasement*, Wendt's intention was to substantiate the claims made by previous writers and to show that no clear line could be drawn between political and economic appeasement.[10]

Although controversial, Wendt's ideas continue to attract adherents.[11] His thesis is that the supporters of Anglo-German trade and finance continually exercised a considerable influence on the planning and execution of British policy. Wendt places heavy emphasis on the significance of capitalism. In looking for a re-establishment of political and economic trust as a basis for the revival of international trade and world prosperity, City institutions were prominent in regarding Nazi Germany, first and foremost, as belonging to the capitalist system of western Europe. They hoped, therefore, that a natural congruity of business interests would bridge political differences. According to Wendt, so long as the Third Reich wished to continue profitable trading and to remain a credit partner, interested circles were willing to overlook the repulsive and criminal practices of Nazism as an internal German affair.[12] But Wendt goes much further than this. He claims that a fusion of political-business interests between the City – especially the bankers – and the conservative-bourgeois National Government was a step away from being a conspiracy (*Verschwörung*).[13]

According to Gustav Schmidt, another German scholar, Wendt failed to show either the degree to which the articulations of various financial and economic interests were allowed to filter through the Cabinet committee system to infuence the decision-making process, or the grounds on which the government took decisions in favour of 'pro-German' economic interests. Consequently, Schmidt based his study on an encyclopaedic analysis of the ideas and schemes advanced by all those in political circles who could be counted as economic appeasers. Schmidt concludes that the importance of economic factors in influencing appeasement policies should not be overestimated.[14] But an examination of the substance of Britain's commercial and financial links with the Third Reich lies outside the compass of Schmidt's study.

Even today little is known about the interests of British industry and finance in relation to such a vital market as Germany in the inter-war years. In this respect it is important to understand the relationship between domestic structural change and global conditions between the two world wars. Apart from the deep and lasting psychological scars produced by the First World War, the delicate machinery of international economic and financial co-operation was left disrupted and never really recovered. A gradual amelioration in conditions promised a brighter future, but it is doubtful whether the 1920s were ever taken to be a new era in Europe. Indeed, the depression years of the 1930s were readily taken as evidence that the tasks of the preceding decade had not been achieved. International investment was moving to debt-ridden and war-damaged Europe from America instead of following the reverse movement of pre-war days. At the same time, gold flowed across the Atlantic from east to west. Uneasiness over these trends added to the sense of insecurity in important countries, such as Britain and Germany, which had not yet again found their place in the world economy.[15] International economic relations were conducted, therefore, in a climate of great uncertainty and bewildering change. With the rise of economic nationalism the system of multilateral trade and payments began to break down. Barely one-third of the century had passed and it seemed safe to consign to historians the study of how capital, labour and commodities moved freely across national boundaries.

Before 1914 Germany had rivalled Britain as the world export leader. Recovering in the 1920s, Germany had pulled ahead by 1930 and was ranked second to America. In terms of this global picture, Anglo-German bilateral trade was not insignificant. Both countries took a large share of the other's exports, with the trade balance lying in Germany's favour. Along with the Netherlands, Britain was, until 1932, by far the most important export market for Germany. The commodities traded covered a wide range of manufactured and finished goods, especially machinery, and also chemical products such as dyestuffs. Indeed, by imposing import duties in 1920 on a wide range of chemicals, Britain had tried to shut out German competition from the home market.[16] For British exports, especially those of coal, herrings and textiles, Germany was an important market. A White Paper, drawn up by the Board of Trade in 1919, looked to encourage British traders to compete in and secure a proper footing in the developing markets of the late enemy countries which had become open to the whole world.[17] Furthermore, just as in the decades before 1914, the accumulated fees paid to British shippers, insurers, bankers and commodity dealers by German industry provided invisible earnings which probably went a long way to offset the UK's deficit in visible trade with Germany.[18]

The coming of the depression was bound to cut into existing patterns of trade. But in the case of Germany's exports to Britain, the effects of the global downturn were then compounded by the depreciation of sterling and the imposition of British tariffs and Imperial Preference. The net result was that Germany's favourable trade balance declined from over £30 million in 1931 to about £5 million in 1932. French exports to the UK suffered a similar decline. It was not a matter of surprise, therefore, that British policy was far from popular in Europe. Even though Germany had herself imposed an average *ad valorem* 15 per cent duty on all imports as early as 1925, many were encouraged to attribute their political and economic ills to the lack of an empire, both as a source of raw materials and as a market for exports. In 1933 Britain once more assumed the place of the world's second greatest exporter and maintained it. But by the middle of the decade Germany – resurgent under National Socialism – was tending to improve her relative position.[19]

The rise of German industrial power in the second half of the nineteenth century was aided by the facilities London could offer for international trade. There was, in particular, a time-honoured tradition of financial transactions between the two countries. City houses provided finance not only for Anglo-German trade but also for the vast increase of raw material imports into Germany.[20] After 1918 British capital, in the shape of several different kinds of loan from several sources, formed a significant part of Germany's external debt. It was common, up to the Great Depression, for British banks to grant medium-term loans to German states and municipalities. However, the short-term credits made to German banks and industry were more important in terms of volume and function.

The problems of economics which acquired, for the first time, such an importance after the First World War, therefore placed new demands on government for economic management. It is questionable whether policy progressed very far down the road to interventionism during the 1930s. Fundamental change accompanied the depression, not because of any radical reassessment of *laissez-faire* thinking, but because new policies were implemented either on grounds of expediency or because short-term conditions forced them on a reluctant government. Ministers desired to intervene in the affairs of industry as little as possible.[21] Similarly, the role of economic doctrine in policy formation should not be overemphasized. What dictated policy was not official understanding of the tenets of economics but public attitudes. Leading politicians and Treasury officials shared certain fixed principles: the need to avoid risks, governmental retrenchment and an almost Gladstonian desire to reduce the public debt.[22] Theories which challenged this orthodoxy could make little headway; Keynesian ideas had taken to the offensive in the years before 1939 but there were many battles still to be fought.[23]

These qualifications notwithstanding, the 1930s witnessed a complete alteration in the direction of British economic policy and the adoption of entirely new purposes. At the beginning of the decade a *coup de théâtre* was staged. The first act was completely unplanned: with the suspension of the gold standard sterling was no longer fixed against the dollar and depreciated in value. The way was open for Britain to lower the bank rate to 2 per cent and establish a currency bloc based on sterling. Conversely, the second act – protectionism – had been rehearsed on political platforms since the end of the nineteenth century but was contingent on the first act.[24] Britain

imposed tariffs on foreign imports and then, as a result of the Ottawa
Conference in August 1932, Imperial Preference was established.[25] It
is, perhaps, unrealistic to make much of a distinction between foreign
economic policy and the domestic variety; domestic recovery owed a
great deal to the cheap money policy. Nevertheless, the most decisive
changes and the most significant attempts by government to aid
recovery belonged to the external sphere.[26] What is pertinent to this
study, however, is an analysis of what political and business circles in
Britain felt the consequences of those measures to be.

Historians have interpreted the significance of the 1931 financial
and political crisis in several ways. Peter Clarke argues that tariffs, in
the context of the long-run of domestic politics, began to appear less
important as soon as they were implemented.[27] The Conservatives
had been prevented from bringing in protectionism by their election
defeat of 1923. Now, in the guise of the National Government, they
were presented with an opportunity to do so. Britain had
experienced coalition governments before; but the idea that party
considerations should be sacrificed for the greater good of the nation
was unprecedented. If such elevated claims were to have any
practical meaning, Ramsay MacDonald, the Prime Minister, needed
the blessing of the Liberal Party as well as the endorsement of
Baldwin and the Conservatives. The Cabinet decided to disagree
publicly over the kind of protectionism which was to be imposed
and Samuel and Snowden departed in protest over Imperial
Preference. Thereafter, however, unity, or at least the appearance of
unity, between ministers was of paramount importance.[28] Whatever
the nature of opposition in or outside Parliament in the years which
lay ahead, resignations, such as that of Anthony Eden in February
1938, were remarkable precisely because they were so rare.

The surviving National Liberals – Sir John Simon, who held
several high offices of state throughout the 1930s, and Walter
Runciman, President of the Board of Trade – appear to have enjoyed
harmonious relations with their Cabinet colleagues.[29] Cowling
stressed the significance of the class struggle in British politics. He
saw 1931 as a victory for the forces of resistance and declared that,
while liberal opinion remained important, *laissez-faire* was dead and
buried by 1933. Chamberlain, the successful manager of the
Conservative Party, received even the friendly attention of erstwhile
Cobdenites who, in spite of Ottawa, believed in economic
appeasement as the cure for war.[30]

Indeed, it is Walter Runciman who emerges from Philip Williamson's study of the crisis as a pivotal figure. When Runciman accepted the need to impose tariffs as a mechanism to defend the currency and economy, Conservative leaders were able to claim that protection was a 'national' policy. And Runciman's cogent arguments shaped the evolution of government policy thereafter.[31] Tariffs and Imperial Preference were thought of as temporary expedients. In introducing the bill on duties, Chamberlain told the House of Commons: 'We mean also to use it for negotiations with foreign countries which have not hitherto paid very much attention to our suggestions'.[32] Among other things, therefore, tariffs were to be used as a lever to restore 'fair' trade through bilateral agreements. It was particularly important for National Liberals to be able to show how the departure from free trade served the national interest. Sir John Simon justified bilateral trade agreements because they were so successful in securing increased exports for Britain.[33] Similarly, Runciman believed the policy was his special contribution to the Baldwin ministry – formed in June 1935. Runciman so resented any challenge to his authority to make and maintain trade treaties that he almost resigned from the Cabinet when, in 1936, it became divided over issues related to the agreement with Argentina, concluded three years earlier.[34]

As Clemens Wurm asserts, the economic changes had serious consequences for both foreign and domestic policy: Britain became entangled in the contradictions faced by any protectionist country and deep divisions were opened up between different sectors of the economy.[35] The political disorientation which followed the crisis of 1931, together with the constraints imposed by the Ottawa agreements and the needs of industry, all combined to frustrate hopes of breaking down tariff barriers. Later, the 1938 Anglo-American Trade Agreement, although a significant development in trade liberalization, actually confirmed the difficulties created by preference policies. Indeed, by focusing on Britain's commercial links with Germany it is possible to show that far from ending in 1932, Cabinet discord continued unabated as the new trade policies began to make their mark.

If the role of the 1931 crisis is considered in the context of long-term relative decline, it is important to remember that Britain was the only world power of any consequence in the 1920s and for most of the 1930s. Foreign observers continued to be impressed by British

prestige.[36] Cain and Hopkins argue convincingly that the energy
shown throughout the decade in pursuing resurgent imperialist
ambitions hardly suggests that Britain was becoming moribund.[37]
Nevertheless, while protectionist measures provided some respite
from the ravages of the depression, concern over Britain's ability to
command economic resources was no less prominent than it had
ever been. In their annual defence review for 1932, the Chiefs of
Staff noted the revolutionary change in the world situation since
June 1931: the slump, the departure from gold and the general
malaise in Europe were among the factors said to be involved.[38]
Everywhere international investment was cut back in the aftermath
of the financial crisis, capital repayments to creditor countries
exceeded new loans and relations between debtors and creditors
became strained. Because of her dependence on overseas trade,
Britain also relied, more than any other power, on stability in
international affairs. Yet, as Robert Boyce has written, it was obvious
that the 1931 crisis had placed British capitalism at the crossroads:
tariffs signalled the end of an era for the world, but the alternative
to discrimination in international trade was not stability but the
policies of extreme nationalism which increased the risk of war.[39]
The National Government was continually preoccupied with the
thinness of the veneer of British prosperity.

   In addition to this distraction, the culture of domestic politics left
many parliamentarians poorly equipped in the struggle to
understand the significance of the ideology that underpinned
authoritarian governments in Europe. While British statesmen rarely
lacked guile and determination when defending national interests,
they were also essentially pragmatic and moderate – the dominant
values inherent in a parliamentary democracy. Eventually, as the
concept of totalitarianism began to permeate the political discourse
of the 1930s, Nazism came to be linked with communism.[40] In his
recent biography of Baldwin, Williamson shows how the
Conservative leader offered anti-totalitarianism and the need to
rearm in the face of foreign threats as the justification for continuing
with a national government.[41] But advocates of rearmament were
always opposed by arguments about the need for prudence and
stability in order to preserve the nation's economic resources.[42]

   Whereas the desire to help in the economic recovery of Europe
had once seemed admirable and sensible, it was not quite so
appealing in the case of National Socialist Germany. Once Hitler's

régime became established, various assumptions were made by government and influential interest groups in Britain about its nature. As in other areas of government, the administrative apparatus for the collation and analysis of intelligence was inadequate. While the Foreign Office ran the Secret Intelligence Service, each of the three service departments maintained its own independent-minded intelligence section.[43] In 1919 the Cabinet introduced the 'ten-year rule' and, in 1928, it was put on to a continuous basis. For as long as it applied, military chiefs were supposed to assume that Britain would not have to face a major war within the next ten years. The effects on military and defence policy were not necessarily all pernicious. Moreover, as the military-industrial sector continued to absorb a large share of national economic resources, it is possible to assert that Britain was more powerful than is often recognized.[44] Nevertheless, the delay, until 1932, in abandoning the ten-year rule could hardly have helped the experts in intelligence and strategy who had to plan how to resist emerging threats to national security.[45]

Political assessments in Britain came to be dominated by one idea: the course of events in the Third Reich would depend upon the degree of restraint Germany's 'moderates' could exercise over the 'extremists'.[46] On one side of this debate it was argued that a prosperous or 'fat' Germany would be good for British business and would enable the supposed moderates to exercise a stabilizing influence; on the other side it was held that prosperity would only facilitate Nazi rearmament – keeping Germany 'lean' would help, therefore, to preserve the peace in Europe. Armament exports could be proscribed while trade in war *matériel* could, in theory, be carefully monitored. But one of the lessons of the Great War was that most if not all commodities had a role to play in the prosecution of 'total war'.

In an age of economic nationalism, the principles of the free market inevitably fell into desuetude. Britain's business relations with the Third Reich were conducted within and regulated by a framework of several official or semi-official agreements. By far the most important was the 1934 Anglo-German Payments Agreement. Britain felt that it had driven a hard bargain and achieved a settlement more favourable than had any other country in Europe. Germany was allowed to enjoy a favourable trade balance in order to facilitate debt repayment of all kinds. Indeed, alone of creditor countries, Britain accomplished substantial liquidation of its old commercial claims. While the administration of the agreement fell to Germany, pledges were secured for the continued purchase of specific British exports, especially those of the struggling staple industries. Berlin's freedom to alter the terms of trade by means of Germany's comprehensive system of subsidy and licensing was thereby limited, the more so as subsidies for exports to Britain were probably extensive already because of sterling's depreciation. In negotiating the agreement British officials aimed to take up a strong bargaining position by acting as if the country could afford to turn to other export markets which was, of course, doubtful in the extreme. More importantly, Britain and the Empire were an unavoidable source of raw materials for industry in the Third Reich.

For this reason the Payments Agreement has always been criticized as an act of economic appeasement.[47] As hopes of preserving peace slipped away in the late 1930s, the evidence that the Third Reich was using her trade with the UK to build up a war reserve seemed compelling. Later, during war itself, Hubert Henderson, the economist, took issue with the claim that it had been impossible to interfere with this traffic, the significance of which was unmistakable, because this would have amounted to an offence against those principles of the liberal commercial code which still inspired respect. Henderson concluded that there was better reason for holding that the remains of economic liberalism helped the Axis powers to make war than that economic nationalism provoked them to it.[48] That the political complexion of the National Government is best characterized as a form of liberal Toryism is not in doubt.[49] But to suggest that the Payments Agreement was an example of sentimental attachment to an outmoded ideology, or to categorize it as an act of appeasement, is to be cavalier with the historical record. The intention of this book is to show that the agreement was a pragmatic and effective response to the multidimensional problems confronting Britain in the 1930s.

For officials who devised and initiated such bilateral structures there were virtually no precedents to follow. In this respect, as in many others, the corporate influence of the administrative class was at its peak in the 1930s. Although the sphere of government in the legalistic sense remained comparatively small, the Treasury, the Board of Trade and the Bank of England were becoming increasingly involved in domestic industry. The trend continued after 1931 to the extent that large interest groups (employers' organizations and trades unions) accepted the need for formal collaboration with the state in order that some kind of balance might be struck. In an increasingly hostile world, the tendency was for different sectors of society to band together. The change from government by parliamentarians to one dominated by a bureaucracy oriented towards the needs of the economy went forward slowly. Furthermore, the means to co-ordinate governmental business were only just being developed.[50]

The Treasury, especially, occupied a key role not just because of the perennial importance of financial matters but also because the offices of Permanent Head of the Home Civil Service and Permanent Under-Secretary of the Treasury were combined in the person of Sir Warren Fisher. The Second Secretary and Controller of Finance was Sir Richard Hopkins who, as the leading expert on fiscal matters and the principal link with the Bank of England, exercised a degree of influence which was not dissimilar to that of a Cabinet minister.[51] The same was true of Sir Frederick Leith-Ross who, in 1932, left his post of deputy to Hopkins to become Chief Economic Adviser to the government. Leith-Ross was based in the Board of Trade but he was occupied with the aspect of Treasury work which had developed after 1918: economic relations with foreign governments and financial institutions. Government departments tended to distrust most experts, although an exception was made for the financial experts in the Treasury and the Bank of England, with the former deferring to the judgement of the latter over matters of business confidence. After outstanding careers in the Treasury in the 1920s, Sir Otto Niemeyer and Henry Arthur Siepmann both joined the Bank and helped to reinforce the relationship between the two institutions.[52] Compelled to take into account a range of pressures, which included parliamentary opinion, the City, industrial interests, the reconciliation of conflicting departmental interests, as well as the strictly economic needs of the time, the Treasury was predisposed to be cautious in outlook.[53]

In the inter-war years the Foreign Office never recaptured the dominant position which it had held before 1914. Proposals advanced by Sir Victor Wellesley, Deputy Under-Secretary until 1936, caused such acrimony between departments that when the Commercial Diplomatic Service and the Department of Overseas Trade were created they were put under the joint control of the

Foreign Office and the Board of Trade. The new service was
designed to assist the effort to secure export markets rather than to
look for ways to integrate trade, finance and diplomacy. Yet
conditions soon turned the new commercial ambassadors into the
economic advisers of the diplomatic posts to which they were
attached. Wellesley also strongly favoured the creation of an
economic intelligence apparatus that could co-operate with the main
economic departments and advise on long-term policy. Eventually,
the Foreign Office's Economic Relations Section was allowed to
creep into existence in 1933.[54] But, in reaching decisions on
international trade matters, the Board of Trade remained a powerful
arbiter. Inevitably by the mid 1930s the Board's own Commercial
Relations and Treaties Department was becoming more important.

International commercial and financial relations in the years
before the First World War were controlled almost entirely by
businessmen. There was, therefore, little in the way of tradition in
the field of intergovernmental economic relations and the machinery
for economic diplomacy was rudimentary. The Bank of England had
long carried on its own form of financial diplomacy through its
contacts with other central banks; a forum for further co-operation
was provided by the establishment of the BIS. Nevertheless, J.H.
Richardson was able to observe in 1936 that the need for and the
limitations of the co-ordination of economic with political policy
had been discerned only in part. Inconsistencies were frequent and
harmony was accidental.[55] Government certainly depended upon the
business world for information. However, the extent of the
influence enjoyed by business interests with ministers and
government departments over the direction of foreign economic
policy is yet to be clearly defined. Wurm has pointed to the
methodological and theoretical difficulties which confront any
analysis of these issues: while economic and political power work
together in the arena of international relations, the two forms of
power are not identical. Historians writing about the inter-war years
have still to unravel the ways in which the interests of business and
those of the state co-operated or collided in foreign markets and to
establish how far business mobilized state power or vice versa.[56]

In this respect, Watt suggests that while the heads of a few major
British multinationals – such as oil companies – have carried some
weight in terms of foreign policy formulation, the influence
exercised by other industrial concerns has been at best marginal.[57]

One of the more important multinationals was Dunlop Rubber, whose chairman was Sir Eric Geddes, a forceful industrialist who succeeded in restoring the company's fortunes after leaving Lloyd George's Coalition Cabinet in 1921. Consequently, while the British state was directly involved in oil matters for strategic reasons, issues relating to the rubber industry were certain to attract the attention of the National Government. Watt argues, however, that Geddes and Reginald McKenna – Asquith's war-time Chancellor of the Exchequer – enjoyed a degree of success in their commercial lives which was not matched by corresponding political influence. Of the two, McKenna, in representing finance, is reckoned to have been the more influential.[58]

As chairman of the Midland Bank, McKenna was a leading City figure and closely involved in Anglo-German financial matters. British bank loans formed part of Germany's short-term borrowing which was frozen under the Standstill Agreement (*Stillhalte-abkommen*) – a product of the London Conference of July 1931.[59] The intention was to create a temporary emergency measure. But the arrangements, born in such extraordinary circumstances, were maintained throughout the decade. The role of the Standstill in the financial crisis is considered in the works of Sayers and Sir Henry Clay, while the significance of the agreements for Germany has been analysed by Harold James.[60] Examining the Standstill in the Nazi era provides an opportunity to assess the role of British banks which, because of their importance in the national economy and the size and nature of their German commitments, represent an interest group of particular significance. Bankers were always quick to remind the government of the existence of these credits when relations with Germany became especially tense.[61]

The type of commercial capitalism practised by the City of London was naturally favoured by the Treasury and the Bank of England because it acted to reinforce their independence and institutional power. With the retreat from cosmopolitanism and free trade after 1931 and the arrival of conditions which favoured manufacturing industry and agriculture, it would have been reasonable to assume that the influence wielded by the City would diminish.[62] Yet Geoffrey Ingham, in his important study *Capitalism Divided?*, finds little evidence of a fundamental shift in the balance of power. Big business had no political party to champion its interests. The advocates of industrial capitalism continued to occupy a position in the policy-making processes subordinate to that held by the proponents of City-based cosmopolitan capitalism.[63] Similarly, David Reynolds points out that, as the interests of the state and of politically dominant groups within it (the City–Bank–Treasury axis) were global, support for maintaining multilateralism based on London never wavered.[64]

British bankers with commitments in Germany wanted to ensure that they continued to have the full attention of the authorities. To that end, the committee of banks and acceptance houses concerned with the Standstill was reorganized and became the Joint Committee of British Short-Term Creditors, in January 1932. Of all the lobby groups which existed in the inter-war years, the Joint Committee (as it was commonly known) was potentially one of the most powerful. But this was not how it seemed to the bankers. Feeling the need to justify the actions of their institutions which appeared to them to be the subject of widespread public misunderstanding, the reaction of the British bankers was, if anything, a defensive one.

The financial relationship between Germany and Britain in the inter-war years could not, of course, be the usual one between debtor and creditor nation. Although reparations were effectively annulled in 1932, the international payments made by Germany continued to be dominated by the Dawes and Young Loans. These two loans were guaranteed by the governments of the participating states, but it was the public and the financial institutions which subscribed to them. When the Nazis gained power they sought to equate any payment made abroad with one form of tribute or another, and they continually attempted to reduce the service of Germany's international debts, while this jeopardized London's position as the leading centre for international finance. Even so, the City seemed ready to believe Nazi warnings that the effect of any retaliatory action against Germany would be to disrupt, either deliberately or ineluctably, the intricate systems of British capitalism. But it is not possible to say that contemporaries exaggerated the dangers. British financial institutions did not collapse like several of their foreign counterparts. Relatively few insights are afforded to those who seek to probe the state of mind of leading figures in the 1930s. Without doubt, though, insufficient attention has been paid to the significance of the psychological and material effects of the crisis and its aftermath on individuals and institutions alike.

Actors on the economic stage ranged from private entrepreneurs to public companies; what they shared was an instinct to compete with each other in order to have the greatest influence over the making and the carrying out of official policy. Although tariffs affected British industry and commerce in various ways, business in general wanted to see the restoration of 'normal' relations with Germany. With the coming of the Third Reich such aspirations were shown to be utopian and every individual interest group argued that it merited special protection in advance of all others. The National Government was hard pressed in trying to respond both to the complex tangle of demands related to the national economy and to the dictates of foreign policy. Judgement was clouded by the contrasting but seemingly equally valid definitions of national interest. Britain's relations with Germany were certainly made more complex, even convoluted, by the variety of different financial and commercial interests. Some interpretations of Britain's descent from the pinnacle of power in the nineteenth century suggest that the nature of British society has allowed only one form of 'national interest' to be recognized – the securing of short-term profits. Foreign policies have supposedly pursued this objective even at the expense of future ruin.[65]

The problems which Britain's multinational companies, banks and several other commercial and financial interests had to confront in the Third Reich are examined separately in the chapters which follow. This offers an opportunity to see how much influence industrialists, bankers, bondholders, exporters and others were able to exercise with government as Britain tried to maintain commercial and financial relations with the Third Reich. This work is concerned with how financial and economic policy towards Germany was made, how it was executed and what it achieved. More light should be thrown, therefore, on the wider question of how well British institutions responded to the challenge posed by the Third Reich and whether the use of the term 'economic appeasement' aids or hinders historical understanding. Above all, the intention is to consider what the consequences were of doing business with the Nazis. But first, it is necessary to turn to consider the impact of the crisis of 1931.

NOTES

1. For detail on Geddes see below.
2. J.M. Keynes, *The Economic Consequences of the Peace* (Macmillan, 1920), p. 131.
3. S. Marks, *The Illusion of Peace: International Relations in Europe 1918–1933* (Macmillan, 1976), pp. 132–4.
4. N. Branson and M. Heinemann, *Britain in the Nineteen Thirties* (St.Albans: Panther, 1973), p. 17.
5. R.A.C. Parker, *Chamberlain and Appeasement: British Policy and the Coming of the Second World War* (Macmillan, 1993), p. 304. Parker refers to the involvement of banking interests in the attempts which were made to achieve market-sharing and price-fixing agreements with German industry.
6. See, for example, P. Einzig, *Appeasement before, during and after the War* (Macmillan, 1942). Einzig enjoyed both a network of information and the gift of lucid explanation of technical foreign exchange matters. But his works, comprising many books together with articles in the financial press, are not characterized by modesty. For his Churchillian claim that, 'Mine was a lone voice crying in the wilderness', see his autobiographical *In the Centre of Things* (Hutchinson, 1960), p. 177.
7. M. Gilbert, *The Roots of Appeasement* (Weidenfeld & Nicolson, 1967), p. 151.
8. W.N. Medlicott, *Britain and Germany: The Search for Agreement 1930–37* (Athlone Press, 1969).
9. CAB 24/248(104), Appendix 34, 'The Future of Germany'.
10. B.J. Wendt, *Economic Appeasement: Handel und Finanz in der britischen Deutschland-politik 1933–1939* (Düsseldorf: Bertelsmann Universitätsverlag, 1971).
11. For a recent example see S. Newton, *Profits of Peace: The Political Economy of Anglo-German Appeasement* (Oxford: OUP, 1996).
12. Wendt, *Economic Appeasement*, p. 17; see also, B.J. Wendt, '"Economic Appeasement" – A crisis strategy', in W.J. Mommsen and L. Kettenacker (eds), *The Fascist Challenge and the Policy of Appeasement* (Allen & Unwin, 1983).
13. Wendt, *Economic Appeasement*, p. 142.
14. G. Schmidt, *The Politics and Economics of Appeasement: British Foreign Policy in the 1930s* (Leamington Spa: Berg, 1986), pp. 45–7, 384. The work was originally published in 1981 as *England in der Krise: Grundzüge und Grundlagen der britischen Appeasement-Politik (1930–1937)*.
15. W.A. Lewis, *Economic Survey 1919–1939* (Allen & Unwin, 1949), p. 138; see also, D.H. Aldcroft, *The European Economy 1914–1970* (Croom Helm, 1978).
16. See W.J. Reader, *Imperial Chemical Industries: A History, Vol.2* (OUP, 1975), p. 239, for background to the Dyestuffs Act of 1920; also F. Capie, *Depression and Protectionism: Britain between the Wars* (Allen & Unwin, 1983), p. 40.
17. J.H. Richardson, *British Economic Foreign Policy* (Allen & Unwin, 1936), p. 19.
18. P. Kennedy, *The Rise of the Anglo-German Antagonism, 1860–1914* (Allen & Unwin, 1980), p. 295.
19. T 160/729/12829/2.
20. For a full analysis of the financing of bilateral trade through the medium of British and German banks see T 160/534/13460/04, Board of Trade memo. See also Kennedy, *The Rise of the Anglo-German Antagonism*, pp. 47–8, on complaints of protectionists and nationalists in both countries that Jewish financiers were putting their own interests above those of the state. Of course,

some important finance houses (such as Schroders) were staunchly Protestant.

21. L. Hannah, *The Rise of the Corporate Economy* (Methuen, 1983), p. 52.
22. Among the extensive literature the following are particularly relevant: H.W. Richardson, 'The economic significance of the depression in Britain', *JCH*, 4 (1969); C.P. Kindleberger, *The World in Depression, 1929–1939* (Allen Lane, 1973); E.W. Bennett, *German Rearmament and the West, 1932–1933* (Princeton, NJ: Princeton University Press, 1979); G.C. Peden, 'Sir Richard Hopkins and the "Keynesian revolution" in employment policy, 1929–1945', *EcHR*, 2nd Ser., Vol. 36, 2 (May 1983); R. Middleton, *Towards the Managed Economy: Keynes, the Treasury and the Fiscal Policy Debate of the 1930s* (Methuen, 1985); P. Temin, *Lessons from the Great Depression* (Cambridge, MA: MIT Press, 1989); A. Booth, *British Economic Policy, 1931–45* (Hemel Hempstead: Harvester Wheatsheaf, 1989); W.R. Garside, *British Unemployment, 1919–1939* (Cambridge: CUP, 1990).
23. R. Skidelsky, *John Maynard Keynes: Vol. 2, The Economist as Saviour 1920–1937* (Macmillan, 1992), p. 621.
24. J. Tomlinson, *Problems of British Economic Policy 1870–1945* (Methuen, 1981), pp. 116–7.
25. These developments are examined in more detail in Chapter 2.
26. H.W. Arndt, *The Economic Lessons of the Nineteen Thirties* (OUP, 1944), p. 94.
27. P. Clarke, *Hope and Glory: Britain 1900–1990* (Penguin, 1996), p. 177.
28. On the question of relations between leading political figures in the 1930s see N. Smart, *The National Government, 1931–40* (Basingstoke: Macmillan, 1999).
29. R. Bassett, *Nineteen Thirty-One: Political Crisis* (Macmillan, 1958), p. 355.
30. M. Cowling, *The Impact of Hitler: British Politics and British Policy 1933–1940* (Cambridge: CUP, 1975), pp. 6–7, 267.
31. P. Williamson, *National Crisis and National Government, 1926–32* (Cambridge: CUP, 1992), pp. 505–8. A similar point is made by Cowling, *The Impact of Hitler*, p. 42.
32. Parl. Deb.(Commons), 261, 4 February 1931, col. 287.
33. Sir John Simon papers (hereafter MS Simon), Bodleian Library, University of Oxford, 84, fol.5, Simon to Baldwin, 26 October 1936.
34. Viscount Runciman of Doxford papers, University of Newcastle Library, (hereafter Runciman papers), 282, draft letter to Baldwin, 23 October 1936. The letter was not sent because Runciman's plans were adopted by the Cabinet the next day. Runciman was a member of the Cabinet at the declaration of war in 1914 and in 1939 – a unique, if grim, distinction in British politics.
35. C.A. Wurm, *Business, Politics, and International Relations* (Cambridge: CUP, 1993), pp. 50–1.
36. See, for example, J.R. Ferris, '"The greatest power on earth": Great Britain in the 1920s', *International History Review*, 13, 4 (November 1991).
37. P.J. Cain and A.G. Hopkins, *British Imperialism: Crisis and Deconstruction 1914–1990* (Longman, 1993), p. 6.
38. Cited in C. Barnett, *The Collapse of British Power* (Stroud: Sutton, 1984), p. 342.
39. R.W.D. Boyce, *British Capitalism at the Crossroads, 1919–1932* (Cambridge: CUP, 1989), pp. 2, 373.
40. L. Schapiro, *Totalitarianism* (Macmillan, 1972), p. 14.
41. P. Williamson, *Stanley Baldwin* (Cambridge: CUP, 1999), pp. 313–21.
42. See, for example, K. Middlemas, *Diplomacy of Illusion: The British Government and Germany, 1937–39* (Weidenfeld & Nicolson, 1972), p. 12;

P. Kennedy, *The Realities behind Diplomacy* (Allen & Unwin, 1981), p. 255.

43. D. Dilks, 'Appeasement and "intelligence"', in D.Dilks (ed.), *Retreat from Power: Studies in Britain's Foreign Policy of the Twentieth Century. Vol. 1 1906–1939* (Macmillan, 1981), pp. 141–2.

44. For a critical review of these issues see J.R. Ferris, 'The Air Force brats' view of history: Recent writing and the Royal Air Force, 1918–1960', *International History Review*, Vol. 20, 1 (March 1998).

45. W.K. Wark, *The Ultimate Enemy: British Intelligence and Nazi Germany, 1933–1939* (Oxford: OUP, 1986), p. 24.

46. C.A. MacDonald, 'Economic appeasement and the German "moderates" 1937–1939. An introductory essay', *Past and Present*, 56 (1972), pp. 105–35.

47. See Chapter 4 for a detailed consideration of the literature.

48. H.D. Henderson, *The Inter-war Years and Other Papers* (Oxford: Clarendon Press, 1955), p. 290. The paper concerned was written in 1943.

49. M. Pugh, *The Making of Modern British Politics 1867–1939* (Oxford: Basil Blackwell, 1982), p. 273.

50. For a thorough examination of these issues see, K. Middlemas, *Politics in Industrial Society* (Deutsch, 1979); G.C. Peden, *British Rearmament and the Treasury: 1932–1939* (Edinburgh: Scottish Academic Press, 1979). See also, J.S. Eyers, 'Government Direction of Overseas Trade Policy in Britain, 1932–37' (unpublished D.Phil. thesis, Oxford University, 1977) for the observation that the interdepartmental committee was in its infancy.

51. See, in particular, D.C. Watt, *Personalities and Policies: Studies in the Formulation of British Foreign Policy in the Twentieth Century* (Longman, 1965); also M. Beloff, 'The Whitehall factor: The role of the higher civil servant 1918–39', in G. Peele and C. Cook (eds), *The Politics of Reappraisal, 1918–1939* (Macmillan, 1975). The Foreign Office remained outside the realm of Fisher's jurisdiction.

52. Niemeyer was an adviser to the Governors (1927–38) and made a director of the Bank in 1938. He was also a member of the Council of Foreign Bondholders of Germany. Siepmann was Acting Chief of the Overseas and Foreign Department (1932–35) and Head of the Central Banking Section until 1936.

53. F. Leith-Ross, *Money Talks: Fifty Years of International Finance* (Hutchinson, 1968), p. 247; P. Clarke, 'The Treasury's analytical model of the British economy between the wars', in M.O. Furner and B. Supple (eds), *The State and Economic Knowledge* (Cambridge: CUP, 1990), pp. 173–4. See also Middleton, *Towards the Managed Economy*.

54. F.T. Ashton-Gwatkin, *The British Foreign Service* (New York, NY: Syracuse University Press, 1950), p. 19. The author was head of the section.

55. Richardson, *British Economic Foreign Policy*, p. 24.

56. Wurm, *Business, Politics, and International Relations*, pp. 1–2.

57. D. Cameron Watt, *Succeeding John Bull: America in Britain's Place 1900–1975* (Cambridge: CUP, 1984), p. 11. See also Watt, 'The European civil war', in Mommsen and Kettenacker, *The Fascist Challenge*.

58. Watt, *Succeeding John Bull*, p. 47.

59. This is examined in more detail in Chapter 2.

60. R.S. Sayers, *The Bank of England, 1891–1944: Vol. 2* (Cambridge: CUP, 1976); Sir H. Clay, *Lord Norman* (Macmillan, 1957); H. James, *The Reichsbank and Public Finance in Germany 1924–1933* (Frankfurt-am-Main: F.Knapp, 1985). See also H. James, *The German Slump: Politics and Economics, 1924–1936* (Oxford: Clarendon Press, 1986).

61. For an earlier version of this analysis see, N. Forbes, 'London banks, the German Standstill agreements, and "economic appeasement" in the 1930s', *EcHR*, 2nd. Ser., 40, 4 (November 1987).

62. The City's position was under threat even before the Great Depression: while the absolute volume of bills in the London market in 1929 may have been higher than pre-war because world trade volumes were higher at the later date, the returns were lower as the City had to contend with international competition. See, Cain and Hopkins, *British Imperialism*, p. 42.

63. G. Ingham, *Capitalism Divided? The City and Industry in British Social Development* (Macmillan, 1984), pp. 171–90.

64. D. Reynolds, *Britannia Overruled: British Policy and World Power in the Twentieth Century* (Longman, 1991), pp. 301–2.

65. B. Porter, *Britain, Europe and the World 1850–1986: Delusions of Grandeur* (Routledge, Chapman & Hall, 1987), p. 95.

2

Britain's economic revolution and the demise of the Weimar Republic

The depression brought momentous, even iconoclastic, change to Britain. In a bewilderingly rapid succession of events, the gold standard was abandoned, tariffs were instituted and Imperial Preference was established. If the cumulative impact of the changes created a sense of a revolutionary break with the past, the revolutionaries were nowhere to be found. It was impossible to welcome a new dawn while fears of a descent into darkness remained so pervasive. Foreign investors withdrew funds worth more than £350m from the London money market between June 1930 and December 1931.[1] Ralph Hawtrey, the Treasury-based economist, observed soon afterwards that 'Such a panic-stricken withdrawal had never occurred before'.[2] To be at the mercy of the progressive collapse in confidence and consequent international capital flight was a traumatic experience. Richard Fry, the financial journalist, observed in 1945 that:

> Behind us lie such changes as few people would have believed possible. The City had suffered fearful losses. Although the merchant banks and others who had been caught with large assets in Central Europe were enabled to carry on they never recovered their nerve.[3]

Britain had already been badly affected by the general reduction in international trade: between 1929 and 1931 the surplus in invisible items in the balance of payments shrank from £359m to £219m. Within these totals, income from financial and other services declined from £65m to £30m. The diminution of income from British overseas interest, profits and dividends from £307m to

£211m was particularly serious.[4] In these conditions, a number of banking failures could not be ruled out.[5]

Apart from financial shocks, the very political culture of the nation was also profoundly shaken by the storm. With the world standing of British capitalism under threat, the 'moment of truth' had arrived: Ramsay MacDonald, the Labour Prime Minister, formed a National Government with Conservatives – the party of big business.[6] Yet even this political transformation was not enough to prevent further withdrawals from London and thereby save the gold standard.

In the struggle to survive the maelstrom of the world economic crisis, long-term political considerations were not necessarily accorded a high priority. But there was a growing realization in Britain that a reparations settlement was required sooner rather than later in order to give democracy in Germany the chance to see off the danger of dictatorship from either the left or the right. In this sense, British efforts to promote a general pacification of Europe intensified with the collapse of 1931.[7] In the course of the Hoover Year, Britain became increasingly anxious to secure international co-operation to sweep away the tangled web of reparations and war debts. That many economic and political benefits would flow from an early settlement of the problem was taken to be a self-evident truth. Equally, it was assumed that there would be a high price to pay for the failure to achieve a satisfactory solution.

The rise of political extremism in the Weimar Republic rekindled painful memories of the consequences of the Russian Revolution: there was a fear that the Allied powers would be left with their war debts to pay America and a 'Bolshevised' Germany which paid them nothing. With an estimated eight million Germans on the starvation line, all talk of reparations and a political truce suddenly seemed pointless and absurd.[8] But the machinery of international diplomacy had to be kept running while, at the same time, economic multilateralism was breaking down. Indeed, by embarking on an exclusive attempt to win national advantage, Britain herself helped to kill off the old economic order. What emerged was something rather different: a regional trading bloc comprising the Empire and other states closely linked to Britain.[9]

For the moment, there was nothing but uncertainty over what the changes portended. Harold Macmillan felt that he was witnessing the collapse of the solid foundations on which the strength of

Europe and the influence of Europeans in the world had been based.[10] The politicians, officials and private individuals caught up in the crisis could do little other than speculate over the likely consequences of any action they undertook. No one could be sure how the changes in Britain's external economic relations would influence political developments in Germany.

Departure from the gold standard: a victory dearly bought

Affected by the impending financial crisis in Austria, Germany began to experience heavy capital withdrawals in June 1931.[11] On 20 June the Hoover Moratorium was announced; its proposal to suspend all intergovernmental debts met initial resistance from the French government. The central bank credit to Germany for $100m (arranged on 25 June) was used up by 5 July. The next day the Hoover Moratorium finally came into effect. This was not enough to forestall further disastrous runs on German reserves, and on 13 July, with the Reichsbank's legal reserve all but exhausted, the Bank of England was approached for emergency credits. The next day the Darmstädter und Nationalbank closed its doors.

As attitudes in London towards Germany were ambivalent, the reparations and debts question was approached with some caution. The consensus was that Germany had brought the difficulties upon herself, even to the extent of manufacturing a political crisis.[12] Those looking for a conspiracy interpreted the Republic's declarations of bankruptcy as a smokescreen behind which an escape from reparations could be planned. This putative plot had run out of control only with the collapse of the Austrian Credit-Anstalt. But the world could not be saved and Germany punished at the same time. There was no equivocation, however, over the need to restore confidence as soon as possible. Most financial experts agreed that, while a long-term 'political' loan would be inappropriate, Germany did need a combination of a large or even unlimited credit to the Reichsbank, middle-term loans for individual banks, and a continuation of short-term loans and acceptances.

At the London Conference of 20 July 1931 the Reichsbank President Hans Luther was unable to win support for the idea of a new central bank loan. But the $100m central bank credit to Germany, already advanced equally by London, Paris, New York and the BIS, was renewed for a further three months. Private creditors were asked not to withdraw loans from Germany; two months later this was formalized under the Standstill Agreement (see below). Another recommendation of the conference was that Germany's problems should be investigated by a special committee. This was set up under the auspices of the BIS; Sir Walter Layton, editor of *The Economist*, was nominated as one of the experts and Albert Wiggin, of Chase Bank of New York, was made chairman. The committee enquired into the immediate further credit needs of Germany and studied the possibility of converting a portion of the short-term credits into long-term ones.[13]

A report was produced by mid August. It suggested that, if severe economic effects were to be avoided, it would be necessary to replace some of the capital withdrawn from Germany, not in the form of short-term credits which would only increase Germany's difficulties, but by a long-term loan from foreign sources. Germany's credit was not good enough to justify such action, so there was an urgent need to restore confidence. At the root of the problem lay reparations. Although this was an authoritative pronouncement, no instant solutions were on offer: the ball was passed back to the politicians. Given the failure by governments to agree on a common approach it was not surprising that the Wiggins-Layton report was veiled and circumspect over the reparations issue.[14]

The difficulty of withdrawing money from Germany aroused in its turn distrust of the position of those financial institutions which were known to be short-term creditors of Germany.[15] During the summer of 1931 the crisis spread to London which had never acquired a buffer stock of currencies or reserves sufficient to meet the abnormal strains being imposed on the international exchange system.[16] On 21 September the Gold Standard (Amendment) Act was hurriedly passed. The intention was to suspend convertibility for six months.[17] However, Britain had left the gold (bullion) standard never to return.

If the shock waves from the crisis brought about a political earthquake, what was the effect on the financial authorities? Was the departure from gold really such an unexpected and unwelcome development? After all, as co-operation between governments became more difficult and relations between central banks showed signs of strain, Britain's commitment to defend the gold régime at all costs was severely tested. Diane Kunz indicates that, while the

Governor of the Bank of England Montagu Norman and his senior colleagues may have privately come to the conclusion by the summer of 1931 that the gold standard was doomed, the manner and timing of its demise was actually determined by British actions.[18] Yet, according to Kunz, the authorities chose to portray suspension as bowing to the inevitable because it freed them from any guilt over what they had done; there did not have to be any questions over whether they had taken the coward's way out.[19] This provides an insight into the circumstances in which the gold standard was abandoned. Yet, what developed in the years which followed was precisely such a sense of guilty responsibility over the way in which devaluation affected Germany.

Similarly, in her study of Sir Charles Addis, Roberta Dayer points to the decision on 9 July by the Bank of England's Committee of Treasury to stop supporting the Reichsbank with further credits. This, it is argued, was a gamble to force the issue of war debts and reparations which willingly put the gold standard at risk. Furthermore, the defence of sterling in the weeks which followed is held to be a careful camouflage for the start of a new and independent monetary policy. Addis, one of the directors of the Bank and a leading financier, gave no indication of surprise or dismay when the *coup de grâce* fell in September.[20] At the very least, the prospect of being forced off gold was acknowledged early in the summer. A Special Committee on Foreign Exchange was established just before the sterling crisis. But it seems unlikely that the Bank of England regarded devaluation as anything other than a disaster.[21]

The crisis had brutally exposed the futility of attempting to achieve both domestic and external stability. In aiming to stabilize the domestic economy, devaluation was preferred to further doses of internal deflation, but only in the sense that it seemed the lesser of two evils. Devaluation was not a planned act of policy; it was foreseen by few and desired by fewer.[22] With the sudden and catastrophic end to Britain's struggle to maintain the gold standard, one of the pillars of the international financial system itself had collapsed. The British-led attempt to return to the normality of the pre-war order had ended in national humiliation. Gold was abandoned with extreme reluctance, for it represented, as Cain and Hopkins argue, a defeat for cosmopolitanism and the City, and for 'gentlemanly capitalism'.[23]

It was possible, of course, to articulate a philosophy which could embrace a new role for sterling; the relevant arguments had been rehearsed on many occasions. John Maynard Keynes was among those who were able to welcome developments: it was a vindication of the attack which he had mounted on the restoration of gold in 1925. Yet, in the following months, even Keynes was comparatively quiet on public issues, perhaps because the crisis had destroyed all available political vehicles for his ideas.[24] As he admitted at the time, 'most of us have, as yet, only a vague idea of what we are going to do next, of how we are going to use our regained freedom of choice.'[25]

Keynesian ideas were to dominate economic debate by the end of the 1930s. At the beginning of the decade, socialism in one form or another appeared to be the only clear ideological alternative to classical liberalism.[26] In a world which was rapidly abandoning the ideals of liberal capitalism there was little point in pretending that Britain's position could be anything other than uncertain. As Eichengreen puts it, if the crisis was an opportunity to surmount a barrier to the unilateral pursuit of stabilizing action, fears of 'a new inflationary era characterized by financial and political chaos' had first to be overcome.[27] More than ever, predicting the future seemed a particularly risky business. André Siegfried, another contemporary economist, wondered whether Britain would gravitate towards America and further away from Europe. He saw how, for the moment, Britain was hesitating: there was a conflict between those with interests in international trade who called for currency stabilization and industrial interests which desired the stimulus of a fresh depreciation. Siegfried felt entitled to remark that 'the Government, in keeping with the usual British practice, is feeling its way and waiting'.[28]

If national self-interest dictated the departure from gold, consideration of how the decision might affect other countries had, inevitably, to be left until later. Montagu Norman and Sir Ernest Harvey, the Deputy Governor, began the painful and embarrassing task of contacting other central banks. Since Norman had only just returned to London after his prolonged rest, it was Harvey who wrote to Luther:

> It cannot have been easy to appreciate from published accounts of what happened last week how suddenly we were faced with the necessity of suspension. Nothing could be more disturbing and

distasteful to us than that Central Banks should suffer as a result of their association with the Bank of England.

While there had been practically no central bank withdrawals up to that point, Harvey invited Luther to exercise his discretion in deciding whether to withdraw Reichsbank funds from the Bank. Harvey hoped that the day would come when co-operation would be resumed on the basis of the gold standard; nothing else, to his mind, could provide such stability. In the meantime, he appreciated that normal banking relationships were probably going to be interrupted or curtailed.[29]

This tactfully understated the true extent of the damage. The Bank of England had indeed sought to maintain relations of mutual confidence with all its central bank clients based on the idea that they might be relied upon to stand together in all circumstances. Among central bankers, Montagu Norman was especially committed to this philosophy.[30] For that reason, if no other, foreign clients could not be expected to view London's actions favourably. The central bank of Belgium soon withdrew large amounts of funds from the Bank of England and Clément Moret, Governor of the Banque de France, threatened to do the same.[31] His institution had been rendered technically insolvent because of its sterling losses and a considerable proportion of the massive drain of gold which the United States now experienced went to Paris.[32]

Yet Luther intended his reply to convey his warm and sincere sympathy. He regarded it as tragic that the assistance the Bank of England had generously and unhesitatingly afforded the Reichsbank and other central banks in their hour of need had increased the difficulties with which London had had to contend. The Reichsbank would:

> not forget what the Bank of England and what you, dear Mr. Governor, have done for the co-operation of Central Banks. In a time of great disturbance and danger I derive the greatest comfort from the sincere friendship existing between our two Institutions.[33]

There were contemporary reports that the Bank of England encouraged the Reichsbank to consider following Britain off gold. But if there was any prospect of Germany voluntarily abandoning the gold standard it did not last long.[34] The German government was not deterred by the constraints of the Young Plan nor pressure from France. It was rather that Brüning and Luther regarded the British devaluation as inflationary and dangerous.[35] At the end of November 1931 Brüning told Layton that he could not contemplate going off gold except to a definite figure (he did not say what figure) or to sterling if sterling were stabilized. Luther was strongly against any departure from gold.[36]

The stabilization of the exchange rate was just one of the economic policy decisions which Britain was suddenly required to make with the precipitate suspension of gold. The unpredictable way in which the crisis hit London in 1931 had left no time to establish new ground rules and the instruments necessary to manage the currency had not been developed. The Treasury wanted a relatively low value for sterling and was not entirely persuaded by other points of view. Hubert Henderson, the prominent economist and member of the Economic Advisory Council, argued that any substantial depreciation of the pound would aggravate financial insolvency abroad.[37] Keynes made much the same point in *Essays in Persuasion*: Britain had gone some way in solving her own problems by abandoning the gold standard but had made matters worse for countries still adhering to it.[38] It was also widely understood that movements in the exchange rates would pose new problems for Germany. Britain's action had helped Germany in one way: a proportionate reduction took place in all Germany's sterling debts.

Against this there was the danger that the cutting of export prices by Britain (and countries such as Sweden) would make the trade position of Germany so uncomfortable that, in the long run, she would be forced off gold to avoid economic collapse. Sir Frederick Leith-Ross, who was about to become the government's Chief Economic Adviser, observed that, in the meantime, the longer Germany could keep itself on gold so much the better for British exports.[39] But such short-term views worried Robert Brand, the widely respected banker and partner in Lazard Brothers (one of the City houses dangerously exposed by the crisis in Germany). He cautioned that the advantages Britain was gaining from sterling's depreciation might be dearly bought by the additional knocks given to Germany in particular.[40]

Of necessity, however, the management of the domestic economy took priority over the facilitation of international co-operation. Sir Warren Fisher and Sir Richard Hopkins, the leading Treasury officials, laid down secret guidelines to aid the Chancellor of the Exchequer. They did not want to overlook the need for settled and far-reaching international understandings on gold policy, reparations and debts. But they were aware that, until the United States and France shared the same objectives as Britain, merely advocating co-ordination was not going to achieve anything. More than this, Hopkins and Fisher were worried that, by trying to force the pace, difficulties would be accentuated to the point where everything could be lost. Any conference, therefore, was foredoomed to fail.[41] The disastrous World Economic Conference in 1933 was a depressing demonstration of the accuracy of this prediction. It was not until the Tripartite Agreement of 1936 that anything substantial in the way of co-ordination was achieved.[42]

Import duties: playing the other 'trump card'

In the wake of the depression and financial crisis, and the fear and suffering it imposed, a broad alliance drawn from across business interests and the Conservative Party had turned to embrace protectionist ideas. Although the tariff question excited as much passion in 1931/32 as it had done at the beginning of the century, the circumstances were very different. The United States had already introduced import duties of up to 50 per cent – an unprecedented level – under the Smoot-Hawley legislation of 1930. Several other countries followed suit.

The debate in Britain, therefore, was over the scope and nature of tariff reform. Although tariffs formed an important part of the National Government's election platform, the Cabinet had been unable to reach a collective decision on the detail of policy. Although they could do no more than agree to disagree, victory in the elections seemed unstoppable. Against a background of a large deficit in Britain's balance of payments, MacDonald's triumphant second National Government brought in the Abnormal Importations Act and the Horticultural Products Act in November 1931. To stem the flood of imports, the Board of Trade was given powers for six months to impose duties of up to 100 per cent on a wide range of manufactured goods; similar powers were given to the Ministry of Agriculture.[43]

The features of the election campaign which were fixed in the public's mind were MacDonald's all-embracing appeal for a 'doctor's mandate' and Snowden's anti-socialist scare-mongering over 'Bolshevism run mad'.[44] Nevertheless, the Cabinet became fearful by the beginning of 1932 that the government's survival could depend upon bringing forward further tariff legislation.[45] Neville Chamberlain, the Chancellor of the Exchequer, moved the financial resolution of the Import Duties Bill on 4 February. In proposing a system of moderate protection he claimed that an effective instrument was being acquired for negotiations with foreign countries which discriminated against Britain. A general *ad valorem* duty of 10 per cent was announced along with the establishment of the Import Duties Advisory Committee (IDAC). On the recommendation of this body, the Treasury was empowered to impose further duties. Sterling's devaluation and the coming Imperial Conference were two complicating factors which made it judicious to postpone decisions on a more detailed and fixed system.[46]

Tariffs and sterling were becoming, for the Foreign Office, Britain's 'two trump cards in the game of foreign politics'.[47] To play the diplomatic hand effectively required finesse: tariffs could be used as a bargaining tool in the search for a general settlement of political and economic issues such as reparations and armaments. By advancing on a broad basis there was a chance that Britain might win an 'all-in' solution to foreign policy problems. Yet, with the increasing impact of economics on diplomacy, the Treasury and the Board of Trade were bound to count for more in decisions on foreign policy. The Foreign Office feared that if tariffs were imposed unwisely they would serve as a battering ram with the potential to stir up economic warfare. So many dangers seemed to lie ahead that, even in 1931, a sense of foreboding was developing over the future of European civilization itself.

Many in the government were persuaded that tariffs were still needed even though Britain had left the gold standard. They believed that the exchange rate was not capable of achieving external balance and that a large depreciation would undermine confidence in the economy, reduce the value of Britain's external assets and result in inflation.[48] For imperial protectionists, naturally, Britain was moving in the right direction. Leo Amery admitted that there was a tendency to forget that duties were on top of exchange depreciation. But he argued that any 'protective' value gained by depreciation applied to just the gold standard countries and then only so far as those countries had not taken special countermeasures. Amery cited the example of the deflationary measures taken under the German emergency decree of December 1931: the effect was sufficient, supposedly, to neutralize any advantage afforded by the fall of sterling.[49]

In April 1932 the IDAC made its first recommendation. In practice, a 20 per cent tariff was imposed on most manufactured imports. For British exports the fall in the pound helped, at the very least, to ward off the additional shrinkage which would have accrued in 1932. Exports to some countries actually began to revive and Britain's share of world exports increased. By December 1931 sterling's rate had fallen from $4.86 to $3.25; this represented a substantial 40 per cent appreciation for those countries which had not immediately followed sterling.[50] With price falls in raw materials and foodstuffs, devaluation led to an improvement rather than a deterioration in the terms of trade. In competition with the sterling bloc the 10 per cent devaluation of the Reichsmark could not achieve much. Germany rapidly lost her export capacity and her favourable balance dwindled in 1932 to a third of its 1931 magnitude.[51] German exports continued to fall until 1934 when they stood at just half of their 1929 volume; for the UK the comparable figure was 70 per cent.[52]

TABLE 1: INDEX OF BRITISH AND GERMAN PRICES, 1931/32
(third quarter 1931 = 100)

		1 UK wholesale index in gold	2 German wholesale index in gold	3 1 as % of 2	4 UK exports (finished goods) in gold	5 German exports (finished goods) in gold	6 4 as % of 5
1931	I	109.4	103.9	105.3	110.2	107.2	102.8
	II	107.5	102.8	104.6	107.1	104.0	103.0
	III	100.0	100.0	100.0	100.0	100.0	100.0
	IV	78.5	98.2	79.9	75.4	96.3	78.3
1932	I	75.0	93.9	79.9	70.3	94.8	74.2
	II	74.8	93.6	78.9	74.3	92.7	80.2
	III	69.8	87.3	79.9	68.6	87.8	78.1
	IV	66.0	82.6	79.9	65.1	90.6	71.9

Source: Ellis, *Exchange Control*, p. 180.

Defining the status of the international Standstill Agreement

In 1931 British banks had Rm922m short-term money in Germany. The dangerous level of capital withdrawal from Germany was obviously a matter of grave concern to bankers worried about the security of their loans.[53] For many years the City had financed drawers of good standing around the world by means of non-documentary credits.[54] About half of the acceptances advanced in the 1920s were finance bills which did not arise from transactions in goods but were used to extend credit to Germany – particularly the banks – and other central and eastern European countries. This proportion was probably even greater for American banks, many of whom had probably set up in this kind of business only after 1918. The German banks reloaned the money to domestic industry and the municipalities on long-term account. While the development of German industry promoted the growth of exports, some of the loans were used for the improvement of public amenities and even for speculation. If British banks were less exacting in their credit standards, it would seem that they were also less liquid than they had been. On the basis of bank data from 1927, the Macmillan Committee offered a reason for the frozen position of the London market: banks had departed from the pre-1914 ratio of a rough balance of short-term assets to short-term liabilities and, in 1931, the latter were several times the former.

The acceptance houses in particular greatly increased the ratio of revolving acceptances to capital. They were also especially involved in Germany: in the 1920s they took up short-term loans in Paris and New York at 2 or 3 per cent and lent long-term to Germany at rates as high as 8 per cent.[55] At the time, the security on offer seemed to be sufficient. The problems emerged when the German banking system itself was caught up in the financial crisis. Thus British banks faced criticism from the political left for profiteering and from the right for being overextended in Germany. So strong was the attraction of profits that warnings by the German government and the Reichsbank over the volume of credit were ignored. It was even suggested that this attitude helped to cause the crisis itself. Since the run on sterling followed hard upon the heels of the German bankruptcies, it looked as if continental holders of sterling claims had been motivated by knowledge of how exposed the City was by its commitments in Berlin. Yet, as Professor Gregory commented soon afterwards, it was questionable whether depriving Germany of the aid of foreign capital would have improved the European situation; those who condemned the banks for lending to Germany would have been the first to condemn them if no or little lending had taken place.[56]

This aspect of German indebtedness led the Bank of England and its Governor into a course of unprecedented action which stretched past the beginning of the Second World War. The Bank was already involved in the Austrian crisis. Sir Robert Kindersley, Lazards' chairman and a director of the Bank of England, negotiated a debt standstill between the Credit-Anstalt and its foreign creditors.[57] Montagu Norman now felt compelled, albeit reluctantly, to prevent what he took to be the imminent breakdown of Germany's international trading system and the consequent disastrous blow to the chances of world economic recovery. It was this continuing broad concern, rather than a conventional interest in factors affecting City firms, which determined the Bank's involvement. The Bank of England also believed that the lending carried out by London's bankers had been reasonably related to the growth of Germany's foreign trade; if an international collapse could be averted bankers could be left to look after themselves.[58] The view from London was that a large part of the loans which had been made by the US ought never to have been made at all. Above all then, British creditors were considered to have been more prudent than their European or American counterparts – a judgement which returned to haunt the British bankers as events unfolded later in the decade.

Norman stressed the importance of banks' maintaining their credit in Germany; he supposed that attempts to call them in would probably fail anyway and precipitate a worst collapse. But he was not prepared to take direct action. In mid June he told British bankers that he would not take responsibility for the maintenance of German credit.[59] Instead, a committee of clearing banks and acceptance houses agreed upon a policy. Through Norman and Harrison (the Governor of the Federal Reserve Bank of New York), the New York bankers were approached and adopted an identical policy.[60] As the Darmstädter und Nationalbank closed its doors, Norman told the committee on 15 July that renewal bills would not be eligible for rediscount at the Bank of England and that he was not prepared to make advances to houses to carry frozen positions arising out of the difficulties which then obtained.[61] The bankers then sought, at the London conference, to extract a guarantee of German foreign credit from either the German government or industry. Their demands were, however, too ambitious.[62]

When Norman met the committee again, on 25 July, he passed on a request from the Treasury for co-operation in carrying into effect the proposals of the London Conference. These were that the volume of credit already extended to Germany should be retained there and that a special committee should investigate German credit requirements and negotiate with the debtors. However, the major consequence of the conference was, in fact, the renewal of the central bank credit. This ensured that there was no German credit collapse and was the essential prerequisite for achieving the bankers' co-operation.

For when the London bankers asked Norman whether any guarantee would be forthcoming from the British government they were told that this was out of the question, especially as it would have been entirely contrary to the attitude adopted by the government at the conference.[63] Similarly, at a meeting of the American bankers in New York, Harrison emphasized that to connect the duration of the private standstill to the duration of the central bank credit to the Reichsbank was illogical and unjustified. Some of the private bankers held that it would be impossible for them to maintain their loans if the central bank credit were withdrawn. Harrison declared that he had no sympathy whatever with that position and would give no assurances about the extension of the credit at maturity.[64]

Lord Brand (the Lazards' partner) recalled that, when he was in Berlin in August 1931, he telephoned Kindersley to urge him to persuade the British and New York bankers to enter into a self-denying ordinance not to withdraw their credits.[65] The bankers agreed and helped, thereby, to ensure that German banks did not close their doors. Eventually, on 19 September this commitment was formalized when representatives from each of the ten creditor nations signed the Standstill Agreement; it was designed to run for six months. Existing credits were frozen on their original terms but service was guaranteed. Although estimates of the figures vary widely, one authority suggested that the agreement covered between one-third and one-half of Germany's aggregate, short-term debt.[66] Although Germany wanted the credit lines frozen at their level on 13

July, the end of the month was taken as the operative date. This meant that the credit lines were significantly reduced to approximately £300 million. Of this total amount, London institutions had extended some £65 million, comprising £46 million to German banks and about £19 million to German commerce and industry.[67]

Naturally creditors hoped that by treating Germany favourably – both economically and politically – they could ensure that they would not lose too much. But, as James points out, the agreement could operate only if creditors were persuaded that the Reichsbank was prepared to prevent *Devisen* (foreign exchange) from fleeing Germany or being allocated illegitimately for long-term debt reduction.[68] The agreement specified that there was to be no discrimination between the creditors and that the German debtors were to provide the creditors with bills eligible for acceptance. If creditors were not satisfied as to eligibility, the obligation was to be carried as a cash advance. This was to try to ensure that the debts would be represented, as far as possible, by readily marketable bills. Provision was also made for a reduction in the total credit lines: the Golddiskontbank could be required to take over 10 per cent of the acceptance credits.[69]

Although the Governor of the Bank of England was emphatic in rejecting any possibility of a governmental guarantee, Clay maintains that he did promise that if the position of the acceptance houses (or the clearing banks which gave them credits) came into such jeopardy that it constituted a national crisis, he would take it up with the government.[70] This could explain why, throughout the 1930s, the bankers were never slow in issuing warnings that such a crisis was imminent. Norman was not, however, prepared to define conditions for an extension of the Standstill and doubted whether Britain could afford to extend it all.[71]

Sir Frederick Leith-Ross believed that it would be hard to exaggerate the vital importance to Britain of securing the restoration of Germany's credit before the termination of the Standstill. This was in the interests not just of the City but of the whole commerce of the country. Leith-Ross admitted privately that it was also a direct interest of the government: British bankers would certainly argue that they entered the Standstill only at the request of the authorities and would therefore expect the government to secure them against any losses which arose as a result. Leith-Ross did not accept this argument unreservedly. But he saw what an extremely awkward matter it would be for the government if commercial obligations, which should have been naturally self-liquidating, could not be met because of the demands made on Germany by her reparations creditors. At the same time, he recalled how, under the Young Plan and the Hague Agreement, the Versailles Treaty provisions which made reparations a first charge on German assets had been definitely abrogated.[72]

These predictions were quite accurate. When Leith-Ross met the bankers in November it emerged that they did indeed expect the government to secure suspension of reparations until German commercial credit was completely restored. But Leith-Ross was intransigent: he told the bankers that the government had only proposed the Standstill scheme for consideration and that if the bankers had had a better idea it was up to them to have put it forward.[73] Philip Snowden, Lord Privy Seal in MacDonald's second National Government, was disturbed at this position. He, at least, felt himself to be under a moral obligation to the bankers: he thought they had been given a tacit assurance that there would be a *pari-passu* settlement of the reparations issue.[74] These differences in interpreting the circumstances which gave rise to the Standstill left the status of the agreement ill-defined and a matter of controversy for the rest of the decade.

As soon as the Standstill Agreement was signed the creditors started to fret over the question of renewal. Next to no progress was being made at governmental level in finding a solution to the reparations problem before the end of the Hoover Moratorium. Consequently, for the benefit of the Treasury and ultimately the British Cabinet, the newly-formed Joint Committee analysed the issues surrounding the Standstill.

They reminded the authorities that the City had for many decades financed German trade to a large extent by means of acceptances. Before the First World War this was done partly by the acceptances of the big German banks with their active branches in London. Subsequently it had been carried out by the joint stock banks and the acceptance houses. There were no figures available to show whether the amount of sterling acceptances for German account were larger after the First World War than before. It was certain that before the war they were considerable. Like Montagu Norman, bankers did not regard the amount of acceptance credits covered by the Standstill as excessive for London to have granted an important country such as Germany with her vast international trade. The business had operated for many years on a large scale with safety; credits were granted partly to the strongest banking institutions and partly to the best commercial firms with whom London had had business connections over a long period. Apart from affirming the quality of their loans, the bankers were also keen to deny that London institutions, in doing nothing more than to transact their normal business with Germany – essential for the smooth working of British and world commerce – had made exceptional profits.

British bankers were aware that additional loans had been made to fill the vacuum of working capital in Germany since 1918, but they had little idea how large the figure was. Such circumstances had produced a situation in the London market which the bankers thought was, quite simply, 'unprecedented in times of peace'. With the exception of the outbreak of war in 1914, unparalleled developments in the outside world threatened for the first and only time to cause serious difficulties. London's bankers believed that they had faithfully fulfilled their undertaking, but that the risks they were running in agreeing to maintain credits had become more fully apparent. It had become public knowledge that out of the total short-term indebtedness of Germany there was a very large sum not covered by the Standstill Agreement; the debts due to London bankers and acceptance houses represented a small fraction of that total. The committee was worried, therefore, that other creditors had received preferential treatment.

What the bankers feared most, however, was that they would be sacrificed to political exigencies if the British government allowed the reparations issue to imperil economic conditions. Commercial claims would then be subordinated to political debts and private creditors would continue by all means possible to withdraw their money from Germany and refuse to give any fresh credit. The committee predicted that the results would be disastrous in world terms and fatal to any hope of further reparations payments. The bankers called on the government to be prepared to stand behind its nationals if political difficulties made it necessary to extend the Standstill.[75] One version of the bankers' memorandum even asserted that foreign creditors proposed not to renew the Standstill unless, in the words of the Wiggin-Layton committee, 'the international payments to be made by Germany will not be such as to imperil the maintenance of her financial stability'. A further stipulation was that the German government would have to arrange some satisfactory scheme for postponing the payment of foreign short-term debts from German debtors outside the Standstill.[76]

Negotiations for the renewal of the agreement laboured therefore under the dual problem of reparations and Germany's other debts. This was an opportunity which the German government quickly tried to exploit, declaring that it would be impossible to pay short-term debts at the expiry of the Standstill given the new higher estimates (Rm28-29 billion) of total foreign indebtedness.[77] The obvious corollary was that reparations, too, could not be resumed.

Relations between the ten creditor countries themselves were far from harmonious, although many difficulties were successfully tackled by an arbitration committee set up by the BIS. British banks wished to limit the renewal arrangements to the safeguarding of bank credit. For while they had lent money direct to German industry, it was not so much as the French and especially the Swiss and the Dutch had. The American creditors were irritated because they thought the British had made excessive profits.[78] Americans felt that their interest rates had been just and reasonable and that the costs to German credit-takers had been less than for similar credits granted by other countries.[79] Because of the fall in sterling, which was widely expected to be only temporary, German debtors had attempted to take advantage of what looked like a unique opportunity to repay sterling debts. Indeed, whether the Standstill had laid the basis for a dismantling of German exchange control cannot be known: Britain had left the gold standard a few days after the agreement was signed, the Reichsbank lost Rm66m in *Devisen* in the following week and exchange control was tightened.[80]

Brand became a member of the British Joint Committee and one of the British nominees on the Joint Committee of Representatives of Foreign Bankers' Committee (of Germany). On one of his frequent visits to Berlin he wrote to Sir John Simon, the Foreign Secretary, on the prolongation of the Standstill. Brand repeated that the bankers needed to be satisfied that creditors outside the Standstill were not going to be repaid. He thought that he had grasped a simple truth – which all short-term creditors would be able to see if gradually educated – that a liquidation policy, or attempts to get debts repaid in cash, would be fatal. Instead, Brand believed that the best chance was to strengthen Germany and the Reichsbank so that most creditors would voluntarily leave their money there. The problem was that in the meantime the position was likely to get much worse and it was difficult for any idea to oust the paramount and familiar one in the minds of creditors of squeezing the lemon as hard as possible. Brand also thought that the risks involved would make it impossible to have a long agreement. The great danger for London was that, while Germany would be unable to find the exchange to pay the Standstill credits, German traders would make less and less use of them for various reasons such as the shrinkage of trade and the desire to avoid exchange risks.[81] Although Brand feared a Standstill which was no more than a shell, with Germans owing money but not producing the bills to make London's machinery work, the problems which lay ahead were to be of entirely different stamp.

Brand and his fellow financiers had reason enough to appear desperate to take initiatives in the crisis: they feared great losses and, in some cases, faced the prospect of seeing their businesses and even their own fortunes wiped out. Lazards was virtually bankrupted by its exposure in Germany. It was for this reason, and perhaps because Kindersley faced personal ruin, that Montagu Norman made an exception: the firm received £3m in support from the Bank of England.[82] A presidential address given by Sir Arthur Maxwell to the Institute of Bankers in November 1931 is indicative of the state of morale in the City. Maxwell asserted that members had nothing to be ashamed of in respect of the German loans. He wanted it to be recognized that, whatever faults his audience possessed, at least Britain had not been made to face the alarming series of bank failures which had occurred in many other important countries.[83]

Apart from Lazards, a further six City houses were most severely affected by the Standstill and left technically insolvent. Kleinworts was one of them. The company's acceptance business was especially hard hit: it fell from an average of £16.2m in 1929–31 to £12.1m by the end of 1931 and reached a low of £8.9m in 1933. The company's acceptances involved in the Standstill represented roughly one-tenth of the amount owed to the London banks generally. At the end of July 1931 Kleinworts had £5.8m outstanding on account of German companies. They also had a further £3.5m outstanding in advances and deposits in Germany and a further £2.7m in municipal loans. Kleinworts' lending-to-capital ratio was also a problem: it seems that it was higher than that of other houses and therefore Kleinworts looked more vulnerable. Certainly, the sum of £12m owed by defaulting debtors in 1931 was nearly four times that of the capital of the partners. The company was forced to take up an overdraft facility of £3.5m granted by the Westminster Bank. The terms were onerous: £2.5m of the total was secured against the private assets of the partners. Although the Bank of England recognized that Kleinworts was alone in having to take exceptional facilities, Norman could not be persuaded to underwrite the arrangement, however much this upset the partners.[84]

Also on the list of acceptance houses facing insolvency was J. Henry Schroder. Just as Chase was the most heavily committed bank in America, so Schroders was in Britain. Thus like Wiggin (Chase Bank), F.C. Tiarks, the Schroders' partner, was obliged to be friendly to Germany.[85] He was also a director of the Bank of England and could keep Montagu Norman informed of developments direct.[86] Tiarks took a leading role in securing the first Standstill and, in association with Brand, he continued to occupy a particularly influential position in the arrangements. Indeed, appointed chairman of the Foreign Bankers' Committee, Tiarks became foremost among the international bankers involved in the Standstill.

In comparison, the commitments of the Midland Bank, the largest clearing bank, appear light. Under the original Standstill the Midland's total commitments as creditors of German banks amounted to just over £3.5m (some £1.5m to Deutsche Bank and £880,000 to Dresdner Bank). Outside the Standstill commitments to German banks amounted to £615,000. By 1938 total Standstill credits to German banks stood at £2.7m and, in response to a Bank of England circular, the Midland returned a figure of £480,000 for its credits to Germany outside the Standstill.[87]

In December 1931 Brand and Tiarks met Flandin, the French Finance Minister, in Paris. A scheme was being taken to Berlin although it was assumed that creditors and debtors would sign nothing until the outcome of the reparations was known. The foreign bank creditors wanted to tell the German government that the Standstill would continue only if the reparations issue was settled. But the French would not agree to this, nor, because of war debts, would the Americans.[88] Nevertheless, on 22 January 1932 the Standstill was renewed; formally known as the German Credit Agreement of 1932 it was designed to run for a year from the end of February.

There was general surprise that all the foreign creditors actually sank their differences, especially as neither of the two most important conditions had been secured: it proved impossible to include the short-term debts of the German *Länder* and municipalities and the reparations conference was postponed until the end of the Hoover Year. But there was an important addition to the agreement – that of clause 10. This 'Swiss clause' (so-called after its proposers) allowed creditors to utilize a maximum of 50 per cent of their advances for purchases of German securities (capital participation). These would, however, remain blocked for five years; this was the origin of one category in the system of 'blocked' marks created by German exchange control. The agreement also provided for a reduction of principal sums by 10 per cent and debtors secured a promise that interest rates would be reduced to some conformity with rates in creditor countries. However, total Reichsmark credits had already been reduced by 20 per cent through repayments and sterling depreciation.[89] The Standstill committee reported that the debts covered by the agreement represented funds which were used for business purposes and used, on the whole, soundly. The acute financial crisis in Germany was blamed on recent excessive withdrawals of capital caused by a lack of confidence which, it was felt, was not justified by the economic and budgetary situation of the country.[90]

The Standstill creditors, ignoring the advice of the central banks, also inserted a provision which gave them the right to terminate the agreement if the Reichsbank was called upon to repay the central bank credit in whole or in part. Luther, President of the Reichsbank, also took the position that any repayment would be difficult. In the light of this, the stance taken by Paris worried London and New York. The Bank of France indicated that, if its statutes were not to be contravened, France's participation in any renewal of the credit depended upon some provision for amortization. Montagu Norman, ever fearful of a German moratorium, resolved to reach a compromise at Basle with Luther and Moret, Governor of the Bank of France.[91] Chamberlain found the French 'very tiresome'; he believed that the bankers would continue to renew the Standstill only if the French decided to be more reasonable.[92] Leith-Ross displayed an even greater condescension. He criticized the Bank of France for behaving in the manner of a pawnbroker. To Leith-Ross this was an absurd attitude which seemed to arise from a parochial conception of banking policy rather than out of a desire to press Germany over reparations.[93]

The British government realized that all the creditors would have liked to get out of the Standstill if they could, but thought that it was typical that only the French and the American ones appeared to be doing so. The French had made desperate efforts to extract their money from Germany; the Banque de Paris was said to have got back 40 per cent of its money in the course of the first Standstill year.[94] The liquidation of the Standstill gathered pace as more and more methods of payment behind it were found. Indeed, the assumption that the Americans would otherwise try to recall all their credits seemed to be all that was keeping the agreement going.[95]

It was difficult to find an acceptable rate of interest to charge German debtors. The London committee tried to persuade the City's banks and acceptance houses to reduce the rates. But several banks considered that the minimum 5 per cent on German short-term credit was too low: 6 per cent was proposed – 2 per cent above bank rate.[96] At the same time, the City was incensed at the Reichsbank's attempts to force a reduction by refusing transfer facilities for interest on loans running at rates above 7 per cent.[97] Yet the fear of a moratorium made international investors, as well as central bank governors, especially nervous. The creditors cut the rate to 6 per cent for bank loans and to 7 per cent for non-bank loans; in July, the rates were further reduced to 5 and 6 per cent, respectively.[98]

At the Standstill conference held in London on 1 July 1932 the creditors agreed that the prerequisite for the termination of the agreement was the freeing of the German exchange; this, in turn, depended on the decisions which were just then being taken at Lausanne. When the time was ripe an attempt would be made to reduce the amount of financing by releasing in succession large blocks of credits. More than half of the total outstanding credit granted by Britain was thought to be recoverable (even in the event of a financial collapse by Germany), although it was not clear how this was to be done. Paradoxically, London credits granted to Germany would probably have increased in the event of the abolition of the Standstill, for even in 1932 some fresh credits had been arranged.[99]

The loans to municipalities and *Länder* became the subject of their own Standstill in April 1932 – the German Public Debtors'

Credit Agreement. Like the main Standstill, it was made for one year and was to be renewed annually; it also provided for a 10 per cent reduction in the principal sum. Kleinworts were the main participant. In late 1931 a representative of the bank confided to the Foreign Office that British firms had been 'let in' over municipal short-term loans; no one had realized how heavily the German towns were borrowing or that such short-term loans were going to be used for long-term purposes. It was unusual for a firm to ask a municipality what it intended to do with the money when borrowing for three months, presumably because the town had sufficiently good credit. The Foreign Office was amazed at this avowal of how business was done; so feeble did it sound to them that they thought the French were justified in saying that the English financial houses had only themselves to blame for being in such a mess.[100]

In the course of 1932 attention began to focus on how the Standstill in conjunction with German exchange control affected Anglo-German trade. Credit lines open under the Standstill were supposed to be utilized in the usual fashion. The German importer asked a German bank into which he had paid the necessary funds and which had an open reimbursement account with a British bank, to draw on the latter. Once the bill had been accepted by the British bank it was discountable anywhere and the British exporter could thus obtain payment immediately. But the embargo placed by the Brüning government on payments abroad had begun to affect international trade. The embargo was not quite complete – German manufacturers were allowed in 1932 to buy foreign currency to a small extent of the value of goods imported in 1930–31. Nevertheless, selling British goods became almost impossible and German importers were compelled to turn to domestic substitutes, even if inferior. The British export trade to Germany was badly damaged.[101]

The German authorities contended that the Reichsmark balances blocked under the Emergency Decrees – Sperr marks – could not be used to pay for normal exports, existing trade debts or British governmental payments, for this would be to deprive the Reichsbank of foreign exchange.[102] Instead, the balances could be used solely for the payment of so-called additional exports (*Zusätzliche Exports*) from Germany. Broadly defined, these were goods which could not normally find an export market – prices were set as low as possible but the equivalent goods produced outside Germany were still cheaper. British goods would then, of course, have met with increased competition from German ones.

As far as Standstill funds were concerned, the German banking committee pointed out that these too could be used in Germany only for long-term investment, as under clause 10, or to facilitate additional exports. The use of Standstill monies to settle German claims would negate the essential purpose of the agreement which was to protect the foreign exchange situation of Germany.[103] Indeed, the great difficulty in transferring or exchanging Standstill money proved clearly that the Standstill had become an institution by which the Reichsbank protected the foreign deposits of the German banks.

In the months before the collapse of the Weimar Republic exporting became more and more difficult for Germany; trade barriers, the fall in the price of commodities and the stabilization of the mark at dollar prices were all contributory factors. Most significantly, the depreciation of sterling was a particularly harsh blow for the exporter trying to conduct business with Britain in the normal way. The German Economics Ministry (RWM) gave permission, therefore, for exporters to use Sperr marks, obtained at a considerable discount of 20–24 per cent, in part payment for exports. Similarly employed were liquidated, foreign-held, German securities or German bonds in dollars or sterling. They commanded much higher prices inside Germany than abroad, and the German exporter used the difference to cover his loss in respect of sales, mainly to Britain.[104]

There was some sympathy for the German position. British bankers were not unhappy with this 'natural' development of finding buyers of frozen accounts and the continuous efforts in exploiting new methods of using such accounts. By such means, the international trade of Germany was assisted. The only real criticism was reserved for the burden created by German officialdom. Francis Rodd, at the Bank of England, agreed that it was difficult to rail at principles which were fundamental to the Standstill. The problem was aggravated by the diversity of interests involved; commercial creditors could not make their voice heard in Germany. Rodd thought that the bankers would be happy to co-operate, but the machinery did not exist. He confirmed that the liquidation of blocked accounts was taking place – on a very considerable scale – where it served German interests. There was thus a very large market in blocked marks as bankers liquidated, although they did so at a discount. Many transactions were carried out through Zurich at a 22 per cent discount, while Americans were liquidating at 30 per cent, a rate unacceptable for London.[105]

The Board of Trade, however, was not so happy. German policy implied that British holders of blocked balances were to be forced to pay their German debts in sterling, although they were not parties to the Standstill. The Board always took the general line on exchange that British traders should not be placed in a position less favourable than those of any other country and it saw no reason why it should refrain from doing so in this case. A contrasting approach, put forward by the Berlin Embassy, was to explore whether the German authorities could be persuaded to relax exchange restrictions. The Foreign Office supported the proposition that British commercial interests needed help. Some attempt had to be made, independently of bankers, to secure the release of frozen balances held by traders.[106] Yet Britain was in no position to employ either bribery or force. To make matters worse, negotiations for the relief of commercial interests risked running counter to negotiations between the Standstill creditors and the German Foreign Debts Committee.

Reparations and the British economy

Tariffs and a managed currency were the instruments grasped by Britain in an attempt to salvage economic and financial interests from an international order which was breaking down. There was no time to consider how the new politics of economic nationalism might affect developments in the wider world, apart from the British Empire. Besides, by common consent, the issue which far exceeded all others in bedevilling international relations and in undermining the political stability of Europe was war debts and reparations. Without a long-term settlement of these international payments recovery from the world depression could not begin. And, with every passing month of the turbulent Hoover Year, the need to find a solution to the problem became more and more pressing. For Britain, distracted by the need to redefine the national interest, the impact of reparations on the domestic economy also attracted particular attention.

Not least among the many factors weighing against reparations was the marked impact they seemed to have on the UK's balance of payments. Hubert Henderson, the economist, tried to demonstrate how the payment of reparations by Germany was likely to be specially damaging to British industry. Both countries were largely specialized in similar activities and, as Germany could make the payments only by achieving an export surplus, she had to check imports and stimulate exports. In the course of the year before Britain left the gold standard, German exports (11.8 per cent of total world trade) exceeded British exports (10.1 per cent) for the first time.[107] Henderson did not see the need to seek alternative explanations for this trend; like many others he was already convinced that reparations harmed the cause of British exporting and crippled British trade with Germany – a customer of particular importance.

But there were, of course, two sides to the debate. It was said by some that a revival of German industrial competition would endanger Europe, just as in the years leading up to 1914. The French government certainly played on these fears as justification for not ending reparations and accused Britain of adopting Germany's thesis that she was not in a position to pay anything. Sir Roland Nugent, director of the Federation of British Industries (FBI), revealed that his organization strongly objected to complete cancellation.[108] Francis Rodd calculated that reparations payments had not stimulated German exports as much as Henderson maintained; as for imports, he reckoned that the steady fall in world prices had pushed down the value of the trade but that the volume had not declined to the same extent. Rodd was sympathetic, therefore, to the thesis that, once relieved of reparations, Germany would be in a position to capture the world's markets because of her highly rationalized plant and unrivalled productive and marketing organizations. This potential to compete successfully remained so impressive that it seemed to counter the assertion that, on purely economic grounds, Germany would never be able to pay anything.[109]

The Treasury, however, emphatically disagreed with this forecast for three reasons. First, it was useless to suppose that a great nation such as Germany could be held down permanently by the imposition of a foreign tribute. Second, Germany's disorganized economy and necessary dependence on foreign capital would be adequate safeguards against industrial supremacy. Third, at the moment when Britain was abandoning free trade she could afford to look with 'more complacency' upon the dangers of foreign competition.[110] For the Treasury to suggest complacency seems extraordinary; it pointed to the growing doubts over the changes in British external policy. Like Henderson, the Treasury was convinced that the real danger to the British economy arose from the way reparations had forced Germany to dump goods. The crisis had also forced Germany to reduce, by more than half, her imports of British goods. An expanding Germany might be expected, then, to benefit British industry more than threaten it.[111]

Bankers also believed that Germany would be able to pay reparations at some future date. Yet they reasoned that international confidence would be restored only when creditor governments renounced entirely all such hypothetical claims on the future. Of all the charges raised against reparations this was the most serious; by preventing the re-establishment of German credit they inflicted serious damage on Britain's financial sector. Germany's commercial creditors, with the City of London in the lead, looked to the authorities for reassurance that political obligations would not prevent Germany from honouring commercial debts. The markets, supported by the Bank of England, wanted a definite clearance: cancelling reparations would produce a natural inflow of foreign credits while mere postponement would be a signal to withdraw money from Germany in the meantime.[112]

Whatever other talents bankers possessed they could not reasonably claim to have special powers of insight. As one official wryly observed, they were neither politicians nor psychologists. The case made by the bankers was persuasive because the crisis seemed so serious. Creditor governments were facing Germany's willingness to default over reparations and were hardly strong enough to make good their claims. Accordingly, Britain would have to take risks in order to avoid being dragged down in the predicted universal collapse. One of those risks was the possibility of having to resume the struggle with Germany for world markets.[113]

But the very thought of facing German trade competition in the future seemed quite risible. As economic conditions in the Weimar Republic deteriorated, anxious British observers described the situation as irremediable and suggested that the cancellation of reparations would not be enough to restart the machine.[114] Germany's ability to continue unimpaired her service of foreign debt looked increasingly doubtful. With the new British tariff set to accelerate the decline in the Republic's export surplus, the City of London began to wonder whether even interest payments could be maintained.[115]

Brüning's economic policies foreshadowed those which were to be employed, albeit more systematically, by the Nazis. Autarky was rejected in theory, yet many of the individual measures taken were scarcely reconcilable with any other idea. The intention was to prevent the withdrawal of further foreign capital, to remain on gold and to pay debt interest. Attempts were made to reduce payments abroad by cutting down on imports. A default on foreign debt, however, would have cut an important thread connecting Germany with the outside world. Britain feared that it might open the door to the full regulation of trade and a degree of state control scarcely compatible with international capitalism.[116]

In seeking to have intergovernmental payments cancelled or reduced to a minimum, Britain followed the lead taken by the Special Committee of the Young Plan.[117] Some of these experts warned towards the end of 1931 that prompt measures had to be taken in order to avoid the declaration of a moratorium by Germany. Apart from the restoration of confidence which would allow credit to be left in Germany, the balance of payments had to be freed from the transfer of all reparations for several years.[118] Ramsay MacDonald wanted a conference to be held straight away.[119] Under the Young Plan the onus was on Germany to prove that she could not pay; the objective now was to have the onus placed on the creditor powers to prove that she could. On that basis, a compromise with the French government was envisaged: the Hoover Moratorium would be extended by at least three years as a first step towards general cancellation.[120]

France, on the other hand, was most unwilling to follow Britain along this path to a solution. There was, first and foremost, a general resistance to any idea of revising existing obligations. Moreover, as Robert Boyce has shown, the French viewed the Hoover Moratorium and demands for the cancellation of reparations as desperate attempts by the Anglo-Saxon powers to save their own over-exposed commercial banking systems at the expense of placing France's financial stability in jeopardy.[121]

Britain was more than able to repay the compliment: in London, French manoeuvring was held to be outrageous. France benefitted most from reparations and had comparatively few commercial credits in Germany; difficulties in reaching a settlement could be blamed, therefore, on Gallic self-interested obstructionism.[122] France was suspected of manipulating capital flows between financial centres in order to try to create the conditions for her own solution to the German question. The Treasury thought that the French recognized that reparations were dead but did not dare say so.[123] Neville Chamberlain could see that the rise of National Socialism posed great dangers. But he believed that the means to avert them lay in the hands of the unpredictable French: to insist on reparations before commercial credits was 'an extraordinary failure of that logic which is supposed to be their special characteristic',[124] for this kept British financial resources frozen and threatened the stability of the pound which the French were anxious to restore. Chamberlain thought it was absurd to keep the whole of Europe in a state of nervous anxiety, thereby precipitating the rise of Hitler, while making it impossible for Germany to pay any reparations.

Keynes remained passionately committed to the cause of abolition and he, too, held France responsible for the way in which Germany's short-term creditors had fallen into a panic. He endorsed the idea that Germany's future capacity to pay anything to anyone was largely dependent on restoring her credit.[125] He was in close contact with Ramsay MacDonald and, in the pages of the *New Statesman*, in January 1932, came down in favour of the government's policy.[126] As a result, Keynes was said to be hated in France.[127]

The government's perception was that all sections of British public opinion agreed that the existence of international political debts, and the consequent heaping up of gold in France and the United States, had played a considerable part in aggravating the economic crisis. There was no reason, therefore, why Britain should go out of its way to impoverish Germany in order to increase the creditor balances of France and America.[128] These two countries were accused of 'sterilising' gold: instead of allowing for world demand to be stimulated they had brought about widespread deflation by seeking, perversely, to hold down the money supply in their domestic economies.[129] The world crisis heightened Britain's desire to strengthen her own channels of international finance and trade by finding a solution to the reparations problem. This coincided, of course, with German interests. As such, it may be seen as an attempt to prevent French economic hegemony in Germany which brought Britain into competitive conflict with the United States.[130]

In fact, Britain found working with the Americans no less a strain than dealing with the French. While the US administration was thought to be sympathetic, Congress had set its face against debt revision. Consequently, it was assumed in London that some kind of leverage would be required to break the log jam, even though the suspension of 'tribute' was something entirely justifiable.[131] The aim was to pay to America only what was recovered from Germany and Allied debtors. But if receipts from Germany were technically just postponed rather than cancelled the British government did not see how it would be possible to ask Washington for anything more than a temporary suspension of British war debt.[132]

The modesty of the British government's proposals greatly disquieted Montagu Norman. He declared that anything less than a five-year suspension would produce a complete jam over Standstill bills and place the Bank of England in an impossible position. There was no doubt that Norman reflected the view of the market. However, in view of the stance taken by France, the Bank's ideas were quietly dismissed as politically disastrous and financially suicidal.[133]

Indeed, the French government made it clear by the start of 1932 that it would not accept anything beyond a two-year conditional moratorium. On Britain's suggestion the reparations conference was postponed until June. The London market favoured adjournment in the hope that conditions for securing a permanent settlement might be more propitious later in the year.

Yet, to entertain hope on this basis was very dangerous. There was an obvious risk that the Brüning government would be swept away and replaced by a National Socialist combination that would flatly reject any plan or suggestion of payment. The British Ambassador in Berlin warned that the deteriorating political and economic situation could, with justification, be blamed on external factors: trade figures showed the decline in Germany's purchasing power in the world and the progressively restrictive effect of protectionism in other countries.[134] These dangers were understood in London. But in his reply to the Berlin Embassy, Leith-Ross dissembled over the influence of the City authorities: 'You will realize that the attitude of ministers here is necessarily to a large extent influenced by the opinion of the Bank of England as to what the market wants.'[135]

With the postponement of the Lausanne conference until the end of the Hoover Year, the British drive for an early solution ground to a halt. In *The Spoils of War* Bruce Kent argues that there was, in any case, no real effort to resolve the reparations problem in the six months following September 1931 since the Standstill Agreement had taken the edge off Germany's short-term credit crisis.[136] But the diplomatic stalemate exposed Britain's banking interests to further destabilization. The news at the end of January 1932 that the Standstill was going to be renewed, even though a reparations settlement had eluded governments was, therefore, as surprising as it was welcome. Neville Chamberlain put the development down to a widespread belief that, whatever governments might say, the payment of reparations had come to an end.[137] It was self-evident to members of the Cabinet that the twin purposes of a settlement – to improve the economic position of Europe and to reassure the City of London – were mutually reinforcing. In the absence of any settlement, the Standstill was looked to as a possible alternative way of achieving these objectives.[138]

No advance on the diplomatic front could be made in the first half of 1932: America refused to discuss war debts, France refused to discuss cancellation of reparations unless war debts were included, and Germany refused to discuss anything other than cancellation. With elections looming in all three countries, even discussions on a formula for an eventual settlement were rendered nugatory. France believed that a decision should depend upon American action. Britain, on the other hand, took the opposite view but dismissed any idea of acting unilaterally as too dangerous.[139]

The precise way in which Europe was supposed to act in concert to deal with the American debts had to be left, therefore, for the conference itself to consider. This ensured that there would be no clean break at Lausanne: while decisions reached could take effect immediately, they would be provisional and formal ratification would depend upon a settlement with the United States. From Britain's perspective, the advantage in delay was that the seemingly inevitable crisis in transatlantic relations would be deferred for as long as possible.[140] Turning debts into a presidential election issue was thought to be a sure-fire way of stimulating American denunciations of Europe. Consequently, no proposal to end payments to the US would be made until the American elections on 5 November were out of the way.[141] In the meantime, the British government omitted from its budget for the fiscal year 1932–33 all provision for both payments to America and receipts from reparations. The Chancellor's public explanation for this was that these two items were self-balancing and that their amounts were uncertain in the light of future events.[142]

On 30 May Brüning, the German Chancellor, was forced from office. Ramsay MacDonald, disturbed by the news, wanted Britain to lead in Europe and to start at Lausanne. MacDonald thought that it would be simply ridiculous and futile to keep the world waiting on the outcome of the discussions which were to take place at Ottawa. Instead, a 'big mind' was required to deal with all the economic questions.[143] One major concern which Britain had over the new Weimar government was that Schacht would replace Luther as Reichsbank President and then lead the German delegation at Lausanne. These anxieties were lifted when Luther received the confidence of von Papen, Brüning's successor, and it became obvious that Schacht would not go to Lausanne. Ironically, when Schacht did take up the office some nine months later the succession was welcomed in Britain: at least his brand of nationalism was not as extreme as the full-blown Nazi version.

The Lausanne Conference opened on 16 June 1932. Business in the City of London marked time; everyone assumed that failure at the conference would produce a panic reaction. Although the Standstill Agreements and transfer postponements served to hide future losses, a fresh crop of deliberate and unconcealed defaults would have been extremely destabilizing. Nevertheless, for the first time since the start of the depression an intergovernmental conference had given the City a reason to be expectant and hopeful, even if it was a hope bred of despair.[144]

There is a view that the conference did indeed prove to be a diplomatic triumph for MacDonald and that Britain did much to prepare the ground for international financial reconstruction.[145] Certainly, Lausanne bore fruits of a kind: reparations were effectively annulled with the pretence of a final payment by Germany. The British delegation was able to bring about a compromise on the basis of a plan sketched out earlier in the year. Under the Final Act of 9 July Germany was to transfer bonds to the BIS. An accompanying gentlemen's agreement confirmed that payment would only take place if the act were ratified, and ratification itself was made dependent upon a general settlement of debts.[146] Thus everything remained precariously poised. In these circumstances, British statesmen were greatly relieved to hear that the City, at least, was pleased with the settlement. For as Walter Runciman, one of the British negotiators, privately noted, Lausanne was leaving most of the important issues unresolved. He wondered what would happen in the months ahead, especially if America declined to ratify the agreement.[147]

Runciman's suspicions were well founded. Lausanne turned out to be a terminus rather than a staging post. Although conditions remained dangerously unstable, particularly in the Weimar Republic, the momentum behind the construction of a multilateral settlement was soon lost. The news from Lausanne persuaded President Hoover to issue a despatch to the Disarmament Conference to the effect that it was armaments expenditure, not war debts, which had caused the slump in Europe.[148] As for Britain, preparations for the Ottawa gathering – the next great step in the economic revolution – were a major preoccupation long before the Lausanne Conference had even assembled. However noble MacDonald's aspirations, in the course of 1932 the focus of attention shifted away from Europe and its problems.

The aim of the British government at Ottawa was to lower tariffs. But the Cabinet members who attended the chaotic conference struggled to make themselves heard and the results were again disappointing. In terms of economic development, the Empire had advanced some way since the tariff reform campaign at the turn of the century. The Dominions asserted their individual interests above all else; they believed that their infant industries needed protection, even against the UK, while the latter, in turn, was now concerned to protect her agricultural producers.[149] Eventually, Imperial Preference was established in a series of bilateral agreements in which the UK and the individual Dominions swapped mutual preferences and maintained or erected even higher trade barriers against foreign goods. With Samuel and Snowden now looking to resign from the National Government, Runciman was able to comfort MacDonald that he had at least been spared the cruelty of having to pass through the ordeal of Ottawa. Lausanne had seemed in comparison a much more wholesome and dignified affair.[150] Yet, with the collapse in the structures of world trade, even the City, which had been foremost in opposing an extension to tariffs, was forced to accept Imperial Preference and a modicum of protection.[151]

Britain continued to hold the ambition to try to secure reductions in duties by means of bilateral negotiations with particular countries.[152] Herein was recognition, at least, that tariffs had implications for foreign relations. This was one way to promote the cause of general European stability. But the scope was very limited: opportunities would arise only from negotiations over specific trading interests. Indeed, Ian Drummond, the economic historian, has found no evidence that consideration was given to the possible interactions between Ottawa, Lausanne, and the prospective World Economic Conference.[153] The National Government pretended otherwise. France and the United States had agreed at Lausanne that discussions on stabilization should continue: the League of Nations would be invited to convene a world economic conference. This was sufficient for Runciman to claim, in late 1932, that Britain had a 'Conference policy' which linked all of the international gatherings. Bilateral trade negotiations were, apparently, an essential part of that policy and a start had already been made.[154]

Doubtless, Runciman had in mind a development in the long-running story of British coal exports to Germany. The Lausanne Conference gave the President of the Board of Trade a chance to speak about coal restrictions to Konstantin von Neurath, previously Ambassador in London but now German Foreign Minister. The quota allocated by Germany to British coal imports had declined from 420,000 tons per month in October 1931 to 125,000 tons in April 1932. Britain took the reduction as evidence of trade discrimination. This appeared to contravene not only the 1924 Commercial Treaty but also a secret formal declaration, made at the same time, to the effect that the status quo in British coal exports to Germany would be maintained. Rumbold, the British Ambassador, had made repeated complaints to Brüning. The response was to claim that the British emergency duties and the Import Duties Act had in some cases fallen with special severity on German trade. Sterling's devaluation had, at the same time, allowed British exporters to secure advantages in the German market over domestic producers.[155]

By the end of 1932 Britain and Germany had opened negotiations. Germany no longer felt bound by the secret note in regard to coal because conditions had changed so much since 1924. A large proportion of British duties were still said to be 'specially injurious' and reductions were required. Furthermore, the German government highlighted the effect of the pound's devaluation and newly acquired unpredictability: a drop in the level of sterling had the potential to wipe out any concessions obtained from Britain. Giving voice to supposed grievances was an expected part of the bargaining process. In this case, the charges stood up and the British government knew that its negotiating position was not strong. Yet, as the German authorities were anxious to reach an understanding, the way to a compromise was open. The trade agreement was concluded in 1933 (see Chapter 7). But by then the Weimar Republic was no more.[156]

Indeed, the implications of the economic revolution which had swept the world were only just becoming clear. Many in Britain began to question how wise it had been to implement beggar-my-neighbour policies – especially when Germany was one of the neighbours. With the ideological support for Britain's new external policies resting on shallow foundations, a coherent and confident response to the threat posed by the Third Reich could not be mounted.

NOTES

1. A.R. Holmes and E. Green, *Midland: 150 Years of Banking Business* (Batsford,1986), p. 186.
2. R.G. Hawtrey, *The Art of Central Banking* (Longman, 1932), p. 224.
3. R. Fry, 'The work of a financial journalist', *Manchester Statistical Society Paper* (Manchester, 1945), p. 13.
4. C.H. Feinstein, *National Income, Expenditure and Output of the United Kingdom, 1885–1965* (Cambridge: Cambridge University Press, 1972), T.84: invisible items (balance of payments).
5. For an analysis of interwar bank rescues see G. Jones, *British Multinational Banking, 1830–1990* (Oxford: Clarendon Press, 1993), pp. 239–45.
6. Branson and Heinemann, *Britain in the Nineteen Thirties*, p. 12.
7. Reynolds, *Britannia Overruled*, p. 118.
8. T 188/21, note by Leith-Ross, 8 October 1931.
9. A. Booth, 'The British reaction to the economic crisis', in W.R. Garside (ed.), *Capitalism in Crisis: International responses to the Great Depression* (Pinter, 1993), pp. 41–2.
10. H. Macmillan, *Winds of Change 1914–1939* (Macmillan, 1966), p. 282.
11. For Anglo-German discussions on Austria's problems see H. Brüning, *Memoiren 1918–34* (Stuttgart: Deutsche Verlags-Anstalt, 1970), p. 337; also CAB 24/222, CP157. On the June crisis see S.V.O. Clarke, *Central Bank Co-operation, 1924–31* (New York, NY: Federal Reserve Bank, 1967), pp. 186–9; Kindleberger, *World in Depression*, p. 157; K.E. Born, *Die deutsche Bankenkrise 1931* (München: Piper, 1967).
12. FO 371/15210; see contemporaneous comments by Orme Sargent, head of the Foreign Office's Central Department.
13. *The Times*, 20 August 1931.

14. T 188 23, minute by Hopkins, 22 August 1931.
15. Henderson, *Inter-War Years*, p. 99.
16. Lewis, *Economic Survey*, p. 158; L.B. Yeager, *International Monetary Relations: Theory, History and Policy* (New York, NY: Harper & Row, 1966), p. 335.
17. Kindleberger, *World in Depression*, p. 159; S. Howson, *Domestic Monetary Management in Britain 1919–38* (Cambridge: CUP, 1975), pp. 75–82.
18. D.B. Kunz, *The Battle for Britain's Gold Standard in 1931* (Croom Helm, 1987), pp. 133–4.
19. Ibid., p. 188.
20. R.A. Dayer, *Finance and Empire: Sir Charles Addis, 1861–1945* (Basingstoke: Macmillan, 1988), pp. 223–30.
21. P.L. Cottrell, 'The Bank of England in its international setting, 1918–1972', in R. Roberts and D. Kynaston (eds), *The Bank of England: Money, Power and Influence 1694–1994* (Oxford: Clarendon Press, 1995), pp. 100–3.
22. D.H. Aldcroft, *From Versailles to Wall Street, 1919–1929* (Allen Lane, 1977), p. 186; A. Cairncross and B. Eichengreen, *Sterling in Decline* (Oxford: B.Blackwell, 1983), pp. 27, 102.
23. Cain and Hopkins, *British Imperialism*, p. 75.
24. Skidelsky, *John Maynard Keynes*, pp. 397–9; Williamson, *National Crisis*, p. 470.
25. J.M. Keynes, preface to 'Essays in Persuasion' (1931), in D. Moggridge (ed.), *The Collected Writings of John Maynard Keynes*, Vol.9 (Macmillan/CUP, 1972).
26. Temin, *Lessons from the Great Depression*, p. 108.
27. B. Eichengreen, *Golden Fetters: the Gold Standard and the Great Depression, 1919–1939* (Oxford: OUP, 1992), p. 286.
28. A. Siegfried, *England's Crisis* (London: Jonathan Cape, 1933), preface. The work was first published in 1931.
29. Bank of England Archives (hereafter BoE), OV34/81, 28 September 1931.
30. For an overview see H. James, H. Lindgren and A. Teichova (eds), *The Role of Banks in the Interwar Economy* (Cambridge: CUP, 1991).
31. R. Boyce, 'World depression, world war: some economic origins of the Second World War', in R. Boyce and E.M. Robertson (eds), *Paths to War. New Essays on the Origins of the Second World War* (Basingstoke: Macmillan, 1989), p. 76.
32. Kunz, *The Battle for Britain's Gold Standard*, pp. 148, 159.
33. BoE OV34/81, 6 October 1931.
34. James, *The Reichsbank*, pp. 288–91. See also K. Borchardt, 'Could and should Germany have followed Great Britain in leaving the Gold Standard ?', *JEEH*, 13, 3 (Winter 1984), pp. 447–9. Borchardt concludes that there was no political pressure put on Germany by Britain to follow the latter off gold.
35. Kindleberger, *World in Depression*, p. 163; see also FO 371/15211, Berlin Embassy despatch, 28 September 1931, which suggested that the German people as a whole confused devaluation with inflation. For a detailed study of Brüning's reasoning see, T. Balderston, *The Origins and Course of the German Economic Crisis 1923–1932* (Berlin: Haude & Spener, 1993), pp. 319–25.
36. T 188/23; see also H. Luther, *Vor dem Abgrund 1930–1933: Reichsbankprasident in Kreisenzeiten* (Berlin: Propyläen Verlag, 1964), p. 154; Brüning, *Memoiren*, p. 395,
37. S. Howson and D. Winch, *The Economic Advisory Council 1930–1939* (Cambridge: CUP, 1977), pp. 102–5.

38. Keynes, 'Essays in Persuasion', p. 158.
39. FO 371/15211, Leith-Ross to Rowe-Dutton (Berlin), 28 September, and to Sargent, 30 September 1931.
40. Lord Brand papers, Bodleian Library, Oxford (hereafter Brand papers), File 112, letter to H.D. Henderson, 29 October 1931.
41. Neville Chamberlain papers, University of Birmingham Library (hereafter NC), 8/12/2, Treasury memo, 3 October 1931. Chamberlain replaced Philip Snowden as Chancellor after the election on 27 October. According to Fisher and Hopkins, the Treasury's primary objective was to avoid, and to be seen to be avoiding, inflation. The secondary objective was to establish a provisional policy to build up foreign currency reserves, but to postpone judgement on the question of 'pegging' the pound.
42. The Tripartite Agreement came into being when the cycle of devaluations was complete. The immediate challenge was to prevent a reopening of the cycle and to regulate the dollar–sterling rate. See, for example, R. Nurske, *International Currency Experience* (League of Nations, Geneva, 1944), p. 131.
43. W.N. Medlicott, *Contemporary England 1914–64* (Longman, 1967), p. 269. Goods from the Dominions and colonies were excluded.
44. A.J.P. Taylor, *English History 1914–1945* (Harmondsworth: Penguin, 1975), pp. 403–5; A. Thorpe, *The British General Election of 1931* (Oxford: Clarendon Press, 1991), p. 231.
45. CAB 23/70, 5(32) and 6(32).
46. A. Marrison, *British Business and Protection 1903–1932* (Oxford: Clarendon Press,1996), pp. 421–7.
47. CAB 24/255, CP301, 26 November 1931.
48. M. Kitson and S. Solomou, *Protectionism and Economic Revival: the British Inter-war Economy* (Cambridge: CUP, 1990), p. 3.
49. Parl. Deb.(Commons), 261, col.309, 4 February 1932. See also Amery's criticisms in J. Barnes and D. Nicholson (eds), *The Empire at Bay: The Leo Amery Diaries, 1929–1945* (Hutchinson, 1988), pp. 238–9.
50. Kindleberger, *World in Depression*, p. 162.
51. H.S. Ellis, *Exchange Control in Central Europe* (Cambridge, MA: Harvard University Press, 1941), p. 224.
52. Lewis, *Economic Survey*, p. 92.
53. James, *The Reichsbank*, p. 221.
54. For the following section see W.A. Morton, *British Finance, 1930–1940* (Madison, WI: University of Wisconsin Press, 1943), pp. 30–3, 270.
55. See, for example, Schacht's report of his conversation in 1929 with Baron Schroeder in H. Schacht, *My First Seventy-Six Years* (Wingate, 1955), p. 286.
56. T.E. Gregory, *The Gold Standard and Its Future* (Methuen, 1934), pp. 58–9.
57. D. Stiefel, *Finanzdiplomatie und Weltwirtschaftskrise: Der Krise der Credit-Anstalt für Handel und Gewerbe 1931* (Frankfurt am Main: F. Knapp, 1989), pp. 195–6. The Credit-Anstalt was the largest and by far the most important Austrian bank.
58. Sayers, *Bank of England*, pp. 502–5.
59. James, *The Reichsbank*, p. 221.
60. Clay, *Lord Norman*, p. 381. See also Federal Reserve Bank of New York Archives (hereafter FRBNY), C 261.1, cablegrams, Harrison to Norman, 15 July 1931 and Norman to Harrison, 16 July 1931. Harrison's position did not allow him to play such a central role in the American financial system as that played by Norman in the British system.

61. BoE OV34/129.
62. James, *The Reichsbank*, p. 221.
63. BoE OV34/129.
64. FRBNY C 261.12, minutes of meeting, 24 August 1931 and cablegram, Harrison to MacGarrah (BIS), 21 August 1931.
65. Lord Brand, 'A banker's reflections on some economic trends', *The Economic Journal*, 63, 252 (December 1953), p. 769.
66. Ellis, *Exchange Control*, p. 171.
67. BoE OV34/131 and OV34/149. The total was later thought to have been an overestimate (by up to £10m) although it continued in use.
68. James, *The Reichsbank*, p. 218.
69. The Golddiskontbank was a central banking institution set up in 1924.
70. Clay, *Lord Norman*, p. 381.
71. FO 371/15212, letter by Leith-Ross to Sargent, 31 October 1931. See also T 160/436/12630/02/1.
72. T 188/33; FO 371/15212, letter to Sargent, 3 November 1931.
73. T 188/33, note of meeting, 20 November 1931.
74. T 160/450/13050, letter to Leith-Ross, 29 December 1931.
75. CAB 24/255 (306), memo, by Joint Committee; also, T 160/438/12681/01. See C.R.S. Harris, *Germany's Foreign Indebtedness* (Oxford: OUP, 1935), p. 23 for the reference to a letter Brand wrote to *The Times* in 1935, in which he claimed that the amount of short-term money outstanding to Germany in 1931 was probably considerably smaller than the amount in 1914.
76. BoE OV34/149, memo, 30 November 1931.
77. FO 371/15212, memo, by the German Ambassador, 23 October 1931.
78. James, *The Reichsbank*, pp. 227–8. The 'returns' produced by British banks and acceptance houses show that Britain lent direct to German industry.
79. FRBNY C 261.12, letter from F. Abbot Goodhue (Chairman of American Standstill subcommittee) to E.R. Kenzel (Deputy Governor, FRBNY), 2 December 1931.
80. Ellis, *Exchange Control*, p. 171.
81. FO 371/15935/C31, letter dated 30 December 1931; see also T 160/450/13050.
82. Boyce, *British Capitalism*, p. 344.
83. *The Banker*, 20 (December 1931), p. 215.
84. J. Wake, *Kleinwort Benson: The History of Two Families in Banking* (Oxford: OUP, 1997), pp. 243–4.
85. James, *The Reichsbank*, p. 237. F.C. Tiarks was the son of Henry Friederich Tiarks who became a partner in 'Schroeders' in 1871.
86. Sayers, *Bank of England*, p. 503.
87. Group Archives, HSBC Holdings plc, Midland Bank Archives (hereafter MB), 30/190–1, 'Midland Bank's Commitments as Creditors of German Banks' – position at 31 July 1931 and 31 December 1938; note, dated 20 June 1938, of return made to Bank of England.
88. T 160/438/12681/01, memo, by Rowe-Dutton (Financial Advisor to the Berlin Embassy), 10 December 1931.
89. Ellis, *Exchange Control*, p. 178.
90. FO 371/15935.
91. FRBNY, Harrison Collection, 3125.3 and 3115.3, records of telephone conversations between, respectively, Lacour-Gayet (Bank of France) and Harrison, 9 February , and Harrison and Norman, 10 February 1932.
92. NC 18/1/770, to Hilda (Chamberlain's sister), 13 February 1932.

93. FO 371/15936/C1322, letter to Sargent, 10 February 1932.
94. FO 371/15935/C1042, note by Perowne and letter by Leith-Ross to Sargent, 3 February 1932.
95. FO 371/15937, undated despatch to Rumbold (Berlin), seeking confirmation of the accuracy of Sargent's City source – Nigel Law, the former FO official.
96. MB 30/99, Hyde's Diary, p. 180, 21 March 1932.
97. FO 371/15903/C2451, Law to Sargent, 23 March 1932.
98. James, *The Reichsbank*, p. 240.
99. FO 371/15903/C5937, Law to Sargent, 7 July 1932.
100. FO 371/15212, memo, 10 November 1931. See also, MB 30/202, position at 31 March 1939. This showed the total left outstanding under this agreement to be just over £1m (Britain's share coming to £975,000). These were insignificant amounts in comparison with the Standstill proper.
101. T 160/927/12750/2; see letter to British Consulate General, Cologne, from F.Spencer of Fine Spinners Ltd, indicating that the British textile industry was particularly disadvantaged.
102. FO 371/15937/C5771, despatch by Ambassador Rumbold, 2 July 1932.
103. T 160/927/12750/3, letter to Brand, 9 August 1932.
104. FO 371/15937/C8624, memo, no.8 (Financial Series), 30 September 1932, prepared by the Joint Committee at the request of Sir Walter Layton.
105. T 160/927/12750/3, Rodd to Pinsent (Treasury), 9 September 1932.
106. FO 371/15937, Jenkins (Board of Trade) to Pinsent, 26 August 1932; FO 371/15954/C8042, Rowe-Dutton (Berlin) to Leith-Ross, 15 September 1932; T 160/927/12750/3, Pinsent to Siepmann (Bank of England), 1 September 1932.
107. 'German Reparations and British Industry', February 1932, in Henderson, *Inter-War Years*, p. 92.
108. T 160/729/12829/1. Walter Elliot, Financial Secretary to the Treasury, was the recipient of this information.
109. BoE OV34/3, note, 22 January 1932. See also, K. Burk, *Morgan Grenfell 1838–1988: The Biography of a Merchant Bank* (Oxford: OUP, 1989), p. 100. Rodd left the Foreign Office in 1924; he joined the Bank of England in 1929 as an adviser to the Governors and became a partner in Morgan Grenfell in January 1933.
110. T 160/729/12829/1, minute by Hopkins.
111. Ibid. See also, BoE OV34/3, memo, by Leith-Ross, 12 January 1932, 'Germany's Competitive Power'.
112. T 188/21, Leith-Ross minute, 8 October 1931.
113. FO 371/15907/C1262, minute, 12 February 1932.
114. BoE OV34/3, Berlin Embassy reports by Thelwall (Commercial Counsellor) and Rowe-Dutton (Financial Adviser); see also copy of letter, 9 March 1932, Rowe-Dutton to Waley, and note by the Bank of England, 18 March 1932. The Bank did not know quite what to make of Rowe-Dutton: he was thought to be excessively gloomy and alarmingly pessimistic, yet this was said to be natural and well-founded.
115. FO 371/15903/C2030, letter by Nigel Law, 10 March 1932.
116. FO 371/15937/C4550, report by Rowe-Dutton, 12 May 1932.
117. CAB 24/227, memo, by Sir John Simon (Foreign Secretary), for Cabinet on 11 January 1932. The committee, which included four neutrals, met in Basle under the auspices of the BIS. Britain did not contemplate any interruption to the service of the Dawes and Young loans.

118. BoE OV34/148. These opinions formed, in effect, a minority report of the Special Committee.
119. T 160/450/13050; see also T 188/32.
120. FO 800/286, minute by Leith-Ross to Simon, 1 January 1932.
121. Boyce, *British Capitalism*, p. 336.
122. Boyce, 'World depression, world war', p. 70.
123. T 160/729/12829/1, minute by Hopkins.
124. NC 18/1/964, letter to Hilda Chamberlain, 6 December 1931.
125. Brand papers, File 112, 'A Note on the German Riddle', undated, by the Prime Minister's Advisory Committee on Financial Questions. Brand, Keynes, Henderson, Layton and McKenna were all members.
126. *New Statesman*, 16 January 1932.
127. T 160/436/12630/1.
128. T 160/439/12704, minute, 14 November 1931; see also T 160/436/12630/2, minute, 30 March 1932, by Leith-Ross.
129. Parker, *Chamberlain and Appeasement*, pp. 15–16. Parker suggests that the British public did not follow the technical arguments but shared a sense of grievance at French and American behaviour.
130. K. Jaitner, 'Aspekete britischer Deutschlandpolitik 1930–32' in J. Becker and K. Hildebrand (eds), *Internationale Beziehungen in der Weltwirtschaftskrise 1929–1933* (München: Vögel, 1980), p. 21.
131. T 160/450/13050, memo, 28 December 1931.
132. FO 371/15904/C258, minute, 11 January 1932.
133. T 160/450/13050, note of conversation between Leith-Ross, Fisher and Norman, 28 December 1931 and minutes by Leith-Ross, 31 December 1931 and 1 January 1932; see also T 188/32, for further discussions on 31 December 1931 which included Sir Ernest Harvey (Deputy Governor).
134. T 160/437/12630/02/2, Rumbold despatch, 20 January 1932.
135. FO 371/15901/C691, letter to Rowe-Dutton, 13 January 1932.
136. B. Kent, *The Spoils of War: the Politics, Economics and Diplomacy of Reparations, 1918–1932* (Oxford: Clarendon Press, 1989), p. 354.
137. CAB 23/70, 4(32).
138. CAB 23/70, 8(32), 26 January 1932.
139. FO 371/15905/C638, minute by Sargent, 20 January 1932; see also NC 18/1/770, Chamberlain's letter to Hilda, 13 February 1932.
140. T 172/1788, notes by Leith-Ross, 25 and 27 May 1932, for Chamberlain.
141. CAB 24/23a, memo, by Sir John Simon, confirming British policy on 31 May 1932 – the day after Brüning's resignation. See also, CAB 23/71, 37(32), letter, 20 June 1932, from Sir John Simon (at the Lausanne Conference) to Vansittart. Simon expressed his frustration at having to show such constraint at the negotiating table.
142. H. Feis, *1933: Characters in Crisis* (Boston, MA: Little, Brown, 1966), p. 17.
143. FO 800/286, letter to Sir John Simon, 31 May 1932.
144. FO 371/15903/C5806, letter, Law to F.O., 24 June 1932.
145. Williamson, *National Crisis*, p. 497.
146. T 172/1787.
147. Runciman papers, 258, notes by Runciman, 30 June and 1 July 1932.
148. D.Cameron Watt, *Succeeding John Bull*, p. 64.
149. S. Pollard, *The Development of the British Economy, 1914–1980* (Edward Arnold, 1983), p. 122.
150. Runciman papers, 251, letter written from Doxford, 2 September 1932.
151. E.H.H. Green, 'The influence of the City over British economic policy,

c.1880–1960' in Y. Cassis (ed.), *Finance and Financiers in European History, 1880–1960* (Cambridge: CUP, 1992), p. 200.

152. T 160/440/12800/01, Board of Trade memo, June 1932, 'Economic Questions at Lausanne'.
153. I.M. Drummond, *Imperial Economic Policy, 1917–1939: Studies in Expansion and Protection* (Allen & Unwin, 1974), p. 218.
154. Runciman papers, 254, letter to I.H.Tonking (constituency), 29 September 1932.
155. League of Nations, *British External Economic Policies* (Paris, 1939).
156. BT 11/138 /CRT/7082. See, in particular, memo, by Thelwall, 28 December 1932.

3

Britain and the rise of the Third Reich:

dealing with the legacy of reparations

To many people outside Germany, Hitler's appointment as Chancellor on 30 January 1933 did not seem to be an especially important event. Germany's political system was clearly inherently unstable; as alignments were constantly shifting, it was easy to dismiss the sudden influence wielded by the National Socialists as a temporary phenomenon. With British newspapers helping to create the impression that Hitler would not last long, he did not have to be taken too seriously.[1] Rarely, in the early part of 1933, was the attention of the British public focused on events inside the Third Reich. If anything, the new Germany was held to be an alien and relatively unimportant society.[2] Although the disgraceful behaviour of the Nazis towards the Jews was quickly condemned around the world, the prevailing opinion was that Hitler had to be given a chance to settle down, speculation being futile until he had proved himself in office.[3] Among the minority who thought otherwise, working-class movements and intellectuals were prominent. As the grim spectacle of the Nazis' consolidation of power was revealed, Oxford and Cambridge provided a stream of converts to Marxism and communism.[4]

Governing circles in Britain realized, at least, that the electoral success of the National Socialists would create fresh foreign policy difficulties, even though the 'German problem' had been acute for some time. Unless a way out of the impasse could be found, German claims for equality of status and hence rearmament would be difficult to deny. There was an uneasy awareness that opportunities had been lost with the collapse of the Weimar Republic. The Foreign Office was frustrated at what amounted to a failure to co-ordinate policy: the notion of viewing economic concessions as a potential political weapon was too novel to make much headway.[5]

Certainly there was a pronounced reaction inside the British Embassy in Berlin to the rise of Hitler. Given the perilous state of the German economy, Sir Horace Rumbold, the Ambassador, and the experts attached to the Embassy recognized that National Socialism presaged a dangerous future.[6] Reports despatched from Berlin made depressing reading but were highly esteemed in Whitehall none the less: a flow of informed opinion was necessary if some kind of understanding of the new Germany was to be formed. Whether the machinery of government in Britain was capable of producing relevant and appropriate responses was another matter.[7] Elizabeth Wiskemann later recalled how her contacts in Whitehall and at Westminster mostly failed to understand what was happening in Germany in 1933. The reaction of Sigi Waley, a Jewish official in the Treasury, appeared typical to Wiskemann: after hearing accounts of her visits to Germany, he decided that things could not be as disagreeable as her description of them.[8]

Unlike the Bolsheviks in the Russian Revolution, the National Socialists were not intent on smashing the structures of the state when they achieved power. Similarly, although National Socialism proclaimed, on ideological grounds, the rejection of liberalism, it did not serve Hitler's purposes to overturn the fundamentals of financial and economic policy. Pragmatism rather than innovation characterized the first measures taken by the Nazis in the economic sphere. Indeed, fiscal policy was, initially, highly conservative.[9]

Nevertheless, Nazi economics amounted to something more than a simple extension of the basic strategies of the last Weimar governments. Under Dr Hjalmar Schacht, President of the Reichsbank and, from 1934, Economics Minister as well, policies were sometimes extended to their limits. Although a nationalist, Schacht remained conservative and opposed to extreme autarky. This was to provide Göring with an opportunity to build his empire; under his administration of the Four Year Plan, launched in 1936, the economy was further distorted.[10] The result was the construction of an economic system of nationalist *étatisme* that was unique at the time.[11]

Although an economic recovery was soon to emerge, Germany was still in the trough of depression at the start of 1933. The new government was confronted with a completely disorganized capital market, a banking system with little liquidity, a negative amount of net investment and saving, and deplorable conditions in all government finances.[12] It was widely assumed that the future of the régime would depend on its degree of success in dealing with the desperate economic position and that the touchstone would be the curing of unemployment. By mid 1933 total unemployment had declined by a mere half a million from the 1932 peak of six million.[13] Hitler's view of economic priorities showed that the depressed state of the German economy would be something of an advantage to him: the rearmament he planned would not have to compete with other demands on labour and might for a time pass as a form of unemployment relief.

Though the underlying economic realities bore little resemblance to Nazi propaganda images, what struck contemporary observers was the appearance of reflation on an unprecedented scale. Although von Papen had attempted to alleviate unemployment in the Weimar Republic by public work schemes, the Nazis created the impression that a fruitless policy of orthodox deflation had to be completely abandoned and replaced by a vigorous, expansionist, recovery programme. With Germany's reputation for inflation, such rhetoric was bound to precipitate a further flight of capital. The Nazi programme had, consequently, an essential precondition: continuation of exchange controls. Taken as an emergency measure under Brüning, exchange control became, thereby, one of the pivots of the whole system.[14] The policy represented a powerful instrument in the hands of the régime, assuring it of both the potential for maximum freedom in its economic policy and a means of creating isolation in international relations.[15]

But such controls had serious implications for trade and, above all, international debts. There was an immediate warning from the British Embassy that the nationalists were in favour of reducing the service of foreign debt by unilateral action and that the prospect of a default was not going to restrain the Hitler régime from implementing schemes to make Germany more self-sufficient. The Foreign Office considered this refusal to play in international trade to be one of the most important and worrying factors in the European situation.[16]

In spite of these ominous signs, few predicted a sharp deterioration in Britain's financial and economic relations with Germany. It was assumed that, at worst, the atmosphere might become more strained. Yet, in the months which followed, the Nazis sought to give substance to the threats which they had made against Germany's foreign long-term creditors. When the difficulties besetting these bondholders began to escalate, divisions opened up between the different international creditors. Alarmed, Britain and the United States forged a diplomatic alliance to co-ordinate a response to the Third Reich. Co-operation proved to be limited and short-lived: it could not, by itself, arrest the steady deterioration in transatlantic relations.

In the spring of 1934 the Dawes and Young Loan bondholders in Europe and America heard that they too were to be punished. It seemed inevitable, therefore, that Britain would have to take retaliatory action. The ground was prepared for the imposition of a payments clearing system. However, such systems were thought to be highly disruptive of normal patterns of trade and finance. As long as Germany enjoyed a favourable balance of trade with Britain, a unilateral clearing arrangement would have required British importers of German goods to pay their debts to a London office. British creditors, both financial and trade, would then have received settlement of their claims from this office and the balance would then have been remitted to Germany. A bilateral scheme would have required the co-operation of both countries.

As they were revealed, the contortions in Nazi economics left creditors around the world, and most financial experts, bewildered. A despairing Leith-Ross admitted that he struggled to understand why Germany should wish to eschew an instant improvement in the international situation and in her credit-standing. All that was expected in return were commitments to pay Reich loans, fund other loans and treat creditors equally. The alternative, if obligations were not fulfilled, was that Germany would face clearings all round. This, Leith-Ross predicted, would bring disaster to the German economy and perhaps to the Hitler régime – a course of events he, for one, deprecated.[17]

In this was expressed the belief, commonly held in the Western democracies, that Hitler was a stabilizing influence: with his removal central Europe would fall to Bolshevism and the international economy would collapse.[18] The significance of Nazi ideology was continuously and disastrously underestimated. Ultimately, economic activity in the Third Reich was valued by Hitler in terms of what it could contribute to the fulfilment of his annihilationist goals.[19]

As the terms agreed at the Lausanne Conference were never ratified, reparations effectively came to end in 1932. Indeed, the payment made by Germany in 1931 before the start of the Hoover moratorium was to be the last. This seemed to bring few rewards. Instead, Britain was left to deal with the legacy – the attempts by the Reich authorities to dismantle the structure of Germany's long-term debts. As Harold James has observed, the wish of international creditors to unfreeze their debts formed the key element in a strategy of encouraging 'economic appeasement'; in the game of currency control and debt blocking, German economic diplomacy aimed to play off creditors against each other.[20] These tactics caused, of course, great resentment. Negotiations that produced the periodic transfer agreements – settlements over the interest and sinking fund payments (amortization) on Germany's foreign debts – would have to take account of political conditions as much if not more than economic ones. In Britain's case, however, resentment was tempered by some sympathy for Germany's position. For, although the burden imposed by the Versailles Treaty was becoming less onerous, Germany had to contend instead with the consequences of Britain's own economic revolution. The imposition of a clearing system was regarded, therefore, as a sanction of last resort. The mere suggestion that it should be used brought strong opposition from powerful City interests, revealed fundamental differences between financial and commercial interests and produced conflict among Britain's policy-making élite.

The Nazis and international 'tribute'

Once the Nazis were in power, Britain began to search for moderate figures. Men such as Konstantin von Neurath and Lutz Graf Schwerin von Krosigk, the non-Nazi Finance Minister, appeared to fall very much into the category.[21] Other leading figures, such as Schacht, were not so easily categorized. In order to finance the proposed vast schemes of rearmament, drastic changes were needed in the policies of the Reichsbank. Under Luther, an attempt had been made to reduce unemployment through measures such as the *Arbeitsschaffungswechsel* (work-creation bill); these bills were discounted by the Bank and funds were provided for a small-scale programme of public works. But Luther refused to extend the Bank's

credit beyond the legal limit of Rm100 billion. He was replaced by
Schacht who converted the device into an unlimited credit structure
by using bills drawn on an essentially dummy company,
Metallurgische Forschungs Gmbh (Mefo).[22]

Reaction in Britain to the news of Schacht's appointment as
Reichsbank President was mixed. The Treasury approved; as a
former holder of the office and negotiator of the Young Loan,
Schacht promised to provide a certain degree of continuity and
respectability. Governor Norman, who had already done much to
establish a kind of fraternity of central bankers, told Luther in
March 1933:

> I am sad to realise that an association is now to be broken which to
> me (and I hope also to yourself) has been a great pleasure over recent
> years and in times of such uncertainty. (I) assure you that for our part
> we shall endeavour to maintain and further those friendly relations
> which you have done so much to foster.[23]

Norman had every reason to expect that his endeavours would be
successful: Schacht was a longstanding friend and a close
professional relationship continued between them until Schacht was
forced out of office in 1939. At that point, Norman told Joseph
Kennedy, the American Ambassador in London, that for the
preceding 16 years all his information on the German situation had
come from Schacht.[24]

But the Foreign Office view of Schacht was that he was prickly
regarding international issues – just how prickly Britain was soon to
find out, Germany's lack of colonies was identified as a special bee
in his bonnet.[25] On the service of foreign debt, the evidence pointed
to a dangerously simple plan: Germany's favourable trade balance
would be eliminated through autarky and foreign creditors told that
with no export surplus there could be no debt payment. With
Schacht appearing to subscribe to the Nazi propaganda line that the
Dawes and Young Loans were camouflaged tribute, a moratorium by
Germany seemed a strong possibility. To Ralph Wigram, soon to be
head of the Foreign Office's Central Department, these tactics
indicated that National Socialism was a modern but probably less
trustworthy version of the German nationalist tradition.[26] Even
seasoned observers of foreign affairs were slow to diagnose the
pathogenic nature of National Socialism.

In May 1933 Germany's foreign long-term creditors were summoned to Berlin for the next round of talks. Schacht gave an intimation of the possible course of events. He slickly argued that reparations were the cause of Germany's indebtedness; creditors were told that the Reichsbank had been rendered unable to function by the scale of the transfers. On 7 June the Reichsbank announced that in the last resort international debt obligation could be fulfilled only through the movement of goods and services. This statement of the obvious was the warning tremor before the major shock two days later: the Reich authorities declared a moratorium from 1 July on all public and private long-term debts contracted before July 1931. This added the greatest single item to the list of international defaults, just as the World Economic Conference was about to open in London. The devaluation of the US dollar during July then completed the depressing picture of an international monetary system fragmented into different blocs and a world full of high tariff barriers.

The suspension of payments on the Dawes and Young loans was the most serious aspect of the threatened moratorium. In Nazi circles the effective ending of 'tribute' was hailed as a triumph.[27] But prompt threats by the creditor countries to impose clearing systems soon forced a compromise. The transfer of full interest and sinking fund payments on the Dawes and of interest on the Young loan were continued; payments of sinking funds on all other loans were suspended.[28] A *Konversionskasse* was created into which the debts were to be paid and the Reichsbank undertook to make the periodic transfers.

As for the interest quotas which were not transferred, the foreign long-term bondholders were to receive scrip. These scrip marks, in turn, could be sold to the Golddiskontbank for foreign exchange but only at a huge discount of 50 per cent. The justification offered by the Reichsbank was that the other 50 per cent would be earmarked to subsidize exports which would contribute to an increase in Germany's foreign exchange reserves. In other words, it was a way to subsidize so-called additional (*Zusätzliche*) exports. German exporters had, from 1931, received assistance in obtaining cheap marks as an alternative and fairly successful method of deflating costs. Under Hitler, the supply of even cheaper marks increased and the procedure which enabled German exporters to negotiate undercutting transactions was simplified. Scrip marks were added, therefore, to the already large reservoir of blocked marks, such as Sperr marks frozen under exchange regulations and Register marks arising from the Standstill. Blocked marks were traded on foreign markets at considerable discounts as they could be used only inside Germany for one specified purpose or another. The manipulation of the Reichsmark helped to bring about a selective depreciation of foreign-held securities. The intention was to provide another way to subsidize additional exports from Germany: the exporters concerned were permitted to use foreign exchange in order to buy up these securities cheaply and sell them at a profit in Germany. In spite of this, Schacht was able to claim in his memoirs that he did not act unilaterally over the transfer arrangements and that they continued only because they were entirely in accordance with the ideas of the creditors.[29]

In one sense, a substantial German export surplus was prevented by the policy of exchange control. But the pegging of the Reichsmark at gold parity level was also a significant factor in the export equation. Discriminatory exchange measures helped, therefore, to counter the effects of foreign devaluations. Fearing inflation, and for reasons of internal prestige, the Hitler government refused to devalue the mark. The deflation which accompanied other currency devaluations (such as that of the dollar) helped to depress world market prices. These movements intensified the disparity between German export prices and those for the rest of the world. The Reich authorities were able to watch this trend with equanimity; it provided the necessary pretext for unilateral action in reducing the foreign debt service.[30] Schacht never tired of repeating that Germany's ability to pay her debts depended on a favourable balance of trade. He blamed the creditor countries for not importing more.

Although the Foreign Office fretted over the hostile intentions of the Nazis, Britain's financial authorities were not so disturbed. The Treasury agreed that Schacht and the Nazis tried to magnify Germany's difficulties: the reserves had fallen so low partly because of events which lay beyond Germany's control but also through errors in German policy. Bondholders could plead with justification that German credit had been gravely impaired under the Weimar governments. Propaganda against reparations was blamed for causing the flight of capital from 1931; Brüning had shaken confidence and a hoped-for market recovery had then failed to take place because of wild utterances before and continued agitation after the Lausanne Conference. By threatening a default, Germany had depressed the prices of her bonds and then allowed foreign exchange, which should have been used to meet debt service, to be used instead to buy up the bonds at knockdown prices. Following the successes in obtaining a freeze of short-term debts and in settling reparations payments, Germany was now seeking to default on long-term debts.[31] Seen in these terms, Nazi behaviour, although unseemly, was a continuation of the economic nationalism of the Weimar Republic. It was assumed that Schacht's objective was the conservation of the Reichsbank's resources and the rebuilding of a position which would restore the confidence of short-term lenders. As this policy had considerable support in the City of London, the Treasury advised against putting pressure on Germany.

This response caused consternation in the Foreign Office. Sir Orme Sargent, Assistant Under-Secretary from 1933, characterized it as a 'spineless attitude'.[32] By propitiating the short-term creditors – banks and finance houses – Schacht hoped to isolate the long-term ones – the mass of private bondholders – and prevent a common front. A new committee was formed in London to represent the interests of the British long- and medium-term creditors. Sir Arthur Worley, of the British Insurance Association, was appointed chairman, while Sir Edward Reid, of Baring Brothers, and Tiarks, of Schroders, were deputed to represent the London issuing houses. Without the means of retaliation, they were not expected to put up a fight like the short-term creditors.

Although Sir John Simon, the Foreign Secretary, was surprised at the docile reaction in the City and among the public, he reasoned that there was little the government could do if the bondholders had agreed to a bad settlement. Allowing Berlin to impose a moratorium, on the other hand, had serious implications for Anglo-German relations. It would, argued Simon, be a case of using financial default as an instrument of national policy and, as he reminded Chamberlain, 'knowing the Germans as we do, we may count upon it that they will repeat the same tactic in other spheres of international policy.'[33] There was a clear case for making a diplomatic protest at the threat of an apparently fraudulent bankruptcy, regardless of the wishes or even interests of the City of London, and especially in concert with the French government who were pressing for joint action.

With conditions for economic diplomacy changing so markedly, the limits to the administrative competence of government departments needed to be defined. Simmering rivalries now burst out over the question of a protest to the Third Reich. The Governor of the Bank of England, claiming that a decision against diplomatic action had already been taken, argued against intervention. Montagu Norman much preferred to engage in private discussions with Schacht at meetings of the BIS.[34] The reluctance to challenge events direct infuriated the Foreign Office which felt this was a matter for the Cabinet, not the Governor, to decide. Vansittart greatly resented 'this attempted autocracy in matters of high international policy'. Sir Frederick Leith-Ross wanted to fall in with Vansittart's view.[35] Yet, with the future of Germany so uncertain, Britain's financial authorities were unwilling to call Schacht's bluff. The issue was postponed and no action was taken. If necessary, the interests of the long-term creditors would have to be sacrificed.

The 'extraordinary circle' of trade and debts

Doubts over the legality of intervention on behalf of the bondholders was the justification given for inaction. But if the British government was content to see short-term creditors gain some satisfaction while long-term ones suffered, this was not because financiers were favoured at the expense of the individual private investor. As the management of Britain's external economic relations became more complex there were many different interests which expected some form of official representation. It was impossible, of course, to satisfy all expectations. With conditions for certain investors deteriorating sharply, British exporters wondered whether their prospects were anything less than bleak.

Germany's difficulties were not lightly dismissed in Britain. The Reichsbank's position was regarded with understanding, even sympathy, because it was accepted that British policies were a significant factor in limiting German exports. Consideration by Britain of a punitive payments clearing office had contributed to the international pressure which had forced Germany to compromise on the issue of the Dawes loan repayments. But by early July 1933 the Treasury was arguing that a clearing arrangement was worthless given the balance of trade; with the imposition of British tariffs,

German imports had declined dramatically. The same reasoning led to the conclusion that protests to Germany would be ineffective as Britain did not possess a suitable weapon to back them up.[36]

No one could be sure, however, of the effects of Schacht's policies. The Federation of British Industries received complaints that Germany's currency dumping was hitting below the belt and that it had the potential to defeat tariffs. The Treasury expected that the outcry would be such that the British government would be forced to act. But neither the FBI nor the Board of Trade seemed especially concerned by these developments. Once again, there was no diplomatic protest. One inhibiting factor was the perceived effect of the fall in the value of sterling.[37]

The banking community shared this view. Tiarks went so far as to declare that the transfer of sterling by Germany to meet the obligations of bankers and investors had been seriously jeopardized by Britain's depreciation. He argued that the harm to British manufacturers caused by competition through the use of blocked marks was small and should be overlooked. Tiarks believed competition would really only become effective if Germany followed the example of Britain and America and similarly reduced the value of the currency.[38] The exchange rate for sterling certainly declined precipitately, from Rm20 under the gold standard to a level of Rm13 in November 1933.[39] It was open to question whether the cheap-marks procedure, which amounted to a partial depreciation of the currency, was less harmful to British trade than a general depreciation would have been.

Another slant to the currency question was provided by Wilfrid F. Crick, the manager of the Intelligence Department of the Midland Bank, who visited Germany in the autumn of 1933. Crick found it difficult to convince Germans of the theory that depreciation did little more than express the true relation between prices and costs. However, he suggested that Germany used, in effect, three different currencies: one for internal business, one for imports and one for exports (of which perhaps one-fifth of the trade was paid for in discount marks which approximated to the true value of the currency).[40]

The Bank of England, too, was ready to defend Germany's actions. From the debtor's point of view (rather than that of the foreign creditor or industrialist) the *Konversionskasse* and *Zusätzliche Exports* could be said to have their uses: some payment of interest on foreign loans was made possible, the Reichsbank acquired additional reserves of *Devisen* (foreign exchange) and the benefits of currency depreciation in promoting exports and increasing employment were secured with limited publicity.[41] Indeed, complaints about British commercial policy might well have been louder and more sustained. Ashton-Gwatkin, the Foreign Office official, thought that tariffs generally had been extremely severe on German products which had probably been hit harder than those of any other country. Ottawa had damaged German trade with the Dominions while other bilateral trade treaties made by Britain aimed to supplant German goods with British. Ashton-Gwatkin mused that the measure of success was, 'the diminishing German export trade, upon which the payment of money lent by the UK to Germany depends. It is an extraordinary circle.'[42]

Crick was one of many observers to suggest that the régime's continued existence depended upon economic success. German bankers feared that they would be turned out for a more radical alternative if the position did not improve. Crick thought that some highly protective trade policies and advanced monetary experimentation might be in store; external debts might then become subject to even more drastic treatment. But he could not believe that autarky was to be the keynote of Berlin's long-term policy. While a German revival would have made British traders anxious, Crick saw it as an unquestionable fact that a prosperous Germany was the best possible foundation for prosperity in central and eastern Europe. Only by increased exports could Germany resume the full service of her external debt.[43]

Putting the City in a 'blue funk'

In the autumn of 1933 information reached London that the Dutch and the Swiss government were negotiating separate arrangements for their bondholders with the Reich authorities. The Dutch feared that their creditors would suffer unless pre-emptive action were taken. It seems that by smoothing the path for Schacht in Britain and France Montagu Norman had raised the suspicions of Dr Trip, Governor of the Bank of the Netherlands.[44] Despite denials by Schacht, agreements were signed by mid October whereby Swiss and Dutch bondholders were to receive payment of their scrip in full so long as the final 25 per cent was covered by additional German exports to those two countries.

With this the united front of the creditors was broken. As preferential treatment was contrary to Schacht's promises, the British bondholders asked for an official protest to counter the discrimination. The *Financial Times* took up the call on 10 October: Schacht was vilified for showing a 'fraudulent preference' of an unprecedented kind. Discrimination against Britain was regarded as particularly unfair as London's loan market had been an 'indulgent milch cow' for an undernourished Germany. Urging the government to take action, the newspaper reminded readers that Germany's favourable balance of trade was a little treasure which the régime would not willingly expose to blizzards.[45]

But Montagu Norman continued to oppose the threat of a clearing. He regarded the whole episode as a regrettable necessity for Schacht and warned that a stalemate would occur if Britain were offered an agreement similar to the one accepted by the Swiss and the Dutch. In taking City opinion into account, Norman was adamant that the bondholders would not want intervention to prejudice advantages already secured, particularly those relating to the Dawes and Young loans. Thus the Treasury merely questioned whether a debtor was entitled to barter fulfilment of obligations against new trade advantages for himself.[46] The protest was couched in terms which would not cause embarrassment in the event of an impasse; in Foreign Office terms it was *par la forme* only – for domestic public and parliamentary consumption. Britain pointed out that 'additional' exports were already being taken from Germany as the volume of trade was controlled by the normal economic actions of individual buyers.[47] Instructions were despatched to Berlin on 7 November and the protest was accordingly lodged with the German government.[48]

However, the full implications of the scrip scheme were beginning to sink in: Britain was helping to create a fund which was used by Germany to subsidize dumping – a process without precedent in international trade.[49] The exact amount of subsidy made available to German exporters could not be computed although it was believed to be small. According to the Bank of England, this was just what British traders did not like about the system: they could not tell the extent of the competition nor the disadvantage to which they were exposed. The FBI and the National

Union of Manufacturers were soon reporting a rash of complaints.[50] Privately, it was conceded that the stakes would have to be raised and a clearing threatened to secure the full transfer on the scrip.[51]

Discrimination between creditors was at the heart of complaints made at a Reichsbank meeting in December. To make matters worse, the angry British delegates heard the Reichsbank President hint that a further reduction of interest rates was needed. The new arrangements announced by Schacht on 18 December sent shock waves through financial circles in Britain. The plan was to reduce the free-exchange element of the debt service from 50 to 30 per cent. The Foreign Office, believing that it had been opposed by a determined but naive and complacent Treasury, would not accept any blame for the failure to act. Sir Frederick Leith-Ross agreed that Schacht should have disillusioned anyone who still believed in German commercial honesty. Convinced that Germany was in a position to meet all her interest payments but was instead concentrating on building stocks of war *matériel* such as nickel and copper, Leith-Ross sounded an early warning over the purpose behind the restructuring of the German economy.[52]

TABLE 2: ESTIMATED DEBT SERVICE OF GERMANY TO THE UK
FOR 1934 IN £MILLION

Standstill debt interest and commission on £44m	1.6
Municipal Standstill debt interest	0.175
other short-term interest	0.857
interest at 6.5% on £60m long-term debt held in UK	3.9
sinking fund of Dawes Loan	0.628
sinking fund of Young Loan (if paid in paper)	0.144
Total	7.304

Source: T 160 642/8797/04/3, estimate by Waley, Nov.1933; nothing was allowed for invisible imports and exports as there seems to have been no reliable way of computing totals; the assumption was that this balance lay clearly in the UK's favour.

What Leith-Ross wanted, he told Tiarks, was to see London's financial interests join together and present Schacht with an ultimatum: either arrangements satisfactory to creditors as a whole were made or credit facilities would be withdrawn from Germany. Short-term creditors needed to show solidarity with their long-term counterparts; the former had to remember that their turn might come next. Tiarks, like the Governor of the Bank, did not want to blame Schacht for political decisions which had been taken over his head. Tiarks also defended the short-term creditors who, since 1931, had already accepted a 50 per cent reduction in interest and commission charges. He argued that threats to end the Standstill would have no effect because credits were all locked up and subject to transfer restrictions.[53]

Moreover, the continuing uncertainty over international exchange rates meant that the reservoir of sympathy for Germany had not yet run dry. Professor Henry Clay, an adviser to the Governors of the Bank of England, theorized that a partial default on long-term debts was the alternative to Germany's going off the gold standard. Clay argued that Britain could not object to this in principle, unless it could be proved that Germany could find the necessary foreign exchange, because the progress of recovery depended on the writing down of debts. The problem was, rather, the creation of conflict between different types of creditor and the discrimination between countries.[54]

A further protest was delivered by Britain on 22 December. But it merely pointed out that failure to observe the principles of negotiation would tend to undermine the credit of Germany as a whole and make it increasingly difficult to maintain international credit operations.[55] Although relations with Germany hardly evinced seasonal goodwill, protests by Britain continued to be restrained. The assessment made by the *Manchester Guardian* was, therefore, rather overstated: 'It is one of the British Government's objects to force the Reichsbank either to reverse its policy or to face the proof of its political motive.'[56]

Maintaining international credit operations was, of course, a primary interest of the City of London. The Third Reich's actions were jeopardizing the City's position; but the idea of reaching for a clearing system disturbed the City even more. The government had to be diverted from what was seen as an extreme measure of retribution. The short-term creditors complained that they had not been consulted over the likely effect of a clearing on the international character of the Standstill but confronted with a *fait accompli*. Although aware that the interruption of short-term credit to Germany was a weapon, the bankers claimed that very little business was being done anyway; the remarkably good terms offered by Germany indicated that the need was great and the supply very limited.[57] The Joint Committee informed the Foreign Secretary that the City was fearful of a general moratorium on all British financial claims. The impact of this on the Standstill creditors, particularly the acceptance houses, would have been serious.[58]

In emphasizing the international function of London's financial machinery the Standstill creditors might have hoped to take the wind out of the sails of those who – like the Foreign Office – reproached the City for acting against the interests of ordinary British citizens. The Nazis were beginning to draw propaganda value from the existence of groups in the City, said to be Tiarks and his friends, who did not look unfavourably upon the Third Reich and its behaviour over foreign debts.[59] Although financial transactions with Germany might have been in the interests of Britain's foreign trade and credit, it was not too demanding to make a case in favour of relegating those interests to ensure that Britain's international standing was not damaged.

Once again, Montagu Norman engaged in diplomacy behind the scenes with Schacht at Basle. The Bank of England was prepared to satisfy the long-term bondholders for two years by finding that part of their interest which was to be suspended under the new German regulations. To head off a collision Norman was prepared to take the risk (amounting to £500,000) and carry the scrip until it was paid off by Germany. Short-term creditors would have been relieved of their fears over the institution of a clearing and possible retaliation against their interests.

The drawback to Norman's scheme was quickly identified: it would create the impression that the threat of general economic chaos was sufficient to intimidate Britain from taking retaliatory action. Ralph Wigram, at the Foreign Office, thought this would show the Germans once again that, in the last resort, the government would always give in to the pro-German bankers of the City. He could imagine no procedure better calculated to weaken British prestige abroad and encourage discrimination against the nation's interests.[60] These objections (but not opinions about City bankers) were advanced by Neville Chamberlain, the Chancellor of the Exchequer, when he informed Norman that he could not agree to the proposal.[61] When the scheme miscarried, Norman, in conversation with Schacht, apparently referred to 'political difficulties'. Berlin's interpretation of this was that the British government was pulling back at the last minute in the face of Parliament's hostile attitude and after consultations with other governments.[62]

Instead, the Hitler government was informed, in mid January 1934, of Britain's concern over the transfer moratorium. With due diplomatic nicety, the Führer was asked to use his personal influence to find a way out of the problem. While the British Ambassador stressed how great the desire was to avoid a clearing, he also implied that there would be a trade war if Britain was left with no choice but to find a means of self-defence. This appears to have evoked a furious reaction in Hitler and the riposte delivered by von Neurath, the German Foreign Minister, was anything but diplomatic. He declared that Germany would not be intimidated, and that after two months at most not a pfennig would be transferred if the British government continued in its demand for cancellation of the Swiss and the Dutch agreement.[63]

Von Neurath also implied that the creditor nations had missed the opportunity which the World Economic Conference might have afforded the debtor countries for an international revision of the conditions of export and transfer. He employed the familiar argument that Germany's foreign indebtedness was not like that of other countries – the normal outcome of international trade. Rather, Germany's debts resulted from the past political situation and were, therefore, 'political debts'.[64] In resisting the British government's *démarche*, Hitler and von Neurath were prepared to see it not only as a form of extortion on behalf of the British creditors but also as a calculated move to exert general pressure in order to make Germany as tractable as possible, particularly over the disarmament question.[65]

By now finance and politics had become inextricably linked: payment and transfer problems were both the cause and the effect of the deteriorating political atmosphere. And finding a solution to the transfer question now became an issue of primary diplomatic importance for Britain. At the same time, it seemed doubtful that the principle of equal treatment in settling debts could be respected in any agreement. Thus, in preparing for the resumption of the negotiations in Berlin at the end of January, creditors planned to press for an end to discrimination or, failing that, a separate agreement with Germany. The Treasury found the German reply to the British notes of December quite indigestible. Great exception was taken to the idea that Germany's problems were special because so much could be attributed to the need to find foreign exchange for reparations. This implied that the Nazis had a moral responsibility to prevent payment. Sir Warren Fisher, in the Treasury, surveyed German history from the time of Frederick the Great and concluded: 'the Norman–Schacht conversations are shown more and more to have been unfortunate ... The German attitude in this matter is merely a repetition of her historic procedure'.[66]

However, the emergence of a new trend in Anglo-German trade undermined the obvious argument against action.[67] Buttressed by the knowledge that the balance of trade in favour of Germany had stopped declining, the programme for the instituting of a clearing was drawn up in London on 25 January 1934. In the event there was no need for an immediate decision. At the end of the month a deal was struck in Berlin: discrimination between creditors was to end later in the year; interest payments, however, were to be transferred in the proportions originally proposed by the Reichsbank.[68]

Reactions in Britain to the settlement were mixed. There was relief that a major dispute had been avoided. The Bank of England believed that not one of the clearing arrangements in operation around the world fulfilled the purpose for which it had been formed. Instead, trade was retarded. The Bank also wanted to avoid the responsibility for running any clearing office; technical knowledge other than that of central banking was required and there was a danger that relations with the commercial community would be damaged.[69]

Similarly, Chamberlain revealed in a letter to his sister Hilda that he had had an anxious time over the dispute. He had thought it most dangerous for Britain to allow herself to be bullied, but threatening Germany with a clearing had:

> put the City in a blue funk and the Chairmen of the 5 banks with other magnates proposed to come and tell me of the awful disasters which might follow. But before they could come we had a brilliant triumph. The Germans surrendered on both points. They agreed to give up discrimination and abandon their claim to unilateral decisions without consulting the creditors.

Chamberlain was able to reassure Hilda that, although the public might never hear how this great success was the reward for his boldness, he could, none the less, enjoy full satisfaction in the result.[70]

Yet the settlement was clearly a compromise and the more sceptically minded wondered how long it would survive. The bruising process of dealing with the new Germany had left its mark. One Foreign Office proposal was that Parliament should legislate for general powers to impose clearings. Taking pre-emptive action would have armed Britain's negotiators with an effective weapon and denied the domestic opponents of clearings the time to become even more powerfully organized. The plan impressed neither the Treasury nor the Board of Trade. Chamberlain assumed that the warning Britain had given to potential defaulters would be sufficient. He did not want to ask for general powers when there was no specific case in mind and Britain was engaged in negotiations with other countries where she had no desire to threaten a clearing. In the light of this, Simon, the Foreign Secretary took, characteristically, the path of least resistance.[71] He told his officials that to draw up a bill specifically aimed at Germany would be unnecessarily provocative. At the same time, he was persuaded that taking general powers *in vacuo* threatened the most serious domestic and parliamentary reactions and was not merely a piece of useful and innocuous machinery.[72]

The Foreign Office was far from jubilant for another reason: the negotiations had confirmed just how difficult it was to carry out policy. Relations with the City authorities were thought to be in urgent need of an overhaul. To officials used to working with other government departments by means of close personal contact rather than through official letters, the Bank was wrapped in mystery. The lack of co-operation was a long-standing grievance; repeated attempts to find a remedy had been largely unsuccessful. Sargent noted:

> In spite of all our efforts Mr Montagu Norman continues to carry on his own foreign policy, certainly without consulting the Foreign Office and without, I suspect, taking even the Treasury very much into consideration. The present dispute with the German Government affords indeed a glaring instance of this independent action by the Bank of England for the settlement .... was almost wrecked not so very long ago by the sudden intervention of Mr Norman.

Sargent reasoned that, until some system of collaboration existed, the Foreign Office would always be exposed to the danger of being tripped up and double-crossed. Vansittart saw Norman as:

a misguided though pleasant person. His methods seem to me intolerable, and I wish the country were well rid of him – though I suppose that such sentiments are heresy in his City Cenaculum. I have tried keeping in touch, but it has not worked. We must leave him to the Treasury – if they will deal with him.[73]

To Vansittart, the City was guided too much by purely commercial considerations – the 'short view' – and failed to appreciate the weighty political issues involved in financial relations with Germany.[74] With the Foreign Secretary reluctant to face the task of winning over Cabinet colleagues, the beleaguered officials began to reflect on how to educate the public to the German menace.[75]

The limits to Anglo-American co-operation

Relations between the leading democracies, already strained by the 1931 crisis and the Lausanne Conference in 1932, deteriorated rapidly over the abortive attempt to achieve financial stabilization at the World Economic Conference, held in London, in 1933. Britain, France and America became so alienated from each other that a state of virtual war existed in their economic relations.[76] Watt points out that no one in the new American administration understood the degree to which the National Government's proposals for stabilization represented the last stand of economic internationalism in Britain. Injured pride, mutual suspicion and feelings of personal betrayal characterized attitudes on both sides of the Atlantic.[77] The German bondholder question gave Britain and the United States an opportunity to administer balm to the wounds. In both categories of Germany's foreign debts (long- and short-term) America was ranked first in the list of creditor nations. Of the total long-term debt – estimated in 1933 at Rm10.265 billion – just over half was owed to American creditors.[78]

Herbert Feis, economic adviser to the American government, had received the usual categorical assurance from Schacht that he would not sanction any policy that discriminated between different creditor nations.[79] The preference shown to the Swiss and the Dutch was bound, therefore, to cause great offence. The new Nazi practice, carried out in America as elsewhere, of buying up bonds at prices depreciated by declarations that there was no money to pay interest, inflamed feelings all the more. But, unlike Britain or, indeed, Switzerland and the Netherlands, America was not in a position to threaten retaliatory action. German imports from America (especially cotton and other raw materials) were considerably greater in value than German exports. Washington was also conscious of a substantial difference between British and American bondholders: the former were well organized while the latter were poorly represented. It was clearly in America's interest to respond immediately and positively to a request by Britain, at the end of 1933, for a co-ordinated, formal diplomatic protest to be made in Berlin.[80] The State Department promptly instructed Ambassador Dodd, in Berlin, to make a protest identical to the one issued by the British Embassy. Extended collaboration with Britain over the question of preferential treatment was then authorized as it was 'important to maintain a unity of judgement'.[81]

Washington was not, however, completely free of doubts about London's intentions. After all, the British, like the Swiss and the Dutch, were in a position to be bought off by the German government. Furthermore, the sympathies of the Governor of the Bank of England for the German scrip practices were well known. The State Department feared that Norman and Schacht would work out some plan of conciliation which did not include American interests. On 19 January 1934 President Roosevelt personally instructed Dodd to tell Hitler that if discrimination continued a serious demand would arise in America for practical action 'to which the American Government could not lend a deaf ear'.[82]

Britain was presented with an opportunity, therefore, to show consideration to Washington. There was particular anxiety over the effect of a clearing on transatlantic relations: Germany was thought capable of defaulting completely to the United States, hoping thereby to embroil the latter with Britain. The American government's vigour in supporting Britain's stance, in spite of the dangers, was greatly appreciated in London. Indeed, in seeking to consolidate opposition to any compromise, the Foreign Office sought to influence Britain's press to be as outspoken as their American counterparts with their references to fraudulent bankruptcy.[83]

The Reichsbank and the long-term creditors were scheduled to meet in Berlin in the spring of 1934 for the Transfer Conference. No one expected the negotiations to be easy; but serious divisions began to emerge before the conference between the creditors themselves. The Swiss and the Dutch representatives strongly urged the British to abandon what they regarded as sentimental objections to discrimination. They wanted Britain to join with them in insisting that Germany should pay 100 per cent to all creditors who bought German goods and only cut down payments to America with whom her balance of trade was so unfavourable.[84]

The contention that the arrangements made by the Swiss and the Dutch were not discriminatory because they were based on extra purchases of German goods was not one which Cordell Hull, the American Secretary of State, was likely to accept. From his side of the Atlantic it seemed that these two small European nations had made a special calculation – tied up with a bilateral trade movement of a limited character – which secured preferential treatment for themselves at the expense of America. Hull thought it impossible to segregate a small part of bilateral trade from the rest of the international trade system, for this ignored invisible items, the results of triangular trade and purchases in third countries. As an example, he cited the way American imports of rubber from the Dutch East Indies created purchasing power in the Netherlands which, in turn, helped the Dutch to buy German goods.[85]

Washington was also wary about the implications of a British suggestion that Germany should pay no cash interest on her long-term debts during the remainder of 1934. Although this was seen as sound financial judgement it was also thought to favour British interests. In America, the bonds were held by some 300,000 small private investors; the British bondholders were the large insurance companies and other financial institutions. While American citizens would suffer a discount on cashing the funding bonds received as part of this settlement, British institutions could afford to leave the bonds lying in vaults for some years. Cordell Hull noted that the situation would not be improved if British and French bondholders secured a settlement in their interests because the Dawes and Young loans had been floated by the J.P. Morgan bank – 'popularly known as the fiscal agents of the British and French Governments'.[86]

In early 1934 the American legal authorities declared that token war debt payments were illegal. As a consequence, Britain fell foul of the new Johnson Act, which stopped foreign powers in default from borrowing in America. This prompted the National Government to turn aside from the prolonged attempt to reach a compromise with the administration in Washington.[87] With the refusal to continue payment of American war debts, mutual anti-pathy deepened.[88] Franklin Roosevelt, who epitomized the ambivalent attitude held by many Americans towards Britain, appears to have concluded by the middle of 1934 that London did not want to co-operate with the United States.[89] It proved impossible to sustain the co-ordination of Anglo-American financial diplomacy in such an atmosphere.

The threat to the Dawes and Young Loans

The international creditors maintained an uneasy truce at the Berlin conference and accepted the inevitability of some reduction in German transfers. But the Long-Term Creditors Committee, meeting in Basle in May, discovered that payments on the Dawes and Young loans were also being threatened once more.[90] Britain was again thrown on the defensive. Neville Chamberlain wanted an immediate declaration that these loans could not be subject to a transfer moratorium, though he still hoped to avoid any reference to a clearing.[91] Nevertheless, any move on the part of the Swiss and the Dutch towards a clearing would have forced Britain to follow suit straightaway. If, on the other hand, creditors were no longer to be treated equally, Britain had to ensure that its creditors would be treated just as well as the Swiss and the Dutch bondholders.

It was suggested to Montagu Norman that City bankers could help by impressing on their German friends that it was no bluff that Britain would impose a clearing if London remained dissatisfied.[92] Chamberlain too saw the need 'to show the Germans that this country means business'.[93] He approved the setting up of an Anglo-German clearing office on a basis which obviated the unpleasant necessity for separate legislation: a general bill was drafted in which Germany was included. Even these legislative steps were far from straightforward. Payments defined as reparations could be collected only by a reimposition of the Recovery Act of 1921; this would have involved abrogating Lausanne and contradicting the diplomatic notes which had just been sent to America.

The Reichsbank announced on 14 June 1934 that a moratorium on the transfer of interest by foreign exchange on all Germany's debts would take effect from 1 July. Foreign creditors were offered ten-year funding bonds bearing interest at 3 per cent. Germany's foreign exchange reserves in 1932 had stood at well over Rm1 billion, thanks to foreign credits; now, just two years later, they amounted to a mere Rm200m.[94] A state of virtual exhaustion, which became the norm from now on, had been reached because imports, not only of raw materials but also of manufactured articles, had increased while exports had declined. Although British experts could only speculate at the time, the shrinkage in gold and foreign exchange reserves was made more spectacular by the Reichsbank itself through the hurried repayment of certain loans.[95] International creditors suspected that Germany was manipulating her foreign exchange reserves to produce timely losses.

Every country in a position to do so started negotiations for more favourable treatment. The day after the Reichsbank's announcement Chamberlain told the House of Commons that he proposed to seek powers to set up an Anglo-German clearing office. The reaction of the Nazi government, informed at the same time, was immediate and aggressive. According to Leopold von Hoesch, the German Ambassador in London, Britain had overlooked the fact that the British Empire as a whole enjoyed a favourable trade balance with the Third Reich. In the event of a clearing, corresponding reprisals against English and Empire imports into Germany were possible, he threatened. This did nothing to deflect the National Government. Chamberlain considered that the Treasury had made a 'most damaging exposure of a fraudulent debtor'. The Cabinet agreed that a clearing would provide some defence in regard to a form of discrimination against Britain which no other defaulting country had attempted.[96]

However, the powerful counsels in London which had previously advised against any clearing system were not among the converted. Governor Norman, regarded by the Treasury as a conciliatory force, was particularly effective in passing on his worries over the dispute. Sir Richard Hopkins, for example, realized that preparations for a clearing were inevitable but wondered what Hitler would do in turn about the Standstill. No one knew whether the City would continue to hold Standstill bills. Yet the mere contemplation of having to pass legislation which put them into cold storage and guaranteed the Governor against loss upon them was enough to scare Hopkins.[97]

Norman was strongly supported by the London joint stock banks. He acted as intermediary between the Joint Committee and the

Chancellor of the Exchequer. Beaumont Pease, the committee's chairman, told the Governor that bankers were apprehensive lest conditions arose which might make it impossible to continue with the operation of the Standstill. Maintaining the credit facilities covered by the Standstill was, the bankers argued, of the first importance for all those with an interest in Germany's economic stability. This included British bondholders and merchants. Beaumont Pease warned that the bankers who looked to the Reich authorities for provision of the foreign exchange necessary to meet the obligations of German debtors would be compelled instead to look to a clearing for support. It would then be very embarrassing if, at any time, the clearing did not show a surplus.

Seemingly bankers never tired of pointing out that the Standstill was entered into at the express request of governments represented at the London Conference of July 1931. The intention had been to stop the continued withdrawal from Germany of banking facilities of all kinds, and thus avert a general economic breakdown. Bankers were proud that this had proved effective in preserving for Germany facilities which were essential for her trade. They felt that their actions had been not only in their own interests, but also those of the medium- and the long-term creditors, and in accordance with the policy of the British government.

The Joint Committee backed up their case by describing, in a detailed memorandum, the role of the several different kinds of bank credit involved in Germany's foreign trade. The intention behind this analysis was to show how any clearing would upset the balance of limitations and obligations undertaken by both sides and to deter government from interfering in an area of business which was always technical and sometimes highly complex. For the bankers did not see how credits, with such a high volume of daily transactions, could be excluded from a clearing. A further objection was that sterling payments to the Reichsbank might be delayed, interrupting the flow of foreign exchange necessary to procure the continuation of credits. The acceptance houses feared that they would be placed under an enormous strain if the Standstill broke down and no alternative arrangements had been made. Bills worth £34m, payable within three months and mostly discounted on the London market, would not have been renewed at maturity.[98]

In defending its own interests, the City was quick to advance a credible economic argument against clearing mechanisms. They were in their nature destructive of anything except bilateral trade and particularly destructive of the trade of most industrialized countries which, like Germany, bought and sold in different and separate markets. Reinforcing the economic rationale was an assessment of political risk. Imposition of a clearing would, it was said, create an hostile environment over the question of debts, and extreme elements in Germany would be given grounds for default.

The bankers appeared to forget that a clearing was being considered only because a German default was imminent. They also overlooked, of course, the ways in which National Socialism had begun to destroy multilateral trade. The Treasury estimated that the amount of trade financed by Standstill credits was, in any event, small enough to render the problem a negligible one. Moreover, under the clearing proposed, British exports to Germany were to be excluded and a large proportion of the sterling derived from the sale of German goods to the UK would remain at the disposal of the Reichsbank. Foreign exchange would then be available to cover bills at maturity. The Treasury also compared the £34m of British capital under the Standstill to £60m in long- and medium-term loans.[99]

With the bankers' protestations failing to make much of an impact, rumours of a powerful anti-City influence in the Treasury began to circulate. Nevertheless, the government had to be careful that it was not accused of favouritism towards high finance.[100] Chamberlain wrote to the Governor in an attempt to pacify the banking community. The Chancellor stressed that, while the government felt that it had no option but to obtain clearing powers, Britain had clearly not taken the lead as France, Switzerland and Holland had already obtained similar powers from their legislatures. Although Chamberlain agreed that any clearing should be as limited in scope as possible and that the maintenance of the Standstill was desirable for both Germany and Britain, he claimed that he did not envisage any problems with a scheme.[101]

Privately, the government was less self-assured. Chamberlain knew that a clearing would disturb trade, but he confessed that he did not know what else to do to ensure that Britain was not left out of retaliation against the potential 'swindlers'.[102] Hopkins reluctantly agreed with Norman that an agreement extracted from the Germans would be a political triumph of a far higher order than the imposition of a clearing, and also far better for British industry.[103] The obvious point was not made: the extent of a political triumph would depend on the terms of any agreement and on how smoothly it worked in practice.

What British industry wanted was payment for its exports to Germany, something which was becoming increasingly difficult. Debts had piled up because of the successive reductions in exchange quotas; some trades – the herring exporters, for example – were in a dire condition. The London Chamber of Commerce informed the Chancellor that a proportion of its members had already stopped shipments because the problems had intensified. One trade of great importance to Germany was the import of oil seeds, oils and fats. The biggest supplier was a British company which was demanding a change of attitude by the German government. The importers could not obtain confirmed bankers' reimbursements and so there was no security for the fulfilment of contracts. Business had come to a stop.[104] A reduction in trade to Germany might have improved the prospects of sterling payment for those who continued to export, but the UK's balance of payments would have suffered.

It was not obvious to British industry, therefore, why it should join the opposition to a clearing. The London Chamber of Commerce considered it unfair that the government should undertake to collect, first and foremost, the debts of bondholders from a clearing.[105] The National Union of Manufacturers went further and suggested that it would be both inequitable and injurious if the operation of a clearing were to place a heavy burden on British trade just for the purpose of relieving certain bondholders. Exporters feared that their problems would be magnified rather than solved if Germany were left with even less sterling at its disposal. This pressure compelled the Department of Overseas Trade to admit that a clearing which settled just bondholders' claims fell far short of what commercial interests were expecting. The latter did not want negotiations confined solely to the issue of the Dawes and Young loans; assurances were sought that both current and outstanding trade debts would be liquidated from the proceeds of German exports.

Nevertheless, the Treasury did not want to appear to be influenced by the commercial sector any more than by banking interests. Britain would get what it could by way of a settlement of old trade debts. In the meantime, it was hoped that British traders would quietly sell their blocked marks at a discount, just as they had been willing, in many cases, to make a sacrifice to get out of other countries in which they had been stuck.[106] This was an extraordinarily relaxed position to take over the imposition of what amounted to a German tax on British exporters, especially when trade was still depressed.

Then, towards the end of June 1934, the Nazi authorities decided to ignore all previous exchange permits and to ration exchange in accordance with the amount available on any one day. There was a growing realization that trade debts would have to be given priority immediately after the Dawes and Young loans.[107] Beset with anxieties, the National Government pressed ahead with the tactic of preparing for a clearing. Parliament hurriedly passed the Debts Clearing Offices and Imports Restrictions Bill. It provided for a 20 per cent *ad valorem* duty on imports. Another new technique in the art of British commercial diplomacy had been acquired.[108] The Act received the Royal Assent on 28 June. The intention was to publish the order in the newspapers of 2 July and then start the operation three days later if, in the meantime, no agreement had been reached.

With this legislative lever to hand, Britain should have been able to secure particularly favourable terms. If the German delegates in London were put under pressure, they were probably relieved to have been out of the way of the murderous purge of Röhm and associates just then taking place throughout Germany. The talks were quickly concluded and on 4 July the Anglo-German Transfer Agreement was signed. Britain agreed not to exercise her newly created clearing powers. In return, the Reich government confirmed the provisions of the Berlin Transfer Conference of 29 May 1934.[109] In effect, discrimination between creditors was to end and sterling was promised for the purchase of Dawes and Young coupons. Interest on loans other than these two was to be paid in 3 per cent funding bonds (with the proviso that bondholders were entitled to put forward a claim in the event of discrimination). Amazingly, no direct provision at all was made for the liquidation of debts due to British traders. One of the German delegates, Dr Berger, simply gave an undertaking that negotiations on exchange and commercial payments would commence without delay.

For that reason, Paul Einzig, the journalist, fulminated against the agreement. Naturally, those concerned with the Dawes and Young loans were delighted; bankers in general were pleased that the application of the new Act had been suspended. But exporters feared that the agreement had been concluded at their expense; they remained at the mercy of Schacht.[110] Nevertheless, the government's determination was widely praised in the City: bankers were ready to admit to the value of the method which first placed 'the British boot firmly on the Teutonic face'. Relief that economic warfare had been put off for the time being was tinged with pessimism as German credit had been very effectively undermined.[111] While Schacht was now widely regarded in London as a purveyor of calamitous policies, he was said to justify himself by claiming the support and approval of Montagu Norman. The latter was alleged to have spoken of how indifferent he was to the fate of the long-term creditors and how he would back Schacht in every way possible to keep Germany's short-term position satisfactory. The Governor apparently revealed how much he admired Schacht as a great banker and a great man. Whether this affected Norman's desire to protect Britain's financial interests was another matter: Leith-Ross wanted to place on record that, as much as a clearing was disliked and feared, the Governor and his officials had given loyal and valuable assistance in its preparation. Yet, convinced by Schacht that the alternative to Nazism was Bolshevism, Norman was said to be obsessed with the idea that moderate parties in all countries – and with them democracy – were doomed.[112]

As for the Foreign Office, a fundamental shift in policy was necessary to meet the challenges posed by Hitler's consolidation of power. Officials condemned as erroneous the belief, held continuously since Versailles, that Germany could be conciliated by a policy of unilateral concessions. Likewise, the belief that inadequate concessions by the former allies had produced the Hitler régime was dismissed. The new guiding principle, the Foreign Office insisted, was to be that weakness simply tempted the Germans to overplay their hand. To Vansittart, the Anglo-German Transfer Agreement was a vindication of all that he had said:

> the German climb down on the main point is a triumph for the Foreign Office not only over the Germans but over the other departments of His Majesty's Government, who were distinctly reluctant to talk the only language which Germans understand.[113]

Chamberlain, too, showed resolution in the negotiations. He had doubted whether the Germans would sign the agreement:

> for they bluff so persistently and as a rule so successfully that it was

hard for them to believe that we really meant business. But finally we gave them an ultimatum and they collapsed. Everyone was very pleased and undoubtedly the Government stock went up further.[114]

The sorry and sudden end to Chamberlain's life in 1940 left him no time to defend his own reputation. Recent historical analysis has sought to rescue Chamberlain from the libel that he was stupid or ignorant.[115] The shrewd and successful tactics which he employed in the first half of the 1930s were a powerful demonstration of the negotiating skills of the businessman-politician. But although Chamberlain understood how, in dealing with the Nazis, the stakes would be raised to the highest possible level, ultimately he lacked the insight to comprehend that, to Hitler, the rules of the game meant nothing.

NOTES

1. R. Graves and A. Hodge, *The Long Weekend: A Social History of Great Britain 1918–1939* (Hutchinson, 1985), p. 267.
2. R. Griffiths, *Fellow Travellers of the Right* (Constable, 1980), p. 9.
3. For the confused attempts of the press to be 'fair' to the new Germany see for example, A. Scharf, *The British Press and Jews under Nazi Rule* (OUP, 1964), p. 35.
4. R. Skidelsky, *John Maynard Keynes, Vol.2*, pp. 514–16.
5. Medlicott, *Britain and Germany*, p. 4. Medlicott was unable to find any evidence of Sir Warren Fisher's alleged attempts to prevent the Foreign Office from strengthening its economic side. Foreign Office venom was reserved for the Bank of England.
6. Sir Eric Phipps replaced Rumbold in the summer of 1933.
7. K.G. Robbins, *Munich 1938* (Cassell, 1968), p. 46. Robbins plays down the strength of reaction in official quarters to the Nazi election.
8. E. Wiskemann, *The Europe I Saw* (Collins, 1968), p. 38.
9. H. James, 'Innovation and conservatism in economic recovery: The alleged "Nazi recovery" of the 1930s', in T. Childers and J. Caplan (eds), *Reevaluating the Third Reich* (New York, NY: Holmes & Meier, 1993), p. 124.
10. For an expert analysis of how Schacht and his conservative allies in business and the military were to lose this power struggle see R.J. Overy, *Goering: The 'Iron Man'* (Routledge & Kegan Paul, 1984).
11. A. Barkai, *Nazi Economics: Ideology, Theory and Policy* (Oxford: Berg, 1990), p. 10. On the continuities in policy from Weimar Republic to Third Reich see E. Teichert, *Autarkie und Grossraumwirtschaft in Deutschland 1930–1939* (München: Oldenbourg,1984).
12. C.W. Guillebaud, *The Economic Recovery of Germany from 1933 to the incorporation of Austria in March 1938* (Macmillan, 1939), p. 32. After visiting Germany, Guillebaud, a Cambridge economist, emphasized what he took to be the solid economic achievements of the régime in solving the twin problems of mass unemployment and stagnation. See D. Welch, *The Third Reich: Politics and Propaganda* (Routledge, 1993), p. 59.

13. B.H. Klein, *Germany's Economic Preparations for War* (Cambridge, MA: Harvard University Press, 1959), p. 3.
14. Arndt, *Economic Lessons* , p. 157.
15. Ellis, *Exchange Control*, p. 40.
16. FO 371/16693/C1188, minute by Ashton-Gwatkin.
17. T 160/590/8797/05/3, minute by Waley to Leith-Ross and note by latter.
18. For further examples see A.P. Adamthwaite, *The Making of the Second World War* (Allen & Unwin, 1979), p. 43.
19. See Overy, *Goering*, p. 51, for Hitler's comments in 1936 on how economic life had to serve exclusively the German people's struggle for existence. See also, I. Kershaw, *The Nazi Dictatorship: Problems and Perspectives of Interpretation* (Edward Arnold, 1993), pp. 57–8.
20. James, "Innovation and conservatism", p. 128.
21. For background see, I. Kershaw, *Hitler. 1889–1936: Hubris* (Allen Lane, 1998), pp. 370–2.
22 . G.L. Weinberg, *The Foreign Policy of Hitler's Germany: Diplomatic Revolution in Europe 1933–36* (Chicago, IL: University of Chicago Press, 1970), p. 30; see also W.A. Boelcke, *Die Kosten von Hitlers Krieg: Kriegsfinanzierung und Kriegserbe in Deutschland 1933–1948* (Paderborn: Schöningh, 1985), p. 17.
23 . BoE OV34/83, letter, 20 March 1933.
24 . National Archives, USA (hereafter NA), 862.50/1040, telegram, Kennedy to Secretary of State, 27 February 1939.
25. FO 371/16693.
26. FO 371/16695/C4949.
27. FO 371/16696/C5106 and C5438, report by Pinsent.
28. Guillebaud, *The Economic Recovery*, p. 63.
29. Schacht, *My First Seventy-Six Years*, pp. 315–16.
30. Ellis, *Exchange Control*, p. 60.
31. T 160/465/8797/01, memo, by S.D. Waley, 19 June 1933; FO 371/16696/C5584.
32. FO 371/16697/C6025.
33 . FO 371/16697/C6046, letter, 5 July 1933.
34 . T 160/465/8797/01, Leith-Ross to Vansittart; FO 371/16699/C8678.
35 . FO 371/16697/C6493 and C6691.
36 . T 160/465/8797/01.
37 . T 160/642/8797/04/1, memo, by Waley, 9 August 1933.
38 . Ibid., memo, by Tiarks, 'Zusätzliche Exports', 30 August 1933.
39 . *Financial Times*, 21 November 1933.
40 . MB 30/207, Crick's report on visit to Germany, September/October 1933. Crick went on to be a General Manager of the Bank (between 1947 and 1961) – at the time a unique distinction for an economist.
41 . T 160/642/8797/04/1, Bank of England memo, 6 September 1933. It is interesting to note how much had changed with the onset of the Great Depression: Britain's return to the gold standard – just eight years earlier – produced an overvalued pound which damaged the chances of a recovery in exports.
42 . FO 371/16700/C9561.
43 . MB 30/207, Crick's report of visit, September/October 1933.
44 . NA 862.51/3713, report by US Legation at The Hague, 11 October 1933.
45 . *Financial Times*, 10 October 1933.
46 . T 160/642/8797/04/2, note of Norman/Hopkins meeting, 17 October 1933

and minute, Phillips to Hopkins, 28 October 1933.

47. FO 371/16700 C9637.
48. DGFP, Ser. C, Vol.2, Doc.103, pp. 179–80.
49. T 160/642/8797/04/3, Ambassador Phipps to Simon, 31 October 1933 and Pinsent to Waley, 9 November 1933. Frustrated officials suggested that in the last resort, discriminatory tariffs might prove the only, if brutal, way to move Germany, even though that option was debarred under the 1924 Anglo-German Commercial Treaty.
50. Ibid., Bank of England to Waley, 28 November 1933.
51. T 160/642/8797/04/4. An interdepartmental meeting was held on 1 December 1933 with Colonel Colville (Board of Trade) in the chair.
52. T 160/642/8797/02/1; also T 160/642/8797/04/5.
53. BoE OV34/195, correspondence of 28 and 29 December 1933.
54. Ibid., note by Clay. Prominent as a Professor of Economics at Manchester, Clay was an influential Adviser.
55. FO 371/16702/C11241.
56. *Manchester Guardian*, 1 January 1934.
57. T 160/642/8797/04/6.
58. T 160/642/8797/04/7, letter from Stopford (Secretary, Joint Committee) to Simon, 25 January 1934. Commitments had declined from the original £65m to £54m, with actual availments totaling £43.6m, although repaid credits were held open for redrawing if desired.
59. T 160/602/8797/04/6, Pinsent to Rowe-Dutton, 8 January 1934.
60. FO 371/17675/C315, minute by Wigram to Vansittart, 16 January 1934.
61. NC 2/23A, Political Diaries 1933–36, 22 January 1934.
62. DGFP, Ser. C, Vol.2, Doc.204, p. 382.
63. Ibid., Doc. 196, p. 382.
64. Ibid., Doc. 200, p. 387.
65. Ibid., Docs. 193 and 197, pp. 380–3.
66. T 160/642/8797/04/7.
67. T 160/642/8797/04/3, Board of Trade returns (unadjusted). Germany's export surplus for each quarter of 1933 was assumed to be: I – £566,000; II – £859,000; III – £1,502,000; IV – £2,400,000.
68. This was 30 per cent cash and 70 per cent scrip (with the Golddiskontbank redemption rate increased from 50 to 67 per cent of face value).
69. BoE OV34/198, memo, 27 January 1934.
70. NC 18/1/859, 3 February 1934.
71. On this issue see, for example, D. Dutton, *Simon: a Political Biography of Sir John Simon* (Aurum Press, 1992), p. 170.
72. FO 371/17676/C749, minutes by (i) Sargent, 2 and 9 February, (ii) Vansittart, 13 February, (iii) Simon, 16 February 1934.
73. FO 371/17676/C749, minutes, 1/2 February 1934.
74. FO 371/17677/C1232, 22 February 1934. Vansittart looked to enlist the support of Fisher to bring about a change in the attitude of the Governor and the City.
75. FO 371/17742/C1590, 27 March 1934.
76. For a critical account of Britain's position see P. Clavin, 'The World Economic Conference 1933: The failure of British internationalism', *JEEH*, 20, 3 (Winter 1991). Clavin also shows how Germany was frustrated by Britain's apparent failure to acknowledge the damage caused by the Ottawa agreements. See also P. Kennedy, *The Rise and Fall of the Great Powers: Economic Change and Military Conflict from 1500 to 2000* (New York, NY:

Random House, 1987), pp. 333–6.

77. D. Cameron Watt, *Succeeding John Bull*, pp. 66–8.
78. NA RG59/862.51/3704, report by US Commercial Attaché (Berlin), 1 September 1933.
79. NA RG59/862.51/3698, telegram, Cordell Hull to Dodd (Berlin), 9 October 1933.
80. NA RG59/862.51/3782, letter from Lindsay (British Ambassador, Washington) to William Phillips (Acting Secretary), 23 December 1933.
81. NA RG59/862.51/3789, telegrams, 29 December 1933 and 15 January 1934.
82. NA RG59/862.51/3806, telegram, 19 January 1934.
83. FO 371/17675/C77. The news department of the Foreign Office asked, unofficially, the 'important' newspapers to drop hints about the possible institution of a clearing. A uniform approach was avoided, however, in case it gave rise to accusations of a conspiracy. The tone of the press in January 1934 suggests that Fleet Street was only too happy to co-operate.
84. T 160/590/8797/05/1, minute by Sir Warren Fisher.
85. NA RG59/862.51/3930A and 3931, telegrams from Cordell Hull to Swiss and Dutch Legations, 10 and 11 April 1934.
86. NA RG59/862.51/4007, memo, by Cordell Hull, 14 May 1934; see also RG59/862.51/4019, report by US Chargé d'Affaires (Berlin), 16 May 1934.
87. B.J.C. McKercher, *Transition of Power: Britain's Loss of Global Pre-eminence to the United States, 1930–1945* (Cambridge: CUP, 1999), pp. 172–6.
88. Boyce, 'World depression, world war', pp. 85–8.
89. D.Cameron Watt, *Succeeding John Bull*, pp. 80–1.
90. T 160/590/8797/05/2, telegram from Pinsent (Berlin) to Treasury, 18 May 1934.
91. T 160/590/8797/05/1.
92. BoE OV34/198, Leith-Ross to Governor, 13 June 1934.
93. T 160/590/8797/05/3, letter to Runciman, 4 June 1934.
94. Guillebaud, *Economic Recovery*, p. 64; G. Stolper, *The German Economy 1870 to the Present* (New York, NY: Harcourt, Brace & World, 1967), p. 114. In the first six months of 1934 *Devisen* reserves deteriorated so rapidly that they did not exceed 2.5 per cent of note circulation.
95. Ellis, *Exchange Control*, p. 200.
96. T 160/590/8797/05/3; CAB 24/249, 169, memo by Chamberlain and Runciman, 18 June 1934.
97. T 160/590/8797/05/3, 12 June 1934.
98. T 160/534/13460/08, letter by Beaumont Pease to Governor, 21 June 1934 with enclosed memo. See MB 30/189 for the aforementioned letter in draft form, 20 June 1934, which asserted that, in the event of any difficulties, the government would have assumed a great responsibility towards those bankers and merchants in need of help. See also BoE OV6/290 for Stopford memo, 12 June 1934. This assumes the worst: a clearing would lead to a breakdown of all arrangements for dealing with German debts internationally with consequent competitive grabbing by the several creditor countries. Deprived of the purchasing power for essential imports, Germany would be reduced to a state of economic chaos.
99. T 160/534/13460/08, minutes by Waley and Leith-Ross, 23 June 1934.
100. FO 371/17682/C3805, letter, Law (the FO's City informant), to Sargent, 15 June 1934.
101. T 160/534/13460/08, 28 June 1934.
102. NC 18/1/876, letter to Ida (Chamberlain's sister), 22 June 1934.

103. T 160/590/8797/05/4, memo, 27 June 1934.
104. T 160/534/13460/04, Frank Fehr & Co., to Chancellor, 11 July 1934.
105. Ibid., London Chamber to Chancellor, 27 June 1934.
106. T 160/534/13460/06.
107. Ibid., Waley to St.Quinton Hill (Board of Trade, Commercial Relations and Treaties Department).
108. E.V. Francis, *Britain's Economic Strategy* (Jonathan Cape, 1939), p. 272.
109. Cmd 4640.
110. 'The German agreement: robbing Peter to pay Paul?', *Financial News*, 6 July 1934. Einzig also highlighted the extent to which German imports had been financed by new commercial credits outside the Standstill. Most banks had been unwilling to grant new credits to Germany, yet exporters had continued to ship goods on a credit basis. The longstanding connections between British exporters and German importers meant that the former had been willing to deliver goods against book credits, or bills drawn upon them and accepted by the importers. See also T 160/522/12750/02/3; the Treasury simply dismissed the article as a reflection of the views of some of the less reasonable members of the London Chamber of Commerce.
111. FO 371/17684, information from Nigel Law.
112. T 188/77, Leith-Ross to Foreign Office, 11 July 1934. Leith-Ross had been given the letter which alleged that this conversation took place at the Bank of England on 9 June 1934.The identity of the writer was not revealed in order, presumably, to maintain maximum confidentiality.
113. FO 371/17684/C4611, C4613 and C4699, minutes by Sargent, Wigram and Vansittart.
114. NC 18/1/878, letter to Ida, 7 July 1934.
115. Parker, *Chamberlain and Appeasement*, pp. 9–10.

4

Britain's trade and payments with the Third Reich: 'economic appeasement'?

If the Anglo-German Transfer Agreement of July 1934 allowed British bondholders an opportunity to relax a little, British exporters to Germany continued to wait anxiously for assistance. This finally arrived in November of that year in the form of the Anglo-German Payments Agreement, signed after extremely difficult negotiations. Of all the economic and financial arrangements Britain made with the Third Reich, the Payments Agreement was by far the most important. It established an official framework for regulating economic relations and it was to remain in operation largely unchanged until the outbreak of war. It has even been linked with the Anglo-German Naval Agreement, concluded six months later, as one of the two pillars of British policy towards the Third Reich.

Was Britain wrong to choose a bilateral agreement as the instrument with which to implement the policy of maintaining trade with Nazi Germany without increasing credit commitments? In all the arrangements of this kind made by Germany, the terms secured with Britain were the most favourable. Under the trade ratio agreed, the Third Reich was able to go on collecting the considerable proceeds of its export surplus with Britain – so-called free sterling. For this reason Paul Einzig came to regard the agreement as 'the first act of economic appeasement'.[1] Peter Ludlow suggests that, strictly in terms of Britain's national interest, the agreement was not disastrous: it was an example of the National Government's 'sound management'. Britain was the most successful state in Europe in steering her economy through the economic crisis of the 1930s. But seen in terms of its implications for the recovery of the Western European economy and its significance to those who ruled in Berlin, the agreement, according to Ludlow, was destructive of international trade. It provided an early indication that Britain was prepared to pursue its own comfort and security, even at the expense of harming its neighbours and accepting terms laid down by the Third Reich.[2]

This judgement may be challenged on several counts. In the fractured commercial world of the 1930s it was not unusual for states to practise stringent exchange control arrangements. The first German bilateral trade and payments conventions were set up as emergency measures in 1932. Trade could then be conducted on a quota basis. Under National Socialism, the agreement made with Britain was the most important: it provided a blueprint for the many which were to follow with other countries.[3] These arrangements formed a fundamental part of the Nazi strategy to build an autarkic bloc in *Mitteleuropa*.[4]

But another central objective of Nazi economic policy was the progressive reduction in the amount of free exchange available to foreign creditors. It became obvious in 1933/34 that payments between Britain and Germany would have to be controlled in some way: the suffering experienced by British trade and financial interests was widespread. Without a structure which defined and formalized relations, a complete breakdown seemed likely. There were calls for Britain to impose a unilateral clearing system or even exchange controls. The authorities resisted these demands and, after failed experimentation, negotiated a more liberal structure instead.

The formation and operation of the Anglo-German payments system must be seen against the wider picture of Britain's external economic relations. When considering the effect on world trade of any British bilateral agreement, businessmen and politicians alike were in no doubt that clearings were the worst form of impediment. These arrangements were strenuously opposed by Britain throughout the world crisis and, to reiterate the point made earlier, action against Germany would have been taken only as a last resort. The fundamental objection was that clearings injured international trade, especially entrepôt trade – regarded as one of Britain's greatest resources. The Treasury was afraid that once general powers were established there would be continuous pressure to use them in all sorts of cases and that Britain would then find itself trying to conduct foreign trade under a system of perpetual government interference.[5]

At first sight such a robust defence of free trade, when imperial preference had just been embraced, seems curiously anachronistic. But it is precisely the events of 1931/32 which help to explain why clearings were so disliked. Everyone in the political class was conscious of the part Britain had just played in the world economic crisis; some felt that it was a part in which the country could hardly take pride. For the benefit of his Treasury colleagues, Sir Frederick Phillips reinforced a point already made by others:

> No country ever administered a more severe shock to international trade than we did when we both (1) depreciated the £. (2) almost simultaneously turned from free trade to protection. Overwhelming reasons can be given why we were compelled to do these things but the point is we ought not to be too touchy at developments abroad which interfere with us.[6]

This candid confession gives an insight into how self-reproach shaped British policy. A dark cloud of uncertainty and unease started to gather as the implications of Britain's revolution in external economic policy became clearer. By 1934 no one could say that the Nazi régime had been given insufficient time to settle down. Unfortunately, there was very little in its behaviour from which a liberal democratic state could draw comfort. While the collapse of the Weimar Republic could hardly be blamed on Britain's abandonment of the old economic certainties, every opportunity had to be taken to try to preserve a vestige of the collapsing liberal trade structure even, or perhaps especially, in relations with the most illiberal of states.

The rise and fall of the Anglo-German Exchange Agreement for Commercial Payments

British exporters experienced problems in trading with Germany before the Nazis came to power. In commenting on the extent of the injury to British firms in 1932, the Berlin Embassy referred to the possibility of a payments clearing agreement with Germany.[7] Once raised, this idea retained the power to stir up strong feelings for the rest of the decade. Anything which remotely resembled a clearing, or which caused central banks to interfere with the business of merchant banks, immediately aroused the suspicions of London bankers. In his capacity as a director of the Bank of England, Charles Hambro produced the usual theoretical objections to the proposal, and reasons why the Bank would decline to act as agent. These included fear of the 'canalization' of trade, the risk of exchange dumping to the disadvantage of British industries producing for the home market, and depletion of the Reichsbank's reserves. It was also highly desirable for British trade (diversified, changing and largely credit-based), to be as free as possible from bureaucratic control, he argued.[8]

The problem of trade debts was obviously not going to disappear with the collapse of the Weimar Republic. The British Embassy in Berlin decided to advocate some sort of exchange agreement with Germany as an alternative way forward. To the diplomats, bankers appeared to be selfishly pursuing their own interests: Britain was disadvantaged by being the only important European trading nation which did not have this kind of agreement with Germany. Hambro was accused of failing to understand that different types of Reichmark, with various limitations attached to them, commanded different prices. Marks resulting from exchange agreements were commercially free and, because they were used for certain non-commercial payments, were priced higher than the limited blocked marks.[9]

Other attempts were made to persuade the Bank of England that an agreement would not so fetter trade that Britain's business with Germany would soon shrink. The Conservative MP Sir Walter Preston, company chairman and friend of the Governor, pointed out that no one objected to the whole of Russia's trade coming to Britain through the agency of the All Russia Co-operative Society (ARCOS); traders submitted to this condition as they wanted Russia's business. But the Governor continued to be concerned that British exporters would assume commitments without being aware of the uncertainties and risks of *Konversionskasse* marks.[10]

Exchange agreements between Germany and other countries seemed to work well. But they tended to have the effect of diverting trade to those countries and away from Britain. A number of British exporters even sent goods through Holland in order to reach German clients who had exhausted their exchange quotas. An agreement was seen as a gratuitous means of maintaining Britain's position against further damage on the German market. When, finally, the Chancellor of the Exchequer and the President of the

Board of Trade accepted that an agreement was necessary, the Bank of England did not wish to stand out against it any longer. Cameron Cobbold, adviser to the Governors, conceded that their arguments had always been rather thin and that, while an agreement would undoubtedly be a nuisance to the Bank, it would aid some exporters.[11]

But there was to be no immediate relief: the scheme lay dormant while the more pressing affairs of the bondholders received attention. Reports of the hardships and difficulties facing British traders began to mount. Companies always tried to assure themselves that their German customers possessed sufficient foreign currency to cover orders placed. No provision could be made, however, for the rapid reduction which took place in the basic foreign exchange quota, from 50 per cent in February to 10 per cent in June 1934. German customers were unable to pay for anything other than the minimum of imports necessary to keep business going. Although British traders hardly ever bought from and sold to the same German firm, such were their losses that they clamoured to be allowed to offset their credits against their debts, especially as their European competitors enjoyed such an advantage.[12]

Once the bondholders had reached an agreement, the way was open for official trade talks to take place in Berlin. Surprisingly, the Board of Trade was content to have frozen trade debts excluded. Sir Henry Fountain, the Second Secretary, acknowledged that the question was a vexed one which seriously disturbed many traders, particularly the coal exporters and the Lancashire cotton spinners. But neither government wanted to burden the scheme proposed with the additional marks necessary for the liquidation of frozen debts.[13]

An Exchange Agreement for Commercial Payments was signed in Berlin on 10 August 1934. German importers of British goods, having used up their foreign exchange quota (which took next to no time), were now able to pay the balance into a Sonder mark account, opened at the Reichsbank in the name of the Bank of England. Payments into this special account were to be suspended when the balance exceeded Rm5m marks. The Bank of England could make payments out of the account for goods exported from Germany. The agreement was not intended to lead to the alteration in the balance of Anglo-German trade. It also seemed experimental in nature: only two weeks' notice of termination by either side was necessary.[14]

Moreover, the scheme was voluntary. It depended for its success on the extent to which British importers of German goods used the account in paying for their purchases. With Britain importing more than she exported, demand for Sonder marks was expected to be adequate for the scheme to work. New British exports could be financed without straining German foreign exchange reserves.

The financial authorities in Britain realized almost immediately that this was not a satisfactory solution to the problem. Cobbold thought that the Germans hated the agreement and that they would call Britain's bluff and themselves impose a clearing on the Empire.[15] The arrangement was, indeed, so unsatisfactory that it was in trouble within a few weeks. The Bank's fears were realized, but for reasons opposite to the ones suggested: British traders were only too aware of the risks attached to currency transactions. The supply of Sonder marks was greater than the demand. The London Chamber of Commerce reported that many importers were going to avoid speculation in exchange and continue to buy for sterling. A forward market for Sonder marks would have made little difference; German exporters were not trusted to carry out their contracts if the mark depreciated and, in any case, they much preferred payment in freely convertible sterling. Montagu Norman was able to express his general abhorrence of the scheme. Exactly one month after the signing of the agreement the total unsold balance reached Rm7m and payment in Sonder marks for British exports was subsequently suspended.[16]

In the Bank of England, Siepmann and Clay – both advisers to the Governors – clashed over whether the initiative lay with Britain. Siepmann, like Cobbold, questioned the assumption that Germany found Empire raw materials indispensable. By diverting her purchases and threatening a compulsory Empire clearing, Germany might have created endless trouble for Britain. Siepmann recommended, therefore, that commercial arrears would just have to be overtaken by new trade. He also envisaged abandoning the middle- and long-term bondholders to their fate, even though Britain had already done remarkably well, because the doctrine of non-discrimination could no longer be sustained in practice. Siepmann has to be counted among those who were greatly disturbed by the change in external policies. On tariffs, on competitive currency depreciation, and on disarmament he believed Britain had allowed herself to be forced to do harmful things which many people regretted. He had no doubt that there was everything to gain by being 'sensible' with Germany; this involved abandoning the idea of substituting the financial authorities for the original claimants.

In contrast, Henry Clay was fearful of virtually relinquishing control of policy to Schacht, who seemed to be attempting the impossible, and he predicted that Germany's deteriorating trade position would continue to be the governing factor in relations. As a consequence, he believed that the problem of the priority of different British claims would be brought up every few months with each piecemeal settlement exciting fresh ill-feeling. Machinery was necessary, therefore, in order to balance conflicting British claims and to agree with Germany the order in which they should be met.[17]

The suspension of the exchange agreement caused immense frustration in London. Admitting that he was 'desperately gloomy' about the chaotic situation, Leith-Ross also saw the need to forestall complete control of trade by Germany.[18] The Foreign Office, increasingly desperate to prevent Germany from enjoying a potentially dangerous advantage, wanted any new agreement to cover the whole field of economic and financial relations.[19] The political and economic élite in Britain were becoming particularly disillusioned with Schacht. Although he was not held responsible for the economic policies of the Hitler régime, he had seemed to represent the best safeguard against extremism. It was, none the less, in the Third Reich that the world's most extreme form of economic nationalism was being perfected. Schacht was roundly condemned, therefore, as a financial fraudster. His crime was to act on the basis of his allegation that Germany's foreign loans were political just because money had been borrowed during the years of reparations payments. His angry refusal, in public at least, to accept that autarky would reduce the German population to a low standard of living appeared quite irrational and blind. That the rewards for taking the lead in trying to re-establish Germany's political and financial position should be so meagre was greatly resented.[20]

The experiences of British industry from the 1920s revealed a similar pattern. Germany managed to obtain imports without paying for them, first by long-term loans on which the country had defaulted; secondly via unpaid, short-term Standstill credits, and thirdly by failing to carry out promises to exporters. Sonder marks carried the process a stage further: goods were obtained on credit while no assistance was given in the liquidation of the account. The reluctance of the Nazi Party to honour past financial obligations invited comparison with the behaviour of Bolshevik Russia. Exporters in Britain felt compelled to offer extended credit terms. If they tried to demand cash against documents, business was diverted to those countries able to offer more favourable terms involving various forms of compensation arrangements or private clearings. Organizations such as the FBI regarded Schacht's subordination of international trade to the primary object of stimulating German domestic production and employment as amoral patriotism.[21]

Protecting traders or preference for bankers?

In the late summer of 1934 Britain was faced with a problem growing more serious by the day. While the government had shown how reluctant it was to protect the interests of exporters, it had become obvious that an agreement of some kind could not be postponed indefinitely. But the procedure selected had effectively failed almost as soon as it was put into operation and trade was beginning to collapse. The Lancashire spinning industry, owed commercial debts of £400,000 by German importers of cotton yarn, decided to stop further deliveries, even though they feared that they might lose their market share to the Swiss and the Czechs. At the invitation of the importers, a delegation of cotton spinners went to Berlin to try to obtain their money through separate arrangements. Sir Henry Fountain, rather less sanguine than before, warned that Schacht probably intended to divide British interests by satisfying only those whose exports were necessary to Germany.[22]

Indeed, divisions already existed in Britain between some sectors of industry and financial interests, and between industry and the government. Leslie Burgin, the Parliamentary Secretary to the Board of Trade, received a delegation of cotton, woollen and coal interests. Their hostility was taken as an indication of the passion which had been roused in the country. It was the exporters with frozen debts who were the most vocal in complaining that they had suffered discrimination. Burgin reported to Runciman that the position was ugly: the Bradford 'ring-leaders' had no confidence whatever in the government's position or its efforts. The delegation told Burgin that they suspected a preference for finance over commerce. London banks, including Schroders, had just sent representatives to Berlin at Schacht's invitation.[23] Suspicions were aroused because Leith-Ross was also in Berlin to begin preliminary talks. But as soon as his audience had gathered, Schacht staged another *coup de théâtre*: on 19 September 1934 he announced even more stringent foreign-exchange controls. It served the purpose of the Reich authorities to admit that, with such an enormous *Devisen* deficit, Germany's whole quota system of foreign exchange allocation was failing abysmally. Schacht's New Plan abolished all the general exchange permits and subjected all imports to licensing. The few remaining openings for British exporters seemed to be closing rapidly.

Not surprisingly, the Anglo-German discussions began angrily. Leith-Ross tried to convince von Neurath, the Foreign Minister, that the German market was not so strong that other countries would be forced to supply goods on credit rather than not export to Germany at all. He warned that Britain would cut off trade if her exports were reduced and that she would last longer in any competition in suicide. The devious response, furnished by Schacht, was to insist that there was no desire to divert purchases of raw materials from normal channels. It cost nothing to recognize London as the best centre through which to organize buying or to welcome the maintenance of the bills and facilities for international trade offered by the City. Schacht also took the opportunity to recite his mantra: British war debts to America were analogous to the Dawes and Young loans because the latter were incurred in order to pay reparations.[24]

On several occasions throughout the decade Britain assumed that Germany was on the point of economic collapse. In late 1934 Britain expected the inconsistency between Nazi financial and economic policy to produce, at the very least, an impasse and a forced devaluation. This was not particularly unrealistic. According to one leading historian of the Third Reich, the progress of the Nazi economic miracle was then stalling; the public's enthusiasm was fading so fast that, by 1935, the mounting problems were to turn rumbling discontent into visible displays of unrest.[25]

Assumptions in Whitehall about the state of the German economy buttressed the case for a clearing: the Nazis could be taught a lesson because resources for imports and raw materials would be curtailed and unemployment and discontent accentuated. It was hoped that at the last moment the Reich government would recoil in horror at the awful prospect of economic disaster. Significantly, no one suggested that Britain should deliberately seek to facilitate political upheaval and thereby threaten the very existence of the Third Reich. Recent events had proved that disasters could not necessarily be confined to one country. German instability might have precipitated a collapse with serious ramifications for the world economy. And, of course, there was no consensus on the likely effect of a clearing.

Consequently, the British position was largely one of bluff. Leith-Ross predicted in September 1934 that Germany had the capacity to last out a long time on her own resources and could not be blockaded into submission. He cautioned against the mistake of expecting any sudden change in the Nazi régime: 'We should, therefore, do all we can to maintain our trade with Germany so long as we can do so without increasing our credit commitments to her.'[26] Leith-Ross did not feel the need to revise this judgement when he wrote his semi-autobiographical *Money Talks* more than 30 years later. Trade sanctions would have meant restricting British commerce and compounding economic difficulties, while the Nazi Party would have been given an excellent pretext for the anti-foreign propaganda on which it relied to justify the tightening of the belts of the German people. Yet, *Money Talks* does reflect on the way surplus sterling allowed the Reichsbank to finance the import of raw materials such as tin and copper. The Germans feared that in a clearing system Britain might require sterling to be used for the purchase of British-made products.[27] Leith-Ross neglects to add that such a requirement was never seriously contemplated.

That Neville Chamberlain, as Chancellor, should also be greatly exercised by the state of Anglo-German economic relations in 1934 was to be expected. But the source of his frustration was his inability to exploit the situation in order to direct foreign policy. In a private letter in October he put down a revealing early marker to the way British policy-making was to evolve: he felt that he had to try to bring about an understanding with 'another country' but was 'contending all the time with the lethargy of the Foreign Office'. Chamberlain was almost embarrassed at Britain's continued economic improvement while the rest of the world, and Germany in particular, seemed to be continually running downhill.[28] Nevertheless, Leith-Ross was to be allowed a free hand in order to fight the Germans over trade issues as hard as possible.

Many in Britain now argued that the only way to get Germany to make a satisfactory arrangement for existing or future trade debts was through a clearing. At the same time, Berlin's threats to boycott Empire trade, or to impose a clearing based on the Empire, were taken seriously. Schacht constantly criticized British colonial trade practices. Recent analysis has confirmed, however, that Britain was correct to assert that Germany could not show that she was being denied access to colonial raw materials. The volume of German purchases of certain raw materials from the Empire – particularly strategic commodities such as rubber and copper – increased significantly in the period 1932–38.[29] While Britain was careful to give consideration to German complaints concerning the colonial issue, the threats made against Empire trade could not be dismissed: Germany was already attempting to obtain as many raw materials as possible through barter. Consequently, the British Cabinet decided on 3 October 1934 that negotiations with the Nazi government should begin for a bilateral clearing which would operate from 1 November. Although the talks started with the avowed aim of setting up a clearing there was considerable reluctance on both sides to take this step if some other acceptable method could be found.[30]

In preparing the draft order the Treasury estimated the likely outcome of exchange requirements between Britain and Germany for the whole of 1934. It was assumed that Germany would have a balance of £1.5m available as a result of the merchandise transactions between the two countries, including British re-exports. To set against this, however, Germany required some £5m to service UK debts (less than previous estimates). In addition, the total outstanding commercial debt owed to the UK, comprising more than 393 claims, stood at some £4.7m.[31]

The renewed prospect of a clearing propelled the bankers of London on to the offensive once again. This time, the Joint Committee sought to highlight the difference between bankers and traders. The former, it was suggested, had never looked to the government for aid in the collection of their claims, although they continued to fear that this would change when a clearing rendered renewal of the Standstill inequitable or impracticable. Rather, the government had sought the co-operation of the bankers in abstaining from collection, at a time when German capacity to pay was much greater than it had subsequently become. In contrast, debts due to British traders had been incurred at a time when the German economic situation, legislative restrictions and practical limitations affecting the provision of exchange were all a matter of public knowledge. The bankers did not want to appear too unsympathetic: it was just that they wanted to secure as much protection for financial claims as for those of other classes.[32]

However much influence the bankers had with Montagu Norman, and however much respect the latter could command in Treasury circles, Leith-Ross, for one, was not over-impressed by the combined weight. Reflecting on the extent of governmental responsibility for the Standstill, he concluded that in 1931 the bankers had been between the devil and the deep blue sea: without the Standstill arrangement Germany would have imposed a moratorium and the bankers would have been compelled to ask for protection. The effect of the Standstill had been to freeze up that volume of German indebtedness, with really only interest being paid, as the only alternative to a complete breakdown.[33] Although the objective was to liquidate frozen trade debts gradually, German exports did tend to decline under clearing systems and this was a danger for Britain too. The Treasury was persuaded, therefore, that some of the big short-term creditors were genuinely frightened lest the end of the Standstill was in sight. Although correspondence flowed between the Chancellor and the bankers via Governor Norman, each steadfastly refused to accept completely the case put by the other side.

The Payments Agreement and the hidden hand of the Bank of England

A major reason for Norman's concern stemmed from the fact that the Bank of England itself played a significant part in the business of the Standstill. Having decided to encourage and even sponsor London participation in the arrangement, the Bank did everything possible to ensure marketability. The Bank held many of the bills which represented the greatest part of the credits given by London. The Governor's willingness to rediscount these bills was a necessary basis of the system so far as the City was concerned.[34] In the first half of 1932 nearly half of the bills discounted at the Bank were of German origin. Yet the Bank disliked their artificiality, believing that while they circulated the commercial bill was prostituted. One idea was to follow the Dutch central bank and launch an official

1. Anglo-French discussions at Downing Street, 9 April, 1932.
Left to *Right*: Runciman (President of the Board of Trade), Chamberlain
(Chancellor of the Exchequer), Tardieu (Premier), MacDonald (Prime Minister),
Flandin (Minister of Finance), Fleuriau (French Ambassador),
Simon (Foreign Secretary). *(Topham Picturepoint)*

2. At the Lausanne Conference: Ramsay MacDonald, with daughter Ishbel, and
Neville Chamberlain. *(Special Collections, The Robinson Library, University of
Newcastle)*

3. On Board the *Empress of Britain* en route to Ottawa.
Left to *Right*: (standing) Gilmour, Cunliffe-Lister, Lord Hailsham, Runciman, (seated) J. H. Thomas, Baldwin, Chamberlain. *(Special Collections, The Robinson Library, University of Newcastle)*

4. Lord Runciman and Frank Ashton-Gwatkin (Foreign Office) returning from Prague, 16 September, 1938. *(Hulton Getty)*

5. Sir Warren Fisher, Permanent Secretary to the Treasury and head of HM Civil Service, January, 1939. *(Hulton Getty)*

6. Sir Richard Valentine Nind Hopkins, Second Secretary to the Treasury. *(Hulton Getty)*

7. Sir Frederick Leith-Ross, Chief Economic Adviser to the government. *(Topham Picturepoint)*

8. Sir Robert Vansittart, Permanent Under-Secretary to the Foreign Office, leaving his Mayfair, London, home. February, 1934. *(Hulton Getty)*

9. Montagu Norman, Governor of the Bank of England, leaving Southampton for Canada on board the *Duchess of York*, 15 August, 1931. *(Hulton Getty)*

10. Sir Frank Platt, Lancashire Cotton Corporation. *(Topham Picturepoint)*

11. Sir Eric Geddes *(Centre)*, Dunlop Rubber Company, surrounded by the 'Geddes Axe' committee. *(Topham Picturepoint)*

12. Reginald McKenna, Chairman of the Midland Bank. *(Topham Picturepoint)*

13. Sir John, later Lord, Cadman, Chairman of the Anglo-Iranian Oil Company. *(© BP Amoco plc)*

14. Freddie Morris, Deputy Director in charge of Continental Affairs, Anglo-Iranian Oil Company. *(© BP Amoco plc)*

15. Aviation Service of Olex (the German subsidiary of the Anglo-Iranian Oil Company) at Berlin, 1930. (© *BP Amoco plc*)

16. Olex filling station and attendant, Pappenheimstrasse, Marsfeld-Munich. (*Phototechnische Anstalt, Paul Hartlmaier, München 2 SW 5. From the BP Amoco Archive*)

17. Wagons being filled with *Leuna-Benzin*, the synthetic oil produced by IG Farbenindustrie in partnership with Standard Oil and Shell.
(Photo: AKG London)

operation to take the bills off the market. But rather than give an impression of too much government involvement, the Bank opted instead to monitor carefully the implications of Standstill indebtedness. Sayers points out that while the Bank encouraged the 'fiction' that it was proper for these bills to be held in the market, it was also remembered that those firms which were especially dependent on their value might, at some time, need supporting.[35]

In late 1934 it seemed that that time had almost arrived. If the Standstill had broken down the City would have refused to deal in the bills and any default by the acceptors would probably have provoked a crisis requiring intervention by the authorities to avoid a collapse of the London market. On 24 October the chairman of the National Provincial Bank (which carried the accounts of most of the acceptors) was called to the Bank of England and the Governor warned the Committee of the Treasury that the Bank might have to join in a rescue operation for four of the firms. The exposure to all the warnings issuing from the City and to the threats and excuses of the German authorities had a marked effect on Chamberlain:

> I have been having a very worrying time over this Anglo-German negotiation. Horrible possibilities of a German Default and the consequent bankruptcy of some of the great English financial firms have been hanging over me ever since I took office and just lately they have been very menacing.[36]

Meanwhile, the British delegation in Berlin received revised proposals. Schacht, decrying the need for a clearing, had in mind a scheme for liquidating the frozen trade debts (particularly the claims of the herring, coal and textile exporters). Assurances would be given about maintaining British exports on some proportional basis. This scheme involved raising a loan in London using as collateral outstanding sums due to Germany from England.[37] Schacht knew that he could count on Norman's support. The latter, at this stage of the 1930s, was neither concerned about the difficulties of political presentation nor did he entertain suspicions about the bona fides of Germany. Any instrument which was more technically convenient than a clearing was desirable to Norman. Leith-Ross, too, could begin to hope that a combination of Schacht's scheme and the continuation of the Transfer Agreement might enable the government to claim 'Peace with Honour'.[38]

The determination shown in British tactics finally produced a settlement. A clearing was kept in reserve, ready to be imposed if necessary at the last minute. This involved accepting the risk that London's credit business and the raw materials market would suffer direct damage. On 1 November the Anglo-German Payments Agreement was announced. A clearing was avoided once again. Yet, the justification which was offered for not pressing on to obtain safeguards for all payments was that this would have required the institution of novel, cumbrous and expensive machinery which many traders disliked and most bankers detested. Instead, a new technique in British commercial relations had been invented. The President of the Board of Trade, anything but optimistic, warned traders to be cautious. Germany undertook to adjust monthly her imports from Britain to ensure that they amounted to 55 per cent in value of the trade travelling in the opposite direction. If this gave Germany a substantial surplus it also meant, in theory, that the volume of trade was determined exclusively by British initiative.[39]

Under Article 4 of the agreement Germany was bound to make a payment of £400,000 to British trade creditors. Over and above this, the Reich undertook to provide a monthly allocation, provisionally fixed at 10 per cent of the value of German exports to the UK, sufficient to liquidate the outstanding trade debts within one year. German claims on the UK were also to be realized, by a credit operation or otherwise. The phrasing of this last clause was left deliberately vague. Taken together, the terms amounted to a modified version of a clearing. Payments were made in free *Devisen* – an elusive concept under the Nazis – in place of settlement by the offset of clearing balances.

The operation to grant Germany credit was the scheme's most remarkable feature. During the negotiations Schacht had prepared lists of British debtors for the Governor to appraise. The plan was to secure advances from each of the joint-stock banks in respect of the debts owed by their own customers. Norman estimated that the operation would take three weeks and so it was decided to extend credit to Schacht in any case. With this, it appears that the Treasury had been persuaded at the last minute that a clearing could be avoided.[40] Always pessimistic, Norman was frequently autocratic too. He reserved the right to arrange the terms between himself and Schacht and desired written absolution from the ordinary wish of the government that new credits should not be given to Germany.

The Governor confirmed that the Bank of England had been requested to discuss terms for an advance of up to £400,000 in case the Reichsbank needed funds in order to fulfil obligations connected with frozen debts and Sonder marks. Chamberlain readily accepted. While he was not prepared to give a guarantee that any debt incurred by the Reichsbank would be immune from a future clearing, he thought the whole idea was in line with British interests.[41]

Chamberlain not only hoped the Payments Agreement would provide a solution to the difficulties with Germany, he was also delighted with an outcome very much better than the one he had expected. In private, he was generous in his praise for the skills of British officials in calling Schacht's bluff.[42] The agreement was at first well received in public too: the House of Commons greeted it in a positive atmosphere, the City was overjoyed and even traders seemed to be satisfied. But when Schacht made no move in Berlin to commence the credit operation the authorities became uneasy. Britain had been induced to accept the agreement on the understanding that claims on Britain totalled more than £5m. This was sufficient to pay off all the frozen debts. It transpired that the claims comprised up to 8,000 small debts – hardly a good basis on which to raise credit.[43]

Prompted by a telephone call from Cobbold, the Reichsbank proposed to honour its 10 per cent monthly payment to trade creditors by arranging a further credit of £1m with the Bank of England.[44] With the total credit now standing at £1.4m, the question of security had to be taken more seriously. The Bank could justify accepting business only with considerable risk on grounds of public policy. On the other hand, a larger distribution of outstanding debts could be arranged and the Bank was seen as having a better chance than the British government in getting money out of Schacht. Chamberlain and Fisher agreed that the risk was justified.

As trade and government circles began to realize, in late November 1934, that the Payments Agreement was not working well, the euphoria which had accompanied its inception rapidly dissipated. The level of support had almost certainly been based upon relief that a clearing had been avoided. References to a likely breakdown began to appear in the press. The price was being paid for the failure to fix up a relevant and well-defined administrative machinery during the Berlin talks. Although Leith-Ross tried to stop public discussion of the issues, he had serious misgivings over a situation he described as unclear and even 'full of mystery'.[45]

By 4 December Schacht had managed to arrange a credit for £750,000 with the Bank of England. This was to be added to the £400,000 already paid and a sum of £264,000 which represented the 10 per cent allocation for November. The agreement could now start to function. But the ever cautious Norman revealed to Leith-Ross that:

> It is bound to become public knowledge that Germany only makes the payments owing to the advance granted to the Reichsbank. On the other hand the conditions which permitted the advance to be arranged are by agreement held in secrecy between the Chancellor and myself. I think these two points are important: the former may be published abroad; the latter must be hidden.[46]

While knowledge of the advance did become public a day or two later, the conditions were indeed kept hidden. According to a report in the *Financial News*, commercial banking circles were very critical of what appeared to be a straightforward credit to the Reichsbank for a full year, with nobody but the authorities aware of the nature of the debts on which it was secured. There was speculation that the security given would not have been acceptable to a private banking consortium. With the authorities ready to take special measures to expedite payments, it seemed likely that British exporters would be encouraged to sell on credit and that Germany would be financially assisted. The *Financial News* wanted to know, therefore, whether the transaction was in accord with the government's Parliamentary assurances that the extension of fresh credit to Germany was against public policy.[47]

The Foreign Office was certainly not satisfied that the £750,000 advance was in the national interest (as Chamberlain claimed in the Commons on 11 December). Upset at their exclusion from discussions, officials were particularly angry that the nature of the security had been kept secret; they suspected it was little more than a verbal IOU from Schacht. Vansittart was adamant that they should at least have had 'some intelligible explanation' since they were 'not children'.[48] Leith-Ross sought to reassure him:

> I do not know whether you have ever attempted to raise money from the Old Lady, but my belief is that you would find her pockets very

tightly buttoned up unless you could produce extremely good security...and I fancy that however Schacht might treat obligations to other people, he will be extremely anxious to keep faith with the Bank of England.[49]

It is now possible to trace the terms and course of the credit. It was to be for a maximum of one year with interest at variable bank rate plus 1 per cent with repayment in sterling. Security was provided by approved external bills (bona fide trade bills such as the Reichsbank would normally discount), covering the advance with a margin of 10 per cent on sterling bills and of 15 per cent on bills of other currencies. The Reichsbank had to try to arrange that at least 50 per cent of the collateral should always be in sterling bills. By February 1935 the Bank of England thought that the advance was not looking too happy. The shortfall in funds at the end of the term for the repayment of frozen debts was estimated to be £425,000; with the Bank's advance this gave a total deficit of £1.18m. Repayments needed to be increased. Siepmann claimed that he always reckoned the Germans would be this amount short of their undertakings. He immediately contacted Reichsbank director Puhl and £200,000 was swiftly paid back. When the credit balance was reduced later in the year to £150,000 Siepmann was able to note that the situation was 'extremely satisfactory, as was to be expected'.[50]

On the specific matter of the credit, Leith-Ross was not misguided to place his trust in the 'Old Lady'. What is remarkable, though, is just how far the Bank of England was prepared to go to in helping to head off the danger of a clearing system. This was accomplished by the narrowest of margins and only because the Bank facilitated the setting up of a preferred but none the less novel alternative device. Indeed, no one expected the agreement, born after such a painful and protracted labour, to survive for more than a year. There were early complications: the German authorities quickly rejected the original proposal to grant import certificates freely for British wares and started to impose severe restrictions. Nor did the terms granted to British creditors undergo any improvement. In spite of this, the agreement grew into a robust infant. The performance of the agreement was thought to be so satisfactory that it was left, by mutual consent, to run on without modification for more than three years. This was not simply a case of bureaucratic inertia or a natural reluctance to tamper with an arrangement which actually worked. The Bank of England praised the structure as a model of lucidity and simplicity. However, the entire operational responsibility lay with the Reichsbank. The satisfactory results were said to be, therefore, a product of Germany's efficient systems of trade and foreign exchange control.[51]

Yet, with the threat of war looming larger in the second half of the 1930s, it became ever more important for Britain to ensure that external commercial agreements did not operate at the expense of national security. This posed a dilemma virtually impossible to resolve. As Paul Kennedy has shown, Britain hoped to build up her strength and conserve her resources by pursuing economic interests which were best served in a peaceful world. At the same time, the security of the nation required economic as well as military preparations which were likely to be at the cost of trading interests. Of course, what was uppermost in the German mind was, in Kennedy's words, 'A future war, not eternal peace'.[52]

With Hitler's reoccupation of the Rhineland on 7 March 1936 all proposals relating to further agreements with the Third Reich underwent drastic revision. There was even talk of economic sanctions. But the proposition that the Locarno Treaty powers alone should attempt trade reprisals against Germany was quickly ruled out. In Britain the Treasury warned of a potential farce: the Standstill monies would be cut off and, while the Nazi authorities would be free to import whatever they required through dozens of loopholes, Britain's own trade would be damaged. Sir Warren Fisher's opinion of sanctions was that 'Even Alice in Wonderland would regard the idea as lunacy'.[53] It was inevitable that the Payments Agreement would also be called into question. Renewed criticism appeared in Einzig's 'Lombard Street' column of the *Financial News*. The agreement was said to leave Germany with an annual balance of £10m for arms expenditure. But this figure did not take into account British re-exports or the service of several debts. When these payments were included, Germany was left with an unfavourable balance.[54]

Anxieties were eased, therefore, when Germany paid off, relatively speedily, her heavy commercial debts and continued to pay interest in full to British holders of Dawes and Young loans. Altogether, denunciation of the agreement did not appear to be in Britain's interests: a way had been found to settle, for the time being at least, most commercial and financial questions. On this foundation, economic relations with Nazi Germany could be built. There was, for example, a rapid growth in British exports as a result of purchases by Germany of British goods. But this by itself does not explain why the agreement came to be regarded with special favour in some quarters. The useful contribution it appeared to make to good political relations was considered to be just as important. Frank Ashton-Gwatkin, in the Foreign Office, felt able to claim at the end of 1937 that the agreement had led to goodwill and mutual understanding.[55]

The impact of Anschluss

Hitler's annexation of Austria on 12 March 1938 shattered the illusion of goodwill. Suddenly, Britain had to choose between revising the Payments Agreement or renouncing it. The agreement nearly collapsed, but not for political or strategic reasons. Although the Anschluss marked a new and frightening stage in the growing European crisis, London's first concern was what the ending of Austrian independence implied for the upholding of international financial obligations. As the Nazis created the myth that Austria had never been a separate national or economic entity, they naturally claimed as a matter of principle that the Third Reich could not recognize Austrian financial obligations. Berlin's objective was to get international loans written off. The door to recognition of other Austrian treaty obligations could then be kept firmly shut.[56]

Hitler secured gold and reserves of the Austrian National Bank estimated by Britain to be up to £20m, with £80m in realizable foreign securities. But no undertaking was given to honour the service of the Austrian reconstruction loans – the Guaranteed 4.5 per cent Conversion Loan of 1934, the Guaranteed 3 per cent Loan of 1933 and the 7 per cent Loan of 1930. These had been issued under the auspices of the League of Nations and were controlled by the august-sounding Committee of Guarantor States of the Loans for the Reconstruction of Austria. As one of those international guarantors, the British government was liable to pay £675,000 per year in case of total default.

By 1938 Britain remained the only country where the Third Reich negotiated direct with creditors; in all other cases Germany negotiated with the government of the creditor country. If this distinction was quite unreal in the circumstances pertaining in 1934, it was stripped of any meaning by the Anschluss. There was little doubt that negotiations would have to be backed up with the threat of a unilateral clearing.[57] The problems contingent upon imposing such a structure remained the same as in 1934: serious dislocation of trade and termination of existing debt payments. Yet such drawbacks counted for much less: the British government felt that it was confronting a state which had never shown the slightest hesitation in ruthlessly exploiting its politico-economic power. It was assumed that a clearing would harm Britain but do even greater damage to Germany.[58]

Any offer which fell short of unconditional full payment of the service of the loans automatically required the intervention of the international control committee. In the event that the international negotiations failed, Britain planned to approach the Third Reich for a bilateral agreement, as part of the main negotiations over the Payments Agreement. To complicate matters further, the Lever Committee (representing British long- and medium-term creditors of Germany) made informal proposals to the German authorities concerning interest rates for the Dawes and Young loans.[59] So revision of the Anglo-German payments structure to include Austria was linked to the question of Austrian debts and the Dawes and Young loans. An opportunity had arisen for an all-round financial settlement.

Trade between Austria and the UK was roughly balanced through the mid 1930s. Put another way, British exports to Germany and Austria amounted to 70 per cent of the combined export trade of the two states to the UK. An increase in the ratio allocated to Britain under the Payments Agreement from 55 per cent to a notional 65 per cent would still have left the Third Reich with a free surplus of about £3.5m. That such a liberal attitude risked compromising national security had always been an obvious if rarely articulated point: Germany greatly valued free sterling as a means to purchase raw materials. The smooth working of the agreement was now seen as an act of British benevolence which had to be justified.[60] Free sterling could have been used to wipe out debt. But the Bank of England was concerned that the terms for revision should not be pressed too harshly in case Germany reneged on all her existing arrangements for servicing British financial claims; setting a sufficiently low percentage figure would leave a margin for those claims.[61] In spite of this, Chamberlain, the Prime Minister, decided that a 70 per cent allocation was justified on trade grounds.[62]

This was the figure Leith-Ross put to Rudolf Brinkmann at the start of negotiations in Berlin in the last week of May 1938. While the figure was accepted, responsibility for the Austrian loans was denied. Brinkmann was a Schacht protégé, but Göring had made him state secretary in the RWM because of his Nazi convictions. His outrageous behaviour became too much even for the Nazi hierarchy to tolerate; he was spirited away in 1939 on grounds of mental illness.[63]

Leith-Ross wanted to give notice right away that Britain intended to bring the Payments Agreement to an end. The Board of Trade, having secured the objective of 70 per cent, was entirely against denunciation. The Bank of England reasoned that any declaration should come after 1 June by when it would be known whether the Austrian loans were in default.[64] Much to the delight of his officials, Viscount Halifax, the Foreign Secretary, was persuaded by Sir John Simon (now Chancellor) to allow Leith-Ross a free hand in Berlin.[65] The notice of termination (one month) was issued when the Reich authorities repeated that they had no legal authority to pay the Austrian interest instalments.

A bemused Cabinet met on 27 May to contemplate how and why Britain had come to use such a 'steam-hammer' of a weapon, even though it was felt that special account had been taken of German psychology. Discussion was interrupted by news of the German response. Britain was asked to persuade the Dawes and Young loan bondholders to accept a reduction in interest rates; in return, interest on the Austrian loans would be paid in full. This capitulation instantly restored self-confidence in British tactics; Chamberlain was able to recall that it confirmed previous experience of how great firmness was needed in negotiating with Germany.[66] The Cabinet's attitude is all the more surprising given that, just a few days before, Anglo-French firmness had led to the war scare over the Sudetenland.

So many British poltico-economic interests had become wrapped up with the Payments Agreement that denunciation was bound to be seen by many as a doubtful expedient, if not something worse. The Berlin Embassy warned that every opportunity had to be given to the Nazi government before Britain slammed the door and greatly increased the political tensions.[67] In City circles it was naturally the

Standstill creditors who were most concerned that existing financial arrangements should not disintegrate. Thus, in circumstances very similar to those of 1934, Lord Wardington (formerly Beaumont Pease) reminded the authorities, just in case they needed it, that bankers believed the Standstill to be in a special position. An interruption to its service would mean that bills worth some £22m would be taken off the market (thereby depriving Germany of the cheapest money it enjoyed), and bankers would look to the government for the protection they felt they deserved. On the advice of the Bank of England that the proceeds of goods financed by Standstill bills should be exempted from a clearing, all references to the Standstill were left out of the draft Treasury order.[68] The government let it be known through the Bank that it would give the Standstill the same priority as Reich Loans.[69]

A greater weight of opinion, however, believed that the time had come to make a firm stand. The Association of Chambers of Commerce pointed out how much investment capital had already been lost: the Young loan and *Konversionskasse* bonds were quoted at less than £40 per £100, while other obligations were quoted at £25. The Association's members were not only prepared to endure sacrifices for the sake of a clearing, they actually urged the government to set one up, if necessary, in order to see fair play for British investment abroad.[70] Certain bankers apart, the City also appeared solidly in favour of taking the same line. The German technique of depressing the price of a stock and then repatriating the few remaining ones on which payment was made had become sickeningly familiar. The feeling was growing that it had always proved useless, on general political grounds, to make concessions of any kind to Germany. As for a retaliatory switch of trade in raw materials away from the Empire, the City estimated that Germany had already located all the other possible sources of supply.[71]

The international control committee for the Austrian loans assembled in London in early June 1938 and made its protest. With the withdrawal of Italy from this League of Nations body, Leith-Ross became president of the trustees. The German reply represented a further advance in that some payment on the loans was offered but, as before, a condition was stipulated: Britain and the colonies would have to take in more German exports. With this, the international negotiations were deemed to have failed and the Chancellor of the Exchequer was advised, on 13 June, that Britain should immediately move towards a unilateral clearing.[72] The next day the developments became public when the Chancellor announced to the Commons that the Payments Agreement would end on 1 July. Britain calculated that this foreshortened period of notice, albeit mutually agreed, would put maximum pressure on Germany.

The Hitler government wanted, at the very least, to keep the negotiations going. There was a report that Walter Funk, the Nazi fanatic who replaced Schacht first as economics minister and then as Reichsbank president, had delivered an optimistic speech on the possibility of compromise.[73] In late June Dr Wiehl arrived in London to negotiate on the whole range of financial obligations (except the Standstill). Wiehl offered to pay on the Austrian loans but expected a great deal in return: reductions in interest rates on all loans, particularly the Dawes and Young loans, and concessions on trade. With the Lever Committee standing firm, Britain made a counter-offer: revision of the trade allocation under the Payments Agreement to 65 (rather than 70) per cent, with provision for further reductions if requested to ensure sufficient free exchange to meet total financial payments.[74] There was also a suggestion that the Bank of England should advance the sums necessary to make the payments on the Austrian loans. But there was to be no repetition of the events of 1934. The Bank did not like the idea. An advance, even for a short period, would probably have been seen as a political act and made difficulties for the government and the Bank.[75]

In the face of the Third Reich's triumphalism over Austria and aggressive designs on Czechoslovakia, the internecine rivalries that plagued Whitehall erupted once again. Quite suddenly, the Board of Trade decided to object strongly to the priority given to creditors over traders and wanted to resile from the policy of allowing financial claims as the first charge on the clearing. Leith-Ross insisted that the only treatment that Germany understood was the exercise of power without hesitation: last-minute changes would be misinterpreted. He counted the Chambers of Commerce, Fisher at the Treasury, and the widely representative Board of the Midland Bank among those who supported him.[76] Leith-Ross felt that he was being assailed by 'defeatist' Board of Trade arguments. Vansittart was a close ally but he had been kicked upstairs to the post of Chief Diplomatic Adviser; he could do little more than concur with the hope that the Foreign Office would help to defeat the defeatist Board of Trade.[77]

Sir Alexander Cadogan, Vansittart's successor, did not need to be convinced that there were politico-military advantages to be derived from the imposition of a clearing. Cadogan wanted German purchases of essential raw materials to be restricted unless it could be shown that the prejudice to British trade would be so serious that no other consideration could be put in the balance against it.[78] But the Chancellor and the President of the Board of Trade could not resolve their differences over the question of the priority of claims. The Treasury was forced to postpone the announcement of the Clearing Order without any idea of when it was going to be possible to reach some understanding.[79] In the meantime, Wiehl kept up the pretence that new obligations could not be undertaken without the assurance of additional exports to the UK and colonies and that Austrian assets were not available to meet Austrian debts.

Nevertheless, on 1 July – the very last moment – a tripartite agreement was reached between the British and the German government and the Lever Committee. Most of what Britain wanted was secured. Interest rates were reduced but there was to be a full transfer on the Austrian loans. A sliding scale was created for British exports, a large proportion of which were to be of finished goods, to the so-called Greater Reich. In line with the British proposal, it was to be open to Germany to ask for a reduction in Britain's trade allocation if necessary.[80] The Bank of England calculated that Germany would be paying £1m more per year to Britain under the new agreement. Yet, as the amount decreased through amortization, and as Germany would be left with a free surplus of £3m after paying off trade arrears, it was assumed that there would be a margin for an increase at some point in the service of non-Reich commitments.[81]

The threat to impose a clearing had opened the way to the setting up of the Payments Agreement in 1934. The same tactics were used again in 1938 to ensure that Britain's economic interests were protected through a revision of the structure. At the same time, a settlement of the Austrian debt question was secured. In contrast to 1934, however, Britain resorted to tricks to force agreement. Forms printed for the Clearing Office were left conspicuously on a desk at the Embassy in Berlin for an invited German official to spot; it was not long afterwards that Wiehl was despatched to London. When the resumed negotiations still did not go smoothly the official in charge of the embryonic Clearing Office visited the German

delegation and passed in his card.[82] In the allocation of civil servants
to the Clearing Office thought was given to the idea of engaging a
German speaker who could be sent to Germany to gain experience
of clearing methods.[83] Finally, when the conversations became
completely deadlocked on 27 June Leith-Ross took out of his pocket
an order signed by Chamberlain introducing an exchange clearing
on 1 July.[84] These threats to impose a unilateral clearing proved to
be a most effective device, while the complicated formula which was
arranged allowed Germany, at the same time, to save face. The
revision did not escape criticism; in addition to the reduction in rates
the claims of all the Austrian creditors were made subject to the
crippling exchange regulations which applied to German debts.
However, the Board of Trade was satisfied that nothing had been
given away.[85]

In the age of the dictators a new artfulness, if nothing else,
accompanied the defence of British financial and economic interests.
To be taken seriously by the Nazis, British officials were quite
prepared to dispense with conventional diplomatic etiquette. There
was a more serious side to the game of financial diplomacy. The
impact of *Gleichschaltung* on the German authorities so alarmed
Leith-Ross that he identified it as a revolution taking place in the
administration. With Germany's old civil servants swept away and
the Nazi Party in control of the RWM, he believed that the Third
Reich was governed according to the more or less arbitrary decisions
of a few men.[86]

German banking circles were also uneasy at the developments
over Austrian debts. Schacht, too, was probably relieved that he did
not have to participate in the negotiations. By handling the monetary technicalities, the Reichsbank had helped to pave the way for
the Anschluss. Schacht's increasingly desperate attempts to persuade
Hitler of the danger of financial collapse were to end with his
removal from the Reichsbank in January 1939. On these grounds
and because of the ambiguity in his stance on anti-Semitism, Schacht
was able to escape conviction at Nuremberg.[87] His regret at the
expulsion from the Reichsbank of Jewish colleagues, such as Otto
Jeidels, appeared to be genuine. Similarly, Schacht always defended his record of running the German economy on grounds of
patriotism. In the middle of 1938 he privately caricatured Nazi
policy as a compound of the recipes of Lenin and Keynes.[88] There
could be no acknowledgement, of course, that the Soviet Union

provided a model for a centrally-planned economy. Keynes, on the other hand, was widely respected in Germany.[89] And many observers, in Germany and abroad, failed at the time to understand how totalitarian methods enabled Hitler to postpone the day of economic reckoning.[90]

Britain's preparations for war: the trade dilemma

The outcome of the Austrian negotiations was taken as a victory, not just for British policy but also for the supposed moderate Nazis who still had some influence. The Payments Agreement was, according to Ashton-Gwatkin, the ark of salvation for the 'moderates': it stood for what was left of Germany's aspirations for international trade. The revision would, therefore, encourage this 'peace party' just as the May crisis, when Hitler was rebuffed over the Sudeten question in Czechoslovakia, had been a check to the 'warmonger party'. The economic appeasers entertained hopes of a spiralling growth in trade and credits which would lead to marketing agreements with Germany.[91]

Some of the assumptions underlying the Payments Agreement had been questioned by British officials even before the Anschluss. The evident enthusiasm of the German government to preserve the arrangement reinforced fears that the whole basis of British policy was misguided.[92] J.H. Magowan, Commercial Counsellor in the Berlin Embassy, drew attention to how the demands of Germany's economy pressed hard against the general 1932/33 scheme of trade – which Britain had wanted to freeze. In 1936 Germany applied a ratio of 65 per cent (not the 55 per cent due under the agreement) in trading with Britain; in 1937 this rose to 71 per cent. Increases in commodities such as scrap metals, destined for Germany's armaments industries, accounted for the steep rise in British exports.[93]

Following the fateful Munich conference in September 1938 Magowan repeated his criticisms of what he now regarded as a discredited policy. He caused, thereby, a minor sensation in Whitehall. As Germany was 'practically at war' with Britain, he wanted trade relations surveyed afresh in order to give weight to factors other than the purely commercial.[94] This so perturbed the Department of Overseas Trade that Magowan was temporarily recalled to London.[95] Undeterred, he carried on his solitary campaign to show how Germany was able, between 1932 and 1938, to reconstitute imports from Britain.

TABLE 3: ANGLO-GERMAN TRADE 1929–38 IN £MILLION

Year	British exports to Germany	(re-exports)	British imports from Germany	Balance to Germany
1929	60.2	(23.3)	68.8	8.6
1930	44.1	(17.3)	65.5	21.4
1931	32.0	(13.6)	64.2	32.2
1932	25.4	(10.8)	30.5	5.1
1933	24.6	(9.8)	29.8	5.2
1934	22.9	(8.9)	30.6	7.7
1935	28.1	(7.8)	31.8	3.7
1936	27.9	(7.4)	35.3	7.4
1937	31.4	(8.0)	38.8	7.4
1938	28.5	(6.6)	31.9	3.4

Source: compiled from UK Customs and Excise Dept, *Annual Statement of the Trade of the United Kingdom 1932*, IV (1934), *1935*, IV (1937), *1939*, IV (1941).

TABLE 4: GERMAN IMPORTS OF CERTAIN COMMODITIES FROM THE UK IN RM000s

Commodity	Average imports 1932/33	Exchange available in 1937 under Payments Ag. quotas (based on 1932/33 trade returns)	Actual Imports 1937
scrap iron and steel	1,408	1,126	3,900
copper	4,326	3,461	19,876
lead	40	32	1,728
aluminium	932	746	1,959
platinum, palladium and irridium	822	658	5,765
rubber, gutta-percha and waste	102	81	1,575
glycerine	150	120	1,227

Source: abstracted from T 160 821/12750/086, memo, by Magowan, 3 Jan. 1939.

How methodologically sound it was to compare the depth of the slump – 1932/33 – to the peak of the moderately strong recovery in 1937 was open to question: the resumption of some kind of predepression trade pattern might have been expected in any case. What was incontrovertible was the evidence of the significance of access to London's world-wide market in raw materials. The Payments Agreement had come to play an important role in British trade: in 1938 Germany was, after India, the UK's best customer, taking exports to the value of £20.6m. This just exceeded exports to the USA at £20.5m and Argentina at £19.3m. Clearly, Britain provided not only a margin of free exchange but also the best market in which to spend it. A large proportion of these 'gratuitous' German imports comprised strategic raw materials rather than the consumption goods reflected in the spending pattern of the early 1930s. The Nazi authorities depended upon free sterling, therefore, not only for the successful working of their exchange-control system, but also for the purposes of rearmament.[96]

Magowan received generous, if not unqualified, support from the Foreign Office. The strategy of subjecting Anglo-German economic relations to the criterion of national security, rather than the normal peace-time criterion of the trade balance, was thought to be entirely sensible. Denunciation of the Payments Agreement on the grounds of national defence was not difficult to envisage. Yet to close down on the degree of liberty which was still allowed in trade relations with Germany would cause, it was imagined, a great economic shock.[97] Ways to improve Britain's trade with the Third Reich had to be found while the scope for rearmament afforded by the use of London's facilities had to be reduced. Halifax wanted the matter referred to the Committee for Imperial Defence.[98]

According to one recent account, the arguments put up against Magowan were weak and the resistance to change was based on a concern to protect the position of the acceptance houses.[99] But this assessment does not do justice to the complexities of the problem. Abrogation of the agreement would certainly not have been in Britain's wider financial interests: the service of the Standstill and long-term debt was financed by one-quarter of the proceeds of German exports. Apart from satisfying financial morality, Leith-Ross regarded payment of this 'tribute' as one of the best ways of strengthening Britain and weakening Germany. He was unsuccessful, however, in convincing the Board of Trade that fully manufactured goods should take up a bigger proportion of the trade.[100]

The Payments Agreement worked on the understanding that coal would be the main export product to Germany. This tended to crowd out other British goods: combustibles increased from 45.7 per cent in 1934 to 60.3 per cent in 1937 as a share of total British exports to Germany.[101] Yarn and herring were also important raw material exports in terms of value. The Board of Trade wanted no truck with any revisionism which might have led to a loss of market share. Alternative sources for these British commodities could still be found or, in the last resort, replaced by German domestic resources. Furthermore, much of Germany's free sterling was devoted to re-exports and Britain lost out whenever transfers of trade occurred. As the agreement required Germany to take a quantity of manufactured goods rather than all raw materials, the Board suggested that the real question was whether Britain should impose specific export embargoes.[102] This was rather mischievous. Anything so provocative as a trade embargo would have run completely against the grain of Chamberlain's policy.

It might also have been counterproductive. The balance in strategic materials did not automatically lie in Germany's favour. In 1936 and 1937 Britain imported from Germany machinery for manufacturing shells and bombs.[103] Surveying Anglo-German trade in this light, Major Morton, of the Industrial Intelligence Centre (IIC), clinched the argument against change. He did not deny that the Payments Agreement facilitated Nazi war preparations by providing access to London's financial-commercial machine. But this rubbed both ways. Morton pointed out that Britain's most significant imports from Germany were machine tools and machinery, for these items were not easily obtained elsewhere and the progress of Britain's own rearmament programme would have been even tardier without them. Expedience dictated that, at the very least, an alternative source of supply had to be secured before the existing one was cut off.[104]

As Simon Newman has written, Magowan left himself open to the charge that he had underestimated the advantages to Britain in the agreement.[105] The Board of Trade rightly assumed that the Treasury would want to kill off Magowan's ideas. Claiming that the CID had already considered the problem, the two economic departments blocked plans for further discussion. The Treasury's verdict was that abrogation of the agreement and the imposition of a unilateral clearing on Germany would involve difficulties and losses which would impede Britain's war preparations. That was, 'in their Lordships' view ... the essential consideration but it is also the case that such a drastic step would be difficult to reconcile with a policy of attempting to improve political relations between this country and Germany.'[106]

When the Wehrmacht marched into Prague on 15 March 1939 the balance of arguments shifted once more. The Foreign Office, despairing of ever being able to fight its way through the 'tangled undergrowth of Departmental obstructionism', prompted Halifax to initiate Cabinet-level discussions on Magowan's ideas.[107] The Foreign Secretary duly suggested to the President of the Board of Trade, Oliver Stanley, that the deterioration in relations made it advisable to reconsider the position of the agreement. Stanley was reminded that he had himself said in Cabinet that Britain and Germany were virtually in a state of war; consequently, he was asked whether it would be in Britain's interest to maintain the agreement after the outbreak of hostilities. Sir William Brown, Permanent Secretary at the Board of Trade, noted privately and caustically: 'No. And in these conditions it would be in our interests to bomb Berlin. Should we do that now ?'[108]

Stanley rejected the idea of revision until a decision was taken to bring down in ruins the German economy – at whatever cost to British trade and the general peace. But this was misguided to say the least: any opportunity to inflict economic destruction had long since disappeared. Halifax retreated once more. Some solace could be drawn from the rapid fall off in German exports in the course of 1939 and the consequent diminution of free exchange.

But the Third Reich now had little need to maintain international trade. Instead, Hitler had started to plunder the assets of neighbouring states. The Reichsbank organized the seizure or control of the monetary reserves – particularly gold – of Austria, Czechoslovakia and then the rest of occupied Europe. The painful and controversial process of tracking down these and other looted assets, and making restitution, remains incomplete even at the beginning of the twenty-first century.

With the invasion of Czechoslovakia, Britain blocked all Czech accounts held in London. The intention was to exert pressure in negotiations over blocked British balances, non-payment of interest on loans and the freeing of foreign exchange to assist Czech refugees. The problem was that negotiations could not take place because the legality of the annexation was not recognized.[109] On the other hand, some £6m in Czech gold was held in a BIS account at the Bank of England and, by convention, BIS assets were granted immunity. The BIS, under the influence of its pro-Nazi directors and acting on instructions from occupied Prague, asked London to transfer the account to the Reichsbank's BIS account. Neither the Bank of England nor the Treasury had the legal right to refuse the request.[110]

In May 1939 a German delegation arrived secretly in London to discuss the question of Czech assets. They departed empty-handed after questions in Parliament led to a debate on the subject. Nevertheless, the German government agreed, at the end of May, to a further revision of the Payments Agreement to cover debts owing from the Sudetenland. The document was signed on 16 June. However, Britain's impotence in the face of BIS procedures, together with Whitehall's apparent subterfuge, ensured that the gold affair acquired a certain notoriety in the final months of peace.[111] Certainly, the Czech BIS sub-account at the Bank of England was closed. But, contrary to what is sometimes asserted, the gold was never physically transferred. The Reichsbank had given no instructions by the outbreak of war for the bullion to be moved to Germany; the authorities in London were spared further embarrassment and the gold stayed where it was, in the vaults at Threadneedle Street.[112]

The Payments Agreement, therefore, was never renounced. It ran largely unaltered until, like much else, it met its fate and was simply swept away when Britain declared war. In seeking to understand why the system was established and survived it is necessary to focus on the enduring effects of the collapse of multilateralism at the beginning of the decade. The agreement with Germany must be placed, first of all, in the context of general British policy on negotiating bilateral treaties over trade matters. The policy emerged as a result of the 1931 crisis and for the rest of the decade was repeatedly commended by the Cabinet to Parliament and the country.

Nevertheless, the Payments Agreement operated at some cost to Britain in her trade, not only with Germany, but with other countries in north and west Europe too. In view of the drive for exports, the willingness to accept unfavourable trade balances with European states is surprising. The explanation lies in the extreme reluctance to channel international trade through clearings. This had a directly adverse effect on Britain's own trade and indirectly helped Germany to achieve a favourable balance of trade with other European trading nations. As Scandinavian states, for example, were unable to sell in Germany unless they bought there, it was to their advantage to divert orders from Britain to Germany. Sweden spent in Germany a large part of the proceeds of her export surplus with Britain.

On the other hand, bilateral trade agreements with Denmark, Poland, Russia and Argentina all tended to divert trade to Britain at Germany's expense. Above all else, the Payments Agreement was a liberal arrangement which offered, at the same time, some security for long-suffering exporters to the Third Reich and, potentially, other creditors too. There is little substance to the charge that Britain, engaged in an act of appeasement, was looking to make life comfortable for herself at the expense of her neighbours.

NOTES

1. Einzig, *Appeasement*, p. 94.
2. P. Ludlow, 'Britain and the Third Reich', in H. Bull (ed.), *The Challenge of the Third Reich* (Oxford: Clarendon Press, 1986), pp. 151–2.
3. W.A. Boelcke, *Deutschland als Welthandelsmacht 1930–1945* (Stuttgart: W. Kohlhammer, 1994), p. 60.
4. Teichert, *Autarkie und Grossraumwirtschaft*, pp. 31–2.
5. T 160/612/13460/1, minute by Hopkins.
6. T 160/612/13460/2, 30 April 1934. After the departure of Leith-Ross from the Treasury in 1932 Phillips assumed the position of deputy to Hopkins.
7. FO 371/15937/C5771, Rumbold despatch, 2 July 1932.
8. T 160/521/12750/02/1, letter to Treasury, 13 March 1933.
9. Ibid., Thelwall (Commercial Counsellor), to Rowe-Dutton, 3 March and 8 August 1933. The logical conclusion of Hambro's analysis, according to Thelwall, was to suggest that British and Turkish bonds should command the same price because they were both bonds.
10. T 160/521/12750/02/2. Preston was chairman of Platt Brothers & Co., (machinery makers to the textile industry), which was being reorganized and rationalized.
11. Ibid., (i) memo by Thelwall, 21 November , (ii) Thelwall to Waley, 15 December, (iii) Cobbold to Waley, 18 December 1933. In Thelwall's memo, considered too strident for circulation, the Governor was criticized for failing to distinguish between an exchange agreement and a clearing system. See also, BoE OV34/195, Cobbold to Deputy Governor, 18 December 1933. Cobbold was Adviser to the Governors (1933–38) and Acting Deputy Chief of the Overseas and Foreign Department (1933–35).
12. T 160/522/12750/02/3.
13. T 160/522/12750/02/6, draft memo to President (Board of Trade), 6 August 1934.
14. Cmd 4673.
15. BoE OV34/197, memo 16 August 1934. Cobbold appealed to his colleagues not to be misled by Einzig's claims that the government believed a satisfactory

settlement had been achieved.

16. T 160/558/12750/02/01/1, minutes by Phillips, 7 September 1934 and Waley, 3 October 1934; see also T 160/535/13460/010/2.

17. BoE OV34/200, memo by (i) Siepmann, 4 September , (ii) Clay, 10 and 14 September 1934.

18. T 160/559/12750/020/1, memo for Chancellor by Leith-Ross, 13 September 1934.

19. T 188/93, Vansittart to Leith-Ross, 13 September 1934.

20. T 160/714/8797/07/1, unsigned memo entitled 'The Debts Impasse'. Hitler's expansionist policies, with consequent rising demand for raw materials, and domestic politics, resulting in foreign boycotts of German goods, were blamed for exacerbating the transfer difficulties.

21. T 160/534/13460/010/2, letter from the General Economic and Intelligence Division, FBI, 4 October 1934.

22. T 160/534/13460/010/1, Fountain to Runciman, 23 August 1934.

23. Runciman papers, 260, letter by Burgin to Runciman, 19 September 1934.

24. T 160/522/12750/017/1, British Embassy note of Leith-Ross's conversations with von Neurath, 25 September 1934, and Schacht, 26 September 1934.

25. I. Kershaw, *The Hitler Myth: Image and Reality in the Third Reich* (Oxford: Clarendon Press, 1989), pp. 64, 74.

26. T 160/559/12750/020/1, memo 'Trade negotiations with Germany', 28 September 1934 and minutes. See also CAB 24/250, 218.

27. Leith-Ross, *Money Talks*, p. 184. See, too, p. 247 for the claim that he disagreed with those who thought that political difficulties could be solved by removing economic thorns from the flesh. He believed rather that politics in international affairs governed actions at the expense of economics, and often of reason.

28. NC 18/1/891, letter to Ida, 13 October 1934.

29. D. Meredith, 'British trade diversion policy and the "colonial issue" in the 1930s', *JEEH*, 25, 1 (Spring 1996), pp. 54–6.

30. T 160/534/13460/010/1.

31. T 160/535/13460/010/1–2.

32. T 160/534/13460/08, letter to the Governor (Bank of England), 12 October 1934.

33. Ibid., memo by Leith-Ross, 12 October 1934.

34. Clay, *Lord Norman*, p. 449.

35. Sayers, *Bank of England*, p. 508.

36. NC 18/1/893, letter to Ida, 27 October 1934.

37. T 160/535/13460/010/3, Leith-Ross to Treasury and Board of Trade; telegram, Phipps to Simon, 19 October 1934. The proposal was made on 24 October by Dr Ulrich, a subordinate of Schacht.

38. Ibid., Hopkins to Fisher and Chamberlain, 18 October 1934; Leith-Ross telegram to Treasury and Board of Trade, 25 October 1934.

39. Cmd 4726 and 4963. On Runciman's insistence, negotiations had been conducted simultaneously for a clearing, ready to be initialled for inclusion in the agreement. See also, Ellis, *Exchange Control*, p. 211; Richardson, *British Economic Foreign Policy*, p. 78; Arndt, *Economic Lessons*, p. 187.

40. T 177/20.

41. T 160/544/13999/01, Hopkins to Fergusson (PPS to Chancellor), 26 October 1934.

42. NC 18/1/894, letter to Hilda, 3 November 1934.

43. T 160/544/13999/01, Leith-Ross to (i) Fisher and Chamberlain, (ii) Norman,

(iii) Phipps, 8 November 1934, (iv) Pinsent, 16 November 1934.

44. T 188/179
45. T 160/544/13999/01, 1 December 1934.
46. Ibid., Norman to Leith-Ross, 5 December 1934.
47. *Financial News*, 7 December 1934.
48. FO 371/17738/C8738, minutes 11 and 12 December 1934.
49. T 188/79, Vansittart/Leith-Ross correspondence, 17/18 December 1934.
50. BoE OV34/85, note, 7 February 1935, by Peppiatt (Chief Cashier); minutes by Siepmann, 18 February and 12 August 1935.
51. BoE OV34/204, minute by Cobbold, 21 April 1937.
52. P. Kennedy, *Strategy and Diplomacy, 1870–1945* (Allen & Unwin, 1983), pp.103–4.
53. T 160/935/13456/2, minute, 17 March 1936, on 'Report for CID Sub-Committee: Economic Pressure on Germany'.
54. *Financial News*, 29 June 1936; T 160/543/13900/08.
55. Ashton-Gwatkin felt that the Payments Agreement was in the economic world what the Naval Agreement was in the political sphere – a sign of moderation, almost of friendship. This offered an opportunity, he believed, to construct further economic understandings which could pave the way for a comprehensive political agreement with Germany. See (i) FO 371/18851/C7752, memo, 21 November 1935; (ii) CAB 27/599, G(36)2, memo, 28 February 1936; (iii) T 160/743/13999, letter to H.M. Legation, The Hague, 4 December 1937.
56. T 188/215, memo, 29 May 1938; Leith-Ross to Hopkins, 16 June 1938.
57. FO 371/21641/C1966, Leith-Ross to Board of Trade, 17 March 1938. Exporters had to be warned to restrict commercial credit.
58. T 188/214, record of an interdepartmental meeting held at the Treasury, 4 April 1938.
59. FO 371/21644/C4592, memo by Waley, 12 May 1938. In return for a reduction of the Dawes rate from 7 to 5.5 per cent and the Young rate from 5.5 to 4 per cent, the establishment of a sinking fund was proposed.
60. BoE OV34/205, interdepartmental statement of Britsh desiderata submitted to the Chancellor of the Exchequer, 6 April 1938.
61. BoE OV6/290, Gunston to Waley (Treasury), 6 April 1938.
62. T 188/214.
63. P. Hayes, *Industry and Ideology: IG Farben in the Nazi Era* (Cambridge: CUP, 1987), pp. 167–8; D. Marsh, *The Bundesbank: The Bank that Rules Europe* (Heinemann, 1992), p. 130.
64. BoE OV34/205, note, 27 May 1938. Payments on Austria's external debts due 1 April were made, but only because Germany did not revoke Austrian instructions issued before the Anschluss.
65. FO 371/21644/C5223, minute, 27 May 1938.
66. CAB 23/93, 27(38).
67. T 188/215, telegram from Berlin Embassy, 10 June 1938; see also, T 160/769/15447/09, 16 June 1938.
68. BoE OV6/291, letter from Lord Wardington to Bank of England, endorsed by Catterns (Deputy Governor) and recommendation made to the Chancellor, 15 June 1938.
69. BoE OV34/202, note, 16 June 1938, of communication between Cobbold and Tiarks.
70. BoE OV34/206, letter to Sir John Simon, 1 June 1938.
71. FO 371/21645/C6067, letter from Law to Sargent, 17 June 1938.

72. T 188/215, Leith-Ross to Chancellor, 13 June 1938.
73. D. Petzina, *Autarkiepolitik im Dritten Reich*, (Stuttgart: Verlags-Anstalt, 1968), p. 67; *The Times*, 17 June 1938.
74. BoE OV6/291, Leith-Ross to Phillips, 22 June 1938.
75. BoE OV34/206, note by Cobbold, 23 June 1938, of communication with the Treasury.
76. T 160/769/15447/010, Leith-Ross to Sir William Brown (Board of Trade), 21 June 1938.
77. FO 371/21646/C6237, minutes, 24/25 June 1938.
78. FO 21645 C5787, Cadogan to Leith-Ross, 24 June 1938.
79. T 160/769/15447/010, Leith-Ross to Waley, 24 June 1938.
80. Rates on the Austrian 7 per cent and Dawes loans were reduced to 5 per cent with a 2 per cent cumulative sinking fund; rates on the Young and Saarbrucken loans were reduced to 4.5 per cent with a 1 per cent cumulative sinking fund beginning after two years. For details see Cmd 5787 and 5881, Anglo-German Payments (Amendment) Agreement, 1 July 1938; also, BoE OV6/291, memo by Gunston.
81. BoE OV34/206, Gunston to Waley, 6 July 1938.
82. Einzig, *Appeasement*, p. 80.
83. BoE OV6/290, minute, 3 June 1938.
84. Paul Einzig papers, Churchill College Archives Centre, Cambridge (hereafter Churchill College Archives), 1/6, letter from Baron Stackelberg (Foreign Manager, *Financial News*), to Einzig, 5 July 1938.
85. BoE OV6/291, resumé memo, 29 July 1938; Francis, *Britain's Economic Strategy*, p. 324; BT 11/896/CRT8278, minute by Brown, 9 July 1938.
86. T 188/215, memo, 29 May 1938. See also J. Caplan, *Government without Administration: State and Civil Service in Weimar and Nazi Germany* (Oxford: Clarendon Press, 1988), p. 225 for discussion of the effects of *Gleichschaltung* on the civil service.
87. Marsh, *The Bundesbank*, pp. 113–20.
88. T 188/215, memo, 29 May 1938.
89. Barkai, *Nazi Economics*, p. 65. In view of the kind of dirigiste policies advocated by Keynes after the war, Schacht's comment was not too wide of the mark.
90. Schacht's last visit to London while still in office was in December 1938. It was noted that he was distancing himself from the Nazis. He spoke warmly of the Reichsbank, describing it as an island of good men. See T 188/227, minutes by Ashton-Gwatkin, 15 December, and Leith-Ross, 16 December 1938. For the Cabinet's aspirations in relation to the visit see, CAB 23/227, 57(38), 30 November 1938; also, CAB 23/96 60(38), 21 December 1938.
91. FO 371/21647/C7853, minute, 13 July 1938.
92. See, W.G.J. Knop, 'Germany and Europe' in *The Banker*, 46 (June 1938) for criticism of the way Germany had access to raw materials.
93. BoE OV34/205, 23 February 1938.
94. BT 59/540A, memo, 6 December 1938, and personal despatch to departmental colleagues, 7 December 1938.
95. FO 371/22950/C164, minute by Strang, 10 January 1939; see also, FO 371/21648/C15187, minute by Sargent, 17 December 1938. Officials in London thought Magowan to be 'rather rattled and losing his sense of proportion'. However, he was supported by George Ogilvie-Forbes, Commercial Attaché in Berlin.
96. Ibid., memo by Magowan, 7 March 1939.

97. FO 371/22950, Ashton-Gwatkin minutes, 11 and 20 January 1939.
98. T 160/821/12750/086, Foreign Office to Treasury, 20 January 1939.
99. Newton, *Profits of Peace*, p. 92.
100. FO 371/22950/C959, Leith-Ross to Sargent, 24 January 1939.
101. J. Gillingham, *Industry and Politics in the Third Reich: Ruhr coal, Hitler and Europe* (Methuen, 1985), p. 99.
102. BT 11/1045, minute, 31 January 1939. The export of wool direct from South Africa to Germany was one example of a transfer of trade.
103. C. Barnett, *The Collapse of British Power*, p. 483.
104. FO 371/22950, Morton to Sargent, 9 January 1939.
105. S. Newman, *March 1939: the British Guarantee to Poland* (Oxford: Clarendon Press, 1976), p. 84.
106. T 160/821/12750/086, Phillips to Foreign Office, 2 March 1939.
107. FO 371/22950/C2581, minute by Sargent, 19 March 1939.
108. BT 11/1045, minute concerning Halifax/Stanley correspondence, 31 March, 6 and 28 April 1939. Brown replaced Sir Henry Fountain as Second Secretary in 1936 and was appointed Permanent Secretary in 1938.
109. BoE OV34/206, copy of letter by Waley (Treasury) to Foreign Office, 25 March 1939.
110. Francis, *Britain's Economic Strategy*, p. 328; Einzig, *Appeasement*, p. 127; *Financial Times*, 9 June 1939.
111. Einzig papers, Churchill College Archives, 1/8, letter from Einzig to Waley (Treasury), 21 December 1939.
112. FO 371/22952/C7795; Einzig, *In the Centre of Things*, pp. 186–94; A.L. Smith, *Hitler's Gold* (Oxford: Berg, 1996), pp. 5–8.

5

British industry and the Third Reich:
trading in strategic raw materials with the future enemy?

The argument that the economic fortunes of Britain, if not the world, were closely linked to those of Germany was one favoured by many who had studied the development of the international economy. On these grounds the City and the Treasury steadfastly opposed the principle of a clearing arrangement with Germany, for channelling trade and payments in this way posed a serious threat to the interests of British finance. But taking the long-term internationalist view was not an answer to the problem of how to conduct trade, on a day-by-day basis, with potential enemy powers. With the increasingly menacing build-up of armaments by the Fascist states, Britain had to confront the uncomfortable issue of the composition of her overseas trade. British companies exported raw materials, and offered related financial facilities to every corner of the globe including, of course, the Third Reich. According to Gustav Schmidt, studies of appeasement share a common approach to this question: they assume that the British government allowed German subsidiaries of British multinationals, on the basis of short-term credits or cash payment, to import raw materials which were essential for Nazi arms production.[1] One way to test such assumptions is to analyse the business and government strategies which underpinned commercial operations or proposed operations in the Third Reich.

Although there was no real secret about Nazi intentions, rearmament was begun cautiously by Hitler because of the weakness of the economy and because he feared foreign intervention.[2] Nevertheless, the Third Reich soon appeared to be rearming on a considerable scale and at a pace which certainly showed no signs of slackening. In late 1934 the British Foreign Secretary, Sir John Simon, noted in his diary that the day was fast approaching when Germany would be strong enough to repudiate openly the Versailles limitations which she was secretly disregarding.[3] The announcements of rearmament, on a step-by-step basis, led to a series of foreign affairs crises between 1933 and 1936.[4]

As these aggressive intentions were revealed, many observers in the democratic states were persuaded that the only safe course was to try to keep Germany lean. The question of whether the Third Reich could be compelled to abide by the arms clauses of the Versailles Treaty was the first case to be considered by the Committee of Imperial Defence when, in 1933, it turned to examine the problem of exerting peacetime economic pressure on a potential enemy. The one result of any pressure which was predicted with certainty was severe damage to British financial and economic interests.[5] However, the importance of scrutinizing the composition of Britain's trade with Germany was to grow in proportion to the number of German industries devoted to the fulfilment of re-armament orders of one kind or another.

The export of British armaments to Germany was the most obvious trade for the government to proscribe. Indeed, British and French policy was so restrictive that the Third Reich took the opportunity to export its own armaments even to countries which were potentially hostile.[6] Arms exports required a licence. Companies were also expected to stop exporting to countries where the items concerned were being adapted for military purposes. With the British public continuing to cling to the ideals of collective security and disarmament, the view that the manufacture of armaments should be left to the state, rather than the private sector, was not confined to the political left. British manufacturers were acutely aware of how easy it was to acquire or, indeed, reacquire the sobriquet 'merchant of death'. Between February 1935 and September 1936 the structure and nature of the industry was scrutinized in minute detail by the Royal Commission on the Private Manufacture of and Trading in Arms. In particular, industrialists had to defend themselves against the charge that their clients included Fascist régimes.

As one of the world's leading armaments manufacturers, Vickers-Armstrong was constantly called to account for its activities. The annual shareholders' meetings did not always proceed as smoothly as the board might have wished. At the AGM in 1934, a question was raised by Eleanor Rathbone, the Independent MP – best known as the campaigner for family allowances. Her enquiry concerned advertisements that Vickers had placed in the German publication *Militär-Wochenblatt* at the end of 1932. Although the intention had been to reach potential clients in South America, the notices had ceased in 1933. Vickers affirmed that it was not knowingly involved in the rearmament of Germany because the company could not export arms without the complete sanction and approval of the Foreign Office.[7] As part of its evidence to the Royal Commission, Vickers submitted records of the foreign visits made by its executives which indicated that no company official visited Germany after May 1933.[8] The Third Reich seemed, none the less, to offer a climate more favourable than the Soviet Union in which to do business. Among those whom Stalin had just put on trial for sabotaging power stations were six Vickers engineers.[9]

The British public continued to hold suspicions over the activities of leading manufacturers even in the second half of the 1930s. Philip Noel-Baker accused Armstrong-Siddeley of providing the Luftwaffe with the benefits of 16 years of British research by selling aircraft engines to Germany in April 1934. Likewise, the De Havilland Aircraft Company was criticized for its advertisement in the July 1934 edition of *Aeroplane*: listed among the clients that had been supplied with Tiger Moths – used as a training machine by air forces – was none other than the German government.[10] As for Vickers, advertisements for the company could still be seen circulating in Germany in 1935.[11] British armaments and aircraft manufacturers did not face such accusations alone. Big industrial concerns could also come under pressure to reassure shareholders and the public that they had no direct involvement in the arms trade. Imperial Chemical Industries rejected the allegation that the company was involved in poison gas production, although the constituent materials were available for sale to foreign purchasers.[12] As a public relations exercise, ICI's stance was not only clumsy it was also dissembling. Teichova has shown how, even in the late 1930s, the company was carefully protecting its interests in Czechoslovak operations which manufactured explosives among other products.[13]

The identification of armament exports, or exports which can be converted to military use (such as aircraft and chemicals), is relatively easy. To establish a satisfactory definition of war *matériel* and, thereby, to apply this definition to certain categories of export, is much more demanding. An élite group of British strategists were the first to understand that the implications of this approach for the global economy were far-reaching. In 1930 the secretive Industrial Intelligence Centre was established by the CID. The systematic planning which it helped to conduct from 1936 provided the framework for the establishment of the Ministry of Economic Warfare at the outbreak of hostilities.[14] As Robert Young has written, the IIC undertook its work on the assumption that, in the age of 'total war', almost any commodity commercially exchanged in peacetime was capable of being turned directly or indirectly to some military purpose.[15] Whitehall studies of the German war economy were strongly influenced by the notion that industry in the Third Reich would be organized for total war. The IIC considered the raw materials situation to be the most intractable problem facing Germany.[16]

Germany was not well endowed with natural resources; many kinds of raw material had to be imported. Some were of vital strategic importance in themselves, such as oil, or when employed in processes in the armaments industry. Britain became aware in early 1934 that German purchases of raw materials used in the production of war munitions were especially heavy.[17] Although such purchases were not necessarily disclosed in the German custom statistics, the dependence of the Nazi economy on imported raw materials was not a secret; it was self-evident to anyone who cared to undertake little more than a rudimentary analysis of Germany's foreign-trade statistics. An American banker calculated in 1934 that, in terms of total economic consumption, Germany depended on imports for 80 per cent of her iron ore, 92 per cent of her wool, 50 per cent of animal oils and fats, and 100 per cent of cotton, rubber and copper.[18]

As Germany rearmed the shortage of raw materials became so critical that, in 1936, Hitler established the Four Year Plan; its purpose was to increase domestic production, if necessary by synthetic means, in order to make Germany as self-sufficient as possible.[19] It was always recognized that there were limits to what could be achieved through autarky: some dependence on foreign supplies, especially those of strategic importance, could not be avoided. Nevertheless, in many ways indirect rearmament became more important than weapons production and, in these broad terms, war preparation was everywhere in evidence after 1936.[20]

Intelligence on these developments was channelled to Britain. Sir Robert Vansittart established his own secret network which was based around Group Captain Malcolm Christie.[21] Vansittart's fears were fuelled, from the mid-1930s, by the direct access he gained to the situation reports which were compiled by the economic section (*Wehrwirtschaftsstaab*) within the German War Ministry, and the secret speeches by General Thomas, the head of the section.[22] German industrialists also supplied information to their British counterparts which detailed the effect of war preparations; it reinforced the impression of an economy being driven to the verge of collapse.

Historians have considered the reasons for, and the consequences of, the failure to understand the nature of the German economy. Overy refers to conservative groups in Germany that successfully exported their fears of political instability to foreign audiences. There was already in Britain a predisposition to regard the German economy as a fragile structure; National Socialism was seen, therefore, as a crisis-ridden movement that was trying to stave off the consequences of the over-heating of the economy.[23] Peden suggests that the inadequacies of the system of economic intelligence gave rise to the belief in Germany's assumed Achilles' heel of dependence on raw materials; the importance of conventional economic factors in Hitler's decision-making was also vastly over-rated. The Foreign Office argued from the beginning of 1937 that Germany would have to decide within a year whether to limit arms expenditure or embark on a foreign policy adventure rather than face economic collapse. The Treasury was rightly sceptical of this thesis (which dictated that Britain should immediately spend more on rearmament) even if the Foreign Office were right (for the wrong reasons) to urge that a decision was at hand.[24] However, it is also the case that German stocks of raw materials were so low when war came that the Ministry of Economic Warfare could not believe the figures they obtained.[25]

What the German economy needed, Britain could supply. British companies led the world in processing, shipping and selling all kinds of raw material, while the City of London provided the associated global financial resources. Vansittart's agitation over what he saw as Britain's failure to stand up to the Nazis is well known.[26] He found the absence of regulation in the area of raw materials and credits particularly frustrating. Sir Maurice Hankey, the Cabinet Secretary, believed that, in paying too much attention to his secret service intelligence, Vansittart was apt to get jumpy and had 'got on a good many people's nerves'. Although his patriotism, abilities and industry were never questioned, leading members of the Cabinet were looking to make a change at the Foreign Office from 1936.[27] Hankey himself disliked being depressed by Vansittart's forecasts of the dismal time which lay ahead. While Hankey was an advocate of rearmament, he also wanted to avoid any disruption to trade-generated wealth; money was, for Britain, the sinews of war.[28] Vansittart was finally removed at the beginning of 1938 and given the position of Chief Diplomatic Adviser.

In contrast to manufacturers of finished goods, exporters of raw materials to Germany could not ensure that only those industries producing for the civilian market were supplied. In his study of the German economy and Nazi war preparations, H.E.Volkmann pays particular attention to textile raw materials, unvulcanized rubber and motor fuel.[29] British firms were prominent in each of these international trades in strategically vital raw materials. This chapter focuses on three of them: the Dunlop Rubber Company and the Anglo-Persian Oil Company – both multinationals with investments in Germany – and the Lancashire Cotton Corporation which had just been set up to try to revive the fortunes of the industry.

The challenge of guiding the Third Reich towards a liberal prosperity was made all the more difficult by the structure of Britain's economic relationship with Germany. Major British companies, already experiencing difficult trading conditions under National Socialism, looked to the government to protect and advance their interests. At the same time, ministers had to try to decide which trades should be sanctioned and which should be prohibited. It was imperative for Britain to strike the right balance – one which would not place the very safety of the nation in jeopardy.

British industrialists and Nazi Germany

In addition to exports, British industry had substantial interests in manufacturing and distribution within Germany in the inter-war years. While conditions in late Weimar Germany were far from easy, British industrialists became extremely concerned about the security of their investments and the viability of their businesses under National Socialism.

Unilever, the Anglo-Dutch group, had initially invested heavily in German operations in order to circumvent tariffs and supply the biggest edible fats market in Europe.[30] But from 1931 such foreign-owned concerns invested in Germany as an inevitable consequence of the system of blocked marks. When the German authorities began to discriminate in favour of German margarine manufacturers and butter-producing farmers, Unilever's position became peculiarly vulnerable.[31] Amelioration of Unilever's problems was sought by Francis D'Arcy Cooper, its chairman, and Paul Rijkens, the financial expert who looked after continental business and later became a vice-chairman. They met Hitler in Berlin in October 1933 and were reassured by him that foreign-owned companies would not be discriminated against as long as production was not transferred from Germany.[32]

D'Arcy Cooper and Rijkens were just two of the important businessmen taken to Berlin in 1933 by E.W.D. Tennant. Interviews with Schacht and Hitler were easy to arrange as Tennant was friendly with Ribbentrop.[33] Tennant, who had interests in ferrous metals and alloys, was proud of having worked for years with Ribbentrop in an attempt to improve relations between England and Germany.[34] As a self-appointed interlocutor in the world of Anglo-German commerce, he came close to holding a semi-official position of apologist for the Nazi régime. Another British businessman – Frank Tiarks – also tried to use his contacts for propitiatory purposes and he acquired a similar reputation. As one of the leading international financiers of the age, Tiarks had commitments which went beyond the world of finance. He was appointed a non-executive director of the Anglo-Persian Oil Company at the beginning of 1917 and he continued to hold this position until the middle of 1949.

There was nothing unusual about British businessmen visiting Germany. As already indicated, several trade and financial representatives were involved in attempts to resolve specific problems over payments. This demonstrated a pragmatic approach to business and should not be confused with the support extended to the Nazis by fellow-travellers. But in September 1934 the British government was informed that certain leading suppliers of raw materials (including oil, soap, chemicals, metals, jute and rubber) were sending an unofficial mission to Berlin. The delegation, again arranged by Tennant, comprised leading executives from seven British industries; it included a representative from Dunlop but not from ICI. The group was led by Rijkens who claimed that the visit had the blessing of the Board of Trade. This was denied by officials; they disliked the plan and surmised that the German objective was to look for credit on easy terms. It would have been difficult to raise official objection to the visit, so the government was relieved to find that the people involved were 'reputable' and not specifically selected for their pro-German leanings.[35]

Unilever provided an illustration of Germany's policy of attempting to obtain extended credit terms. The company received a proposal from an important German textile concern which sought a large loan in Credit Sperr marks. These marks belonged to the Dutch arm of Unilever. But, as Unilever's London representative delicately put it, such an international concern preferred to refrain from definite negotiations until certain opinions had been obtained. The Board of Trade made its opinion abundantly clear: any such loan would be regarded as a deplorable move. The proposal was dropped.[36]

The unofficial delegation of British industrialists and traders met Schacht and were received by Hitler on 20 September. The British Embassy was furious that Schacht had been afforded the opportunity to sell the line that Germany would shortly be back on her economic feet and all that was wanted was reasonable credit. As some of the businessmen had enjoyed no fewer than seven hours of Schacht's company it stretched credulity to believe that the meetings had been of a purely social nature. The reluctance of members of the mission to be open about any proposals encouraged gossip and rumour to spread. A plan to pay off frozen debts and start up trade again was suspected. Supposedly, this required new credits to be opened at the Bank of England by the Reichsbank (which would deposit collateral made up of balances owned by Germans in England).[37]

Although the discussions seemed vague in character, the objective in Berlin was probably to get a feel for what the big British export firms were prepared to do. But Vansittart wished that a firmer line had been taken initially and that Montagu Norman had been a little more discouraging.[38] The general feeling in Whitehall was that the British mission had served Nazi propaganda purposes. Businessmen could be portrayed as falling over themselves in their eagerness to sell raw materials to Germany. By intervening, the British government could easily be blamed for damaging relations which up until then had been enjoyed in a state of perfect harmony and confidence.

Tennant later claimed that the industrialists drew up and initialled several documents which formed, on the German side, the basis of the Payments Agreement.[39] Rijkens's meetings with Schacht, Wilhelm Keppler, Hitler's economic adviser, and Brinkmann, head of the export division of the RWM, were certainly a success from Unilever's point of view. The Unilever executive pressed for an alternative to investing further funds in Germany. A programme, based mainly in Hamburg, of building ships for Unilever was devised; it allowed the company to bring a considerable amount of its profit out of Germany.[40]

Another result of the mission was the formation of the Anglo-German Fellowship which first met on 11 March 1935.[41] The moving spirits were Tennant and J. Piggot of the British Steel Exports Association. Tennant boasted that the British business magnates had been so pleased with their reception in Berlin that he was able to co-opt them into helping to form and finance the start of the Fellowship. Lord Mount Temple was made chairman and Professor Conwell-Evans became the secretary. Other founder members were Proctor (Overseas Director of Dunlop), Rijkens and D'Arcy Cooper, Sir R. Kindersley (Lazards), Agnew (Shell Transport and Trading), Spencer (Price Waterhouse), A. Guinness (Guinness Mahon) and Evans (C.T. Bowring). Further missions to Germany were planned.[42] Frank Tiarks was also active in the Fellowship. The German counterpart – the Deutsche-Englische Gesellschaft – counted Schacht among its members. Staff exchanges between British and German banks were, therefore, easily arranged.[43]

Supplying rubber: the Dunlop Rubber Company

One raw material which assumed a place of strategic significance in international trade after the First World War was rubber. It was generally accepted that to ensure mobility in wars of the future, armed forces would have to be continuously supplied with motorized vehicles and aircraft which, in most cases, needed tyres. The RWM came to regard unvulcanized rubber as one of the most important raw materials in the entire rearmament drive and war economy and yet, initially, the Third Reich depended entirely on overseas supplies.[44]

German demand for rubber grew rapidly from 1933 and world prices began to reach levels above those of most running contracts. But, in common with most other trades, the problem of German debts had to be overcome. The London-based Rubber Trade Association wanted a united front of British, Dutch and French suppliers to put pressure on Germany. A channel of communication with Dr Hammesfahr, the Third Reich's so-called Rubber Controller, had been opened.[45] But Hammesfahr was derided for trying to pull off a big bluff in relation to synthetic rubber (Buna). Although he claimed that this production process was simple and that the product was remarkable, he remained surprisingly concerned over future deliveries of raw rubber. It was feared that the delegates on the 1934 trade mission, duped by Nazi propaganda, had returned with the firm idea that Germany could satisfy her requirements by ersatz processes. While British officials had a strong desire to see British visitors such as these woken up, they did not want to give Germany the impression that she was being blockaded.[46]

What could not be dismissed so lightly were the consequences of Dunlop's participation in the Berlin visit. For the company was beginning to suffer acute problems with its German subsidiary. Acquired before the First World War, the Deutsche Dunlop Gummi Compagnie AG was kept going after the war because of the potential of the German market. Indeed, the manufacturing plant at Hanau, close to Frankfurt-am-Main, represented a very heavy capital investment.

But in autumn 1934 Schacht decided, as part of his inventory of the whole foreign exchange position, not to give any permits for the import of rubber. Yet stocks across Germany were sufficient to keep manufacturing going for no more than two months. Dunlop was left in an even worse position: with only three weeks' worth of stocks, the Hanau plant was threatened with imminent and indefinite closure.[47] This restriction was just one of many which increasingly limited the ability of the company to trade freely. Paradoxically, Dunlop's German management had welcomed the Nazis' consolidation of power in 1933: after the turbulence of the Weimar era it offered an opportunity to achieve stability and secure the company's profitability. Given the lack of German shareholding interests, Dunlop felt reassured to know that a local Nazi official looked favourably upon the subsidiary because of the absence of Jews in the management.[48]

The Continental Rubber Company, the German national company based at Hanover, helpfully suggested a way forward. The plan was for Dunlop to supply Continental with rubber and other raw materials to a total value of £480,000; Continental would then resell in Reichsmarks one-quarter of the goods to the Hanau subsidiary. Finally, with the Reichsbank guaranteeing payment of the bills, Continental would reimburse Dunlop in sterling at the end of three years. However, the Foreign Office quickly condemned this proposal because of the material's strategic nature. The IIC thought the rubber was needed in connection with the German motorization programme, the military aspect of which could not be discounted. Sir Eric Geddes himself admitted, 'tyres are, of course, by no means merely a peacetime product'.[49]

The issue was, however, even more complicated than making a distinction between products for the civilian market and those put to military purposes. Dunlop was at the centre of an industry which indirectly contributed to rearmament. One historian of the Third Reich, R.J. Overy, suggests that *Motorisierungspolitik* was a major stimulus to industrial revival and re-employment in the critical early years of the régime.[50] Even if Continental's proposal did not amount to direct financing of the German war machine, any acceptance implied, at the very least, support for National Socialism. Vansittart, holding the régime to be dangerous, was adamant that everything possible should be done to 'keep Hitler's Germany lean'.[51]

In London, the Foreign Office, the Treasury and the Board of Trade, in a rare show of unanimity, were all alarmed by the prospect of such a large expansion of new credit. Schacht's behaviour was considered indistinguishable from blackmail and there was an obvious risk that credits would be frozen. Officials wanted Dunlop to be told that, should it embark on such a project, no governmental help would be forthcoming in any recovery operation. The recommendation to the Cabinet was to stand completely aside from the proposition.[52] Nevertheless, the problem of what to do with Dunlop's Hanau investment remained. Furthermore, as the Chancellor of the Exchequer confirmed to the Cabinet on 3 October 1934, the government had no power to stop Dunlop if it decided to proceed. Instead, it was to be made plain that the government disapproved of the scheme and that the entire risk rested with the company. The Chancellor proposed to remind Geddes that a guarantee by the Reichsbank was not comparable to one given by the Bank of England.[53]

This was communicated to Dunlop just as the company received an amended, more favourable, proposal. In crude business terms, Dunlop felt that it would be unwise to turn the transaction down. Indeed, Geddes now regarded Continental as 'our friendly competitor'. He accepted that the government could not accept responsibility. Nevertheless, he still wanted to secure an official blessing or at least understanding that repayments made by Continental would not be prevented in the future by measures such as clearings. Geddes was prepared to engage in special pleading of almost Schachtian proportions. Dunlop claimed that it occupied a unique position among those who traded with Germany: it had been forced to manufacture there by German tariffs. Geddes told the government that Dunlop would suffer enormous losses of plant and skilled manpower if, on 'patriotic grounds', sanction of the scheme was withheld. Leith-Ross appreciated that if the company was prepared to accept the commercial risks involved it would be very hard for the government to tell Dunlop to 'write off this important British investment'. The last thing the government wanted was to stimulate a potentially far-reaching reaction in either country by telling the company to close down the factory for political reasons.[54]

Even so, the Treasury had no desire to see fresh credit being granted to Germany, especially under the kind of pressure being applied and when so many existing credits had been frozen. Continental Rubber might easily have found itself short of foreign exchange as German clearing arrangements with other countries developed. Care had to be taken not to set a precedent which would encourage Germany to seek credit in other directions; the list of traders who would inevitably experience difficulty in receiving payment needed no additions. Granting credits which allowed such easy access to raw materials and severely hampered Britain in negotiations over trade debts was viewed by the Embassy in Berlin as an advanced form of lunacy. The advice of Edwards, the Commercial Counsellor, could not have been less diplomatic: 'If I were a shareholder of Dunlop's, I would suggest that the directors be publicly flayed for considering such a proposal.'[55]

Instead, the government found it very difficult to declare that the tactics of blackmail, which threatened the existence of subsidiary companies operating in Germany, were contrary to the national interest and would be stopped. Chamberlain was unwilling to take such a firm line in the case of Dunlop and sought justification for non-intervention. The transaction was now deemed to be too small and the military use too doubtful and indirect for it to be stopped on grounds of national defence. Such pragmatism was partly determined by domestic political considerations: Geddes was not going to be allowed to tell his shareholders that they had lost their investment because the government had disapproved of the company's proposal. This decision allowed the government to face both ways at once. The idea of British nationals being persuaded by a foreign power to provide credits of an exceptional character, which were needed not for the purposes of the business but for the foreign power's own economy, was condemned. The government would not extend moral support to Dunlop nor would it offer exemption from any action required in consideration of the national interest. At the same time, Geddes was assured that the Chancellor fully recognized that the case of companies with foreign subsidiaries presented special difficulties. Consequently, Dunlop would not have to suffer the intervention of the government on patriotic grounds.[56]

In the final stage of this affair Continental Rubber dropped out of the picture. After conversing with Schacht at Basle, Montagu Norman decided that Proctor had either completely misunderstood the whole matter or had been bluffed by Continental. Schacht maintained that it was not possible for the Reichsbank to give the undertaking which Proctor alleged he had received and that the Hanau subsidiary was, in any case, soon to be guaranteed foreign exchange for its normal imports. As if to confirm the strategic importance of the commodity, Schacht indicated that the German government would look to take over any tyre factory where production had stopped. For whatever reason, Dunlop Hanau now negotiated an agreement direct with the Rubber Controller and the RWM. The company undertook to supply itself with raw materials over four months to a total value of £120,000. Repayment in sterling was to be made by 1937, and so credit was extended for about two years. The Dunlop board believed it to be a prudent investment and Geddes did not relinquish his hope that the government would lend assistance, if need be, in obtaining repayment. The chairman was informed, however, that Dunlop was to be put into a different class to those trades (such as coal, textiles and herring) that were receiving preferential treatment.[57] The Treasury viewed the outcome as unexceptional. Apparently, several similar agreements had been reached without any communication to a government department.

As for Dunlop, Geoffrey Jones has suggested that the company was held hostage in Germany. Sales boomed during the mid 1930s although profits and the range of products were controlled. More capacity was established at the end of 1936. Dunlop's justification for this decision to expand was that friendly relations with Hitler's government depended upon the company's showing just how willing it was to contribute to the motorization of Germany.[58] Further considerable capital expenditure was demanded because the company was forced to switch from natural to synthetic rubber over a two-year period. As one history of the company notes, Dunlop was, to some extent, a victim of its own commercial success. The company continued to build its international reputation for reliable delivery of top-quality products without regard to the ideological complexion of the foreign state where its plants were located or with whom it traded.[59] The facilities based at Hanau were, however, in a class of their own: they had a part to play in helping to prepare the economy of the Third Reich for war. In the absence of any coercion from the British authorities to close the plant, or even encouragement to let production run down, Dunlop was certainly not going to let worries over the nation's security get in the way of protecting this important foreign investment. The company was destined, therefore, to repeat the experiences of the first part of the century. Sir Eric, however, was saved from any embarrassment by his untimely death in June 1937.

It is now clear that the Third Reich delayed production of Buna because the unfavourable price gap between synthetic and natural rubber caused the RWM to abandon plans for plant construction.[60] While technical problems with synthetic rubber had still to be overcome, the world price for natural rubber, even in the mid-1930s, remained at just a quarter of its late 1920s level. The total cost of German rubber imports was far below the bill for fuels and fibres, reaching a mere Rm25m in 1935 and Rm70m in 1936.[61] But reserves of unvulcanized rubber were all but exhausted by 1936 and Germany was to start the war with virtually no stockpiles of natural or synthetic rubber. Military planners in Britain had Nazi economic policies to thank, rather than the strategic foresight of their own government, for creating such shortages.

Supplying oil: the Anglo-Persian Oil Company

As with the harnessing of coal in the nineteenth century, control over the sources and distribution of mineral oil dominated economic life in the twentieth. Among raw materials of strategic importance, oil had assumed the place of *facile princeps* even before the First World War. Without a powerful industrial base the war-making potential of the state was limited. Coal remained a vital factor of production. But the security of oil supplies was of direct military significance and therefore a first consideration for military and other strategic planners. Yet, in line with Britain's general tardiness in preparing for war, detailed oil planning began only with the expansion of the relevant administrative machinery from 1936.[62]

In the debate which took place in Britain in the 1930s over supplying raw materials to Nazi Germany, no commodity or natural resource commanded more world-wide interest than mineral oil. In planning to create critical shortages in the event of war, there was more optimism in Britain over the case of liquid fuels than over any other of Germany's deficiency materials.[63] Both countries were able to exploit vast domestic coal deposits but both were dependent upon foreign sources for oil. Britain, however, enjoyed a massive advantage: the state was the majority shareholder in the Anglo-Persian Oil Company (APOC), one of the world's oil majors in production and distribution.

Anglo-Persian was one of the three European market leaders which supplied Germany with the bulk of her oil imports; the other two were Standard Oil of New Jersey and Royal Dutch Shell. Standard's subsidiary was the Hamburg-based Deutsch-Amerikanische Petroleum Gesellschaft which held a 28 per cent share of the civilian market. Shell's German subsidiary was the Rhenania-Ossag Mineralölwerke AG, with 22 per cent of the market. Nazi rearmament and *Motorisierungspolitik* ensured that the production of petroleum would become the most dynamic element of the Third Reich's energy sector. A rapid increase in the production, refining and distribution of petroleum products was required. At the same time, the oil majors were put under considerable pressure and trading conditions became extremely difficult. For Hitler was also determined to end the dominance of the Anglo-American multinationals in German fuel markets.[64] The development of synthetic fuel, which played a key role in the drive towards autarky, offered a lever. Germany was already advanced in the extraction of oil from coal: IG Farbenindustrie operated a large hydrogenation plant at Leuna, near to Leipzig, and had entered into licensing agreements with Standard during the 1920s.[65] By the time Hitler took power the Leuna plant had demonstrated its capacity to produce about 100,000 tons of synthetic fuel annually. But the cost per litre worked out at about triple the world price for gasoline.[66]

Anglo-Persian's German subsidiary was Olex – the Deutsche Benzin und Petroleum Verkaufsgesellschaft – which held a market share of about 17 per cent. APOC acquired a 40 per cent holding in 1926 and obtained complete control in July 1931. Olex did not trade without difficulty in the Weimar period. In 1932, the company was compelled to negotiate a kind of barter arrangement. Conditions under National Socialism were not expected to be any easier. Nevertheless, Anglo-Persian had no intention of withdrawing from the German market in 1933. Although past performance was poor and forecasts were gloomy, these problems were seen as common to the oil industry as a whole and the market was held to have considerable long-term potential.[67]

In July 1934 Freddie Morris, APOC's deputy director in charge of continental affairs, received a report from Dr Krauss, chairman of Olex. Krauss had been summoned to the RWM, along with representatives from the other two oil majors, and presented with the outline of a scheme. In return for the provision of all current requirements and a large reserve, all on credit with little prospect of much foreign currency payment for five years, German officials indicated that some undertaking would be given to limit production of synthetic oil and to maintain the market for the oil companies. Assurances were given that the idea of complete autarky in oil products was not in any way the policy of the Nazi Party because of the high costs of domestic production.[68] Shell and APOC already had frozen debts amounting to £845,000; the viability of their German investments was now also thrown into question. By the autumn of 1934 the biggest commercial debt owed to Britain was that held by APOC of more than £500,000 for petroleum supplies.[69]

Anglo-Persian, predicting that the German proposition would

hardly go down well in London, was in no hurry to explain it to the Foreign Office.[70] As they played an important role in industrial intelligence, APOC executives and other British oil companies were in a potentially embarrassing position. Major Desmond Morton, head of the IIC, made discreet approaches to the companies to derive accurate information on the location and extent of German underground storage tanks and the overall supply situation.[71] As soon as he was informed, Vansittart certainly became extremely agitated. He called on APOC to organize a united front of the companies to reject the plan and he promised that the Foreign Office would similarly organize a diplomatic front without caring whether offence were caused. This involved asking the Americans to put pressure on Standard Oil, Britain exerting influence over Sir Henri Deterding of Shell, and Vansittart himself approaching the Russian Ambassador. Vansittart dismissed the twin-headed threat of German synthetic production and the separate throwing over of APOC.[72] But he seemed to be unaware that the scheme originated in a meeting between Deterding and Feder, State Secretary at the RWM, and that the head of Rhenania (the Shell subsidiary) had already been acting as an adviser to the Reich government.

Deterding was known to be an admirer of the National Socialists. Indeed, he retired from Shell in 1936 after the London directors became so alarmed at his activities that they approached the British government for help.[73] With the coming of war the search began for guilty men; Sir Henri, who had just died, was named as one of the industrialists suspected of facilitating Hitler's rise to power through financial support.[74] The American consul in Hamburg reported in 1934 that Deterding, because of his fear of the Soviet Union, was favourably inclined toward the German government as a necessary safeguard against the spread of communistic ideas in western Europe. The consul added:

> Sir Henri had contributed fairly large sums to the National Socialist treasury before the advent of the Party into power and since Herr Hitler's assumption of the Chancellorship; he had offered to supply the Reich with all their oil requirements in return for payment in blocked reichsmarks ...

Deterding supported the Nazis in the belief that the alternative would be the downfall of the Reich and a violent swing to the left.

A further consular report of early 1935 claimed that Shell was anxious to obtain a monopoly in Germany. There were also rumours that the company had extended a large loan to the German government.[75]

The lack of solidarity among the companies was a worry for Anglo-Persian. But when the British government signalled its whole-hearted support for rejection of the scheme, with its proposed contracts for a special reserve, APOC became more determined to act – alone if necessary. The company decided that no more than three months' stock would be held. In addition, they resolved to insist upon payment of 90 per cent of the price (cost, insurance, freight) in foreign currencies of the oil delivered to Olex (the latter taking 10 per cent commission). Finally, no contract would be entered into which exceeded two years.[76]

But the resolve lasted just a few days. The oil companies indicated that they would probably continue to supply without getting paid. In Anglo-Persian's judgement, prudence was called for when each of the companies had large amounts of capital locked up in Germany and their businesses were threatened with closure. Of course, some in the oil business had an eye to future profits and were looking to expand rather than contract. Rhenania had taken the commercial decision to invest some £17m in immovable assets. Germany's requirements for oil supplies, in line with the development in aviation and especially motor spirit and diesel oil for the motorization programme, were projected to rise sharply. A comparison of motor traffic utilization undertaken by Shell revealed the scope for expansion in the German market.[77]

TABLE 5: ESTIMATED PETROLEUM CONSUMPTION IN 1933

Population (millions)		Tons
UK	48	3,960,000
France	41	2,500,000
Germany	66	1,500,000

Source: T 160 602/12750/09, memo, by the Asiatic Petroleum Company, 30 July 1934; 'Asiatic' was the old name for Shell's trading company; British officials continued with the usage.

Deterding reported that the Board of Shell, at a meeting in The Hague, had agreed to accept no proposals that were objectionable to the British government. Even so, cash payment for oil deliveries was to be postponed indefinitely. Leith-Ross found this position 'lamentably weak'. Vansittart despaired that, just as empty sacks could not be made to stand upright, government departments could do little if the companies did not have the stuff of resistance in them. The Treasury reasoned that once the companies began looking at the position from a commercial point of view it would be very difficult to change their minds in order to secure a political end. After all, the government directors of APOC were not supposed to interfere with the commercial administration of the company, although they had the right to veto the company's activities if they affected questions of foreign military policy.[78]

Representatives of IG Farben put forward an alternative proposal on behalf of the Reich authorities. The companies would supply oil products to the value of £4m for delivery over five years (with IG having the option to call for the whole delivery in two years), so that a reserve stock could be built up in Germany. With the arrival of each cargo, 10 per cent of the value (free on board) would be paid and the balance remitted in six-monthly instalments over the period of the five years. As an inducement to the oil majors there was the promise of a cartel arrangement to govern selling conditions in the German market.

Anglo-Persian reminded the British government that it had an important distributing organization in Germany and confirmed how it was very anxious to avoid the loss of goodwill. Ministers were well aware that the strategic arguments had to be weighed carefully. In so doing, they found themselves caught between Charybdis and Scylla. Clearly, the position of the Third Reich became stronger in proportion to the level of oil reserves which were established. On the other hand, it was not in Britain's interests to push the Nazi government in the direction of either looking for alternative supply channels or increasing the exploitation of domestic resources. Germany's annual domestic production of natural petroleum was estimated to be 300,000 tons and the authorities were encouraging the discovery of further deposits through subsidies. Furthermore, the trend towards self-sufficiency already suggested a strengthening of the Third Reich's defence position – despite the fact that it implied a diversion of effort from other activities – and a weakening of Britain's strategically vital oil organization. There was a chance, therefore, that the long-term effects of demanding immediate cash payment for supplies would be negative. On 14 November 1934 the Cabinet accepted that there were no clear grounds of public policy on which APOC could be advised to reject the proposal.[79]

While Anglo-Persian, at least, did not carry this scheme through, the oil companies were subjected to continuous pressure to reach some agreement on supplies. The 1934 Payments Agreement stipulated that Germany should produce proof that out of the total foreign exchange allocation there was sufficient for the purchase of British goods in customary proportions. Yet, the oil companies continued to face problems in securing the necessary foreign exchange certificates (*Devisenbescheinigungen*). The German authorities sought to justify this restriction on the grounds that the products were not of British origin, even though it had been agreed previously that oil refined in Britain would count as such. At one point Anglo-Persian threatened to divert cargoes already bound for German ports if the certificates were not forthcoming. The problem had become so severe by the beginning of 1935 that Olex was on the point of shutting down.[80]

APOC knew, of course, that it would be unable to repatriate funds in the event of liquidation; the Reichsmarks would, of necessity, have to find their way to other forms of investment. While the book value of APOC's holding was not great, the capital assets, largely fixed, were extensive. They included 26 depots and 13 service stations on land owned by the company, and more than 200 depots (including aviation depots) and a further 140 service stations on leased land. It is hardly surprising that the management in Britain and Germany hoped that any closure of Olex would be temporary.[81]

Anglo-Persian acted on two fronts: Freddie Morris in London asked for diplomatic representations to be made and Dr Krauss paid a visit to Dr Helmuth Wohltat in Berlin. Wohltat was well known and respected in London for his business career which was concerned with the international trade in oils and fats. But he had recently entered the civil service and had been put in charge of the routine allocation of foreign currency to the several clearing houses (*Überwachungstellen*). Eventually, he became Göring's trade assistant and achieved notoriety for the talks which he held in London with British officials on the eve of war (see Chapter 7).

APOC did not compare favourably with the other oil majors from Germany's point of view. Following the Dutch-German Payments Agreement, Shell had been able to keep payments going between the subsidiary and the parent group by a process of re-exports and large barter transactions. Standard Oil had greatly facilitated its currency position by placing orders in Germany. Wohltat wanted to know why APOC, which had heavy requirements of technical equipment, could not do the same. When he said that he could not imagine that APOC would risk the value of its large German interests by a refusal to supply oil, Britannic House believed that its bluff was being called. The stakes were high for Germany too. Krauss asked the RWM not to lose sight of the far-reaching psychological effects on public opinion of a shut-down by Olex. It was calculated that 2,000 employees would have to look for other jobs. More importantly, 6,000 petrol-pump keepers would have to close their pumps which, Krauss warned, 'would be an all too visible symptom, even in the smallest towns and villages, of Germany's foreign currency and economic difficulties.'[82]

But Olex was far from confident that it would survive. Sir Henri Deterding, who had recently visited Berlin, was expected to take a conciliatory line over the supply of oil products to Germany in view of his past promises. Olex feared a further weakening of its negotiating position. Although APOC might claim that it had done much for German industry, it was becoming clear that Shell and Standard had done more. Olex wondered whether this might justify some relaxation in London's attitude. In view of the potential of the German market, the subsidiary believed that a great deal was at stake for itself and APOC.[83] However, Britannic House was in no mood for relaxation. Olex was told that it was entitled to secure supplies from elsewhere but only in so far as no loss occurred, otherwise London would have the right to object very strongly. As far as the investment of capital in Germany was concerned, APOC did not want to make new commitments given the conditions ruling in the country and while existing funds were being unfrozen. Morris stated: 'there is no likelihood that I can see of our changing our policy, which is "No cash, no oil".'[84]

The other two oil majors certainly did do more for the Third Reich than APOC. Standard Oil entered into a contract with IG (the exclusive purchasing agent in Germany for a number of vital products including oil and rubber) to sell the rising outputs of the Leuna plant. Shell reached a similar agreement in 1935. As a reinsurance against future competition from synthetic fuel, both these majors took a 25 per cent shareholding in IG's Deutsche

Gasolin AG. In strictly commercial terms this decision made sense. By 1939 IG's synthetics factories produced no less than one-half of the petroleum consumed in the Third Reich.[85] Indeed, the policy on autarky was beginning to take effect. German consumption of mineral oils increased by about 56 per cent between 1933 and 1936, and then by a further 24 per cent until 1939. But the proportion of consumption which was foreign-sourced fell from about 75 to just under 50 per cent between 1933 and 1939.[86]

In 1935 the Anglo-Persian was renamed the Anglo-Iranian Oil Company (AIOC). In the months which followed the British government and various industrial interests, particularly the colliery owners, sought to find out more about the developments taking place in German catalytic processes. It seemed as if it might be possible to produce synthetic fuel at costs much less than those achieved by ICI at its hydrogenation plant in Billingham in the north of England. In September 1936 Ruhrchemie AG was visited by W.H. Cadman (brother of AIOC's chairman) and a coal industry representative. Krupps, Mannesmann and Gutehoffnungshutte were the major shareholders in the German company. Unfortunately, the British visitors were not allowed a close inspection of the plant and the general lack of data meant that AIOC did not feel that it could make a decision on the viability of purchasing a licence. Thereafter it became apparent to AIOC that the industrial processes remained so uneconomic that there was no commercial case for the establishment of plants in Britain.[87] This indicates that the Third Reich had little to gain from the British petrochemical industry in the way of relevant scientific or technical expertise; rather, the question was whether it was worth paying for the technology to be transferred from Germany to Britain.

Olex continued to exist from hand to mouth for supplies and attempted to weather the storm by taking steps to cut down deliveries. By April 1936 the company was managing to do no more than keep its petrol pumps going. This represented just 50 per cent of normal trade. All capital and publicity expenditure was eliminated and Olex executives were forced to try to make up the shortfall in supplies by following 'the unnatural practice' of buying oil from Romania.[88] Apart from Russia, Romania was the only state which had been prepared to supply Germany on a Reichsmark basis. This lasted until the Romanian National Bank decreed, in 1935, that shipments were only to be made against 100 per cent free exchange.

Nevertheless, German imports of oil rose considerably up to 1937 and came mostly from Romania. The German-Romanian Payments Agreement provided the solution. It also helped to effect a trade substitution: instead of Britain supplying oil plant to Iran, Germany supplied oil plant to Romania.[89]

Several attempts were made by AIOC and British officials in London and Berlin to secure an allocation of currency under the Payments Agreement for British-supplied oil to Germany. In London an exasperated Morris reminded the Petroleum Department, in September 1936, that the simple facts were that AIOC was a British concern with important interests in Germany. As such, the company felt that it should be one of the first to receive an allocation of significant amounts of foreign exchange. AIOC wanted reassurance that its interests would not be prejudiced in favour of competitors – such as Standard Oil supported by the American administration – which was able to bring barter or compensation business to Germany.[90]

Nevertheless, Olex always struggled to survive, sometimes literally, in the Third Reich. Meanwhile, news reached London of 'a tragi-comedy' taking place in Leipzig. A Luftwaffe machine had taxied across the airfield but had been unable to take off. Defective aviation spirit was held to blame. As the benzene in question had been supplied by Olex from its local depot, the manager was arrested by the Gestapo and thrown into prison pending trial for industrial sabotage. But the quality of the spirit at the oil installation, at Aachen, complied with official regulations. The real 'culprit' turned out to be a few rusty barrels in which the supplies to Leipzig had been delivered. Olex took steps to try to ensure that the company and the manager received no more than a reprimand.[91]

Rumours persisted in Germany and Britain that the Anglo-Iranian was looking to sell the subsidiary. The parent company found it difficult to understand why such ideas should circulate. Although attractive sterling offers would have been considered, such a prospect was not in sight and a disposal of the subsidiary was not sought.[92] Still, as Morris himself noted in March 1939, 'Many producers in Germany would like to get hold of a good distributing organisation such as Olex.'[93] This was why, in spite of all the enduring difficulties, there was such interest in acquiring the subsidiary. It also helps to explain why Anglo-Iranian was prepared to take a long-term view of its asset. Such a policy made commercial sense. The assessment of the potential of the market was borne out by a recovery in Olex's sales even under the burdens imposed by National Socialism. In the mid 1930s Olex's share in the covering of Germany's requirements of mineral oil products was: for motor spirit about 10 per cent, for aviation spirit more than 35 per cent, for gas oil more than 10 per cent, and for kerosene about 25 per cent.[94] By 1938 the total market share commanded by AIOC was about 10 per cent; Standard Oil and Shell remained the clear market leaders with 26 and 22 per cent, respectively.[95] This followed roughly the same pattern as elsewhere in Europe and was not far out of line with the position in late Weimar Germany a few years before.

Following the Anschluss in 1938, all remaining barriers between Austria and Germany were dismantled.[96] Anglo-Iranian realized that it would have to meet competition from both German companies and Shell; London was concerned that an unfavourable situation might develop, particularly in regard to European aviation. For, in this aspect of the business, AIOC's interest was almost entirely concentrated on the 'considerable amount of trade' with Lufthansa and the German air force. As for the motor trade, consumption of benzene was increasing and Anglo-Iranian stuck to the view that important possibilities remained in Germany which represented a large potential market for the future. The expectation was that Olex would soon start to generate surplus marks. Consequently, in order to extend trade the investment of such blocked funds in the purchase of an Austrian oil company was under consideration.[97]

At the outbreak of the Second World War most British investments tied up in central Europe suddenly seemed destined to be lost well before any long-term benefits could be realized. But then clearly the risks had been growing throughout the 1930s. With Hitler determined to prepare the German economy for war, commercial decisions could also carry significant political and strategic implications. Business interests in the Third Reich that were foreign-owned could be made effectively to chose between closure or some kind of co-operation with the régime. Anglo-Iranian's policy was to try to resist Nazi pressure up to but not beyond the point where the Olex organization was likely to collapse. Closure of the business would have left the field wide open for Standard and Shell to exploit; the two arch-rivals might then have gained a massive and irreversible competitive advantage with potentially serious consequences for the British company. Inevitably, therefore,

Olex was caught up in facilitating the Nazi rearmament effort, albeit in a minor and indirect way.

For AIOC was the odd one out among the oil majors. By participating with IG Farben in joint hydrogenation projects, Shell and Standard were afforded both a degree of political protection for the operations of their German subsidiaries and investment opportunities for profits which could not be repatriated. Looked at purely in terms of the oil business, these two companies were well placed: at minimum cost they maintained the option to benefit from the future development of the German market. However, Anglo-Iranian enjoyed no such privileges. This was the penalty to be paid for the failure to contribute either to the Third Reich's strategic reserves or to the drive to achieve self-sufficiency. During the war decisions on military strategy pivoted on the need to secure oil supplies. In this respect, hostilities reduced Olex to little more than a marketing organization; the seizure of the assets by the Nazi state could hardly have helped Germany's war effort. Instead, with Hitler's failure to capture the oilfields of the Caucasus in 1941–42, the Third Reich came to depend upon synthetic fuel in a futile attempt to stave off final defeat.

Supplying textiles: the Lancashire Cotton Corporation

Unlike the oil and rubber multinationals, firms in the textile industry did not own significant subsidiary organizations in Germany. But, in common with the other two commodities, the trade in textiles was subjected to the same critical scrutiny in the interests of national defence. After all, Britain remained the world's leading supplier and the market for cotton and textile products was not exclusively civilian. In the case of the German textile industry, imports accounted for 95 per cent of all the raw materials used in 1928.[98] To meet rising demand, German producers added synthetic fibres to fabrics. However, wool and cotton were never in danger of being replaced. The terrible effects on the German Army of exposure to Russian winters during the Second World War was to demonstrate the inadequacy of clothing made with synthetic products. Textile raw materials represented, therefore, one of the key deficiencies of the Third Reich identified by the IIC before the war.[99]

As the Wehrmacht grew in size in the 1930s, the need to provide uniforms for the enlisted ranks became ever more urgent. Indeed, Volkmann confirms that in the textile sector consumer and rearmament interests clashed and Germany's precarious dependence on world markets was a source of particular anxiety to the Nazi leadership.[100] They had every reason to be anxious. In 1933 imports of cotton and wool cost the Reich Rm570m; in 1935 they took about Rm700 million – a staggering 44 per cent of all foreign exchange expended on raw materials.[101] Yet, by the mid 1930s Nazi propaganda proclaimed that the new Germany would have both guns and butter. Why should Britain help the Third Reich in its hungry search for the raw materials which were necessary to satisfy both civilian and military orders?

The British cotton industry, like most of the staples, was heavily committed to the export market: in 1925 it accounted for 25.8 per cent of total British exports by value. By 1937 this figure had dropped to 13.1 per cent – an illustration of the magnitude of the problem confronting traditional British exports.[102] Along with the coal trade, the export of manufactured and semi-manufactured cotton and textile goods in the nineteenth and the early twentieth century had brought Britain into close commercial contact with Germany.[103] The Great Depression had badly damaged this relationship and British textile exporters continued to experience very difficult conditions even after the Anglo-German Payments Agreement.

Well before the depression struck it had become clear that the cotton industry would never see a return to the position of pre-eminence enjoyed in the nineteenth century. But attempts were made to manage the effects of the decline. Although many firms amalgamated, particularly in the spinning sector of the industry, financial performance remained poor.[104] The Lancashire Cotton Corporation, established in January 1929, was the biggest combination of all. It has been described as a giant corporate oddity which provided emergency support to those clearing banks which were in difficulty because of lending to cotton firms.[105] In drawing up plans for the rationalization of the industry, the cotton manufacturers received advice and assistance from the Bankers' Industrial Development Company which operated under the auspices of the Bank of England.[106] But the LCC did not prosper and the influence exerted by City financial interests was resented in Lancashire. Ironically, the entrepreneur who, in 1931, was asked to investigate the crisis was Sir Eric Geddes.[107] The LCC was reorganized the following year and Frank Platt was appointed a director. This straight-talking Lancashire man was one of the more successful figures in the industry and in 1933 he took over as managing director.

Nevertheless, desperate attempts to rescue the industry continued into the 1930s. These even included a plan to collaborate with the anti-modern trading practices of National Socialism. In 1935 Platt devised a scheme for barter trade between Britain and Germany. The objective was to increase the ability of the company to sell in the Third Reich by trading direct with the users of cotton yarns. Schroders, the merchant bank, told Platt that their Berlin office would be able to make the necessary arrangements with the German exporting interests; these comprised IG Farben, the Steel Trust and Siemens-Schückerts. By way of contrast to the nature of the scheme, Platt's hope that a reduction in selling prices might have stimulated employment in Britain was calculated to appeal to the economically orthodox. He also claimed that compensation agreements were constantly being put to him by his customers; he only wished to systematize a type of business which was already carried on in many instances.[108]

Platt was right in suggesting that there was a movement towards barter transactions. British exporters were no longer sure of getting foreign exchange certificates and the institution of a private clearing would have effected an equal exchange as between German and British products. In principle, the Board of Trade and the Treasury condemned such arrangements. But there was a feeling that the government should not even try to stop Platt.[109] Indeed, as Garside has shown, the government and many of the entrepreneurs concerned had temporarily abandoned any idea of a more far-reaching reconstruction of the industry. It seemed that the only way forward, as always, was to look for a revival of export markets.[110] However, the authorities in both countries had to ensure that barter deals did not begin to impinge upon the working of the Payments Agreement. The German government began, in any case, to forbid most of the transactions involving the direct exchange of German for British goods; they claimed that many goods imported to Germany on barter deals were being priced at inflated levels.

But Platt was not so easily deterred. In September 1936 he put forward a new scheme to sell cotton yarn to Germany. The bankers who were to provide the credit sought approval from the Bank of England. This was forthcoming since the transaction was safeguarded in commercial terms. Indeed, the Bank made it plain that, if a decision were taken to disallow the scheme, they would require some precise indication of the kind of transaction to which no objection would be taken. The Governor wanted to know what commodities and what credit terms would be regarded as normal in the abnormal and unprecedented conditions under which British trade was being carried on with Europe generally and Germany in particular.[111]

It was now the turn of the Board of Trade to raise objections. Nothing was allowed to interfere with the elaborate system devised by the British and German representatives who sat on the consultative committee to oversee the working of the Payments Agreement. Under the 55 per cent ratio, the amount of foreign exchange for each trade was worked out for the succeeding six months. With anxieties over the danger of frozen debts remaining high, the Germans were accused of playing the same game as the Russians – trying to get British goods on larger and longer credit. There was another important reason to veto the new scheme: it enabled the government to avoid any suggestion of favouritism. Relations between Platt's company and its rivals were already dominated by jealously; the rivals alleged that special favours had been shown to Platt because of the influence of the Bank of England. An increase in the Lancashire Cotton Corporation's share of trade would probably have resulted in a corresponding diminution for that of other companies.[112]

The last act in this particular drama was played out some two months later when the company put forward a proposal to sell a modest £50,000-worth of cotton waste to Germany over a year. Hambros Bank was to pay the company in cash and receive the obligations of the Dresdner Bank in nine or ten months. Before 1931 such sales had been effected on 30-day credits. Professor Clay, in the Bank of England, thought that the banks had to be encouraged rather than discouraged to assist industry in this way. With Treasury approval, Montagu Norman wrote to Sir Charles Hambro to say that, while it would be in order to open such a credit, it was important that the credit should represent genuine commercial transactions under normal banking conditions. Six months later the Governor wrote again to give his approval for Hambro to open a non-revolving credit for a further £100,000 on account of the LCC. Hambro did indeed open a credit (apparently for £50,000) and the scheme duly went ahead.[113]

Many commodities had a real or potential role to play in the German rearmament effort and the government had to decide which trades should be sanctioned. Yet, as the Dunlop and Anglo-Iranian experiences show, it was the manner in which British-owned companies were treated by the German authorities which caused most excitement in London; the fact that a raw material was of indirect or even direct military value was far less important. It is doubtful whether the issue of supplying rubber to Germany would have arisen at all but for the difficulties created for Dunlop Hanau. Similarly, although the British government was aware of the strategic significance of textile raw materials, there is no evidence that this dimension of the problem merited even the slightest consideration in the deliberations over the Lancashire Cotton Corporation.

In analysing the links between British industry and the Third Reich, a line may be drawn between manufactures connected in some way with the arms trade and companies involved in supplying raw materials; while the former were under the watchful eye of a public ready to condemn any transgression, the latter drew little, if any, criticism for their foreign operations. In the absence of any particular pressure from popular opinion, government policy continued to concentrate on the need to nurture Britain's fragile economic recovery: anxieties over the implications of German rearmament were outweighed by fears that the imposition of official controls would damage business. British multinationals were largely left to decide for themselves whether to exercise self-restraint and forgo commercial opportunities. The extent to which the same may be said for the way in which the City did business with Germany is examined in the following chapter.

NOTES

1. Schmidt, *The Politics and Economics of Appeasement*, p. 35.
2. R.J. Overy, *War and Economy in the Third Reich*, (Oxford: OUP, 1994), p. 9.
3. MS. Simon, Diaries, fol. 7, 20 November 1934.
4. M. Geyer, 'Military revisionism in the interwar years' in W. Deist (ed.), *The German Military in the Age of Total War* (Leamington Spa: Berg, 1985), p. 126.
5. CAB 47/8, 1118.B, report on 'Economic Pressure on Germany', 30 October

1933. The CID agreed on 6 April 1933 to set up a sub-committee of the advisory committee on trade questions in time of war.

6. C.M. Leitz, 'Arms exports from the Third Reich, 1933–39: the example of Krupp', *EcHR*, 51, 1 (February 1998), p. 153.

7. Vickers Archive, Cambridge University Library, 58.76, extracts from the report of the AGM held on 26 March 1934.

8. Ibid., 57.3. See also, J.D. Scott, *Vickers: A History* (Weidenfeld & Nicolson, 1962), pp. 238–56.

9. A. Bullock, *Hitler and Stalin: Parallel Lives* (BCA/HarperCollins, 1991), p. 316.

10. P. Noel-Baker, *The Private Manufacture of Armaments* (Victor Gollancz, 1936), pp. 47, 195.

11. A.D. Smith, *Guilty Germans?* (Victor Gollancz, 1942), pp. 92, 230.

12. D.G. Anderson, 'British rearmament and the "merchants of death": The 1935–36 Royal Commission on the Manufacture of and Trade in Armaments', *JCH*, 29 (1994), p. 21.

13. A. Teichova, *An Economic Background to Munich: International Business and Czechoslovakia 1918–1938* (Cambridge: CUP, 1974), pp. 287–94.

14. W.N. Medlicott, *The History of the Second World War: The Economic Blockade. Vol.1* (HMSO, 1952), pp. 12–16.

15. R.J. Young, 'Spokesmen for economic warfare: The Industrial Intelligence Centre in the 1930s', *European Studies Review*, 6 (1976), p. 482.

16. Wark, *The Ultimate Enemy*, pp. 170–4.

17. T 160 590 8797/05/1, minute by Sir Warren Fisher, based on a CID paper.

18. NA RG59/862.51/4096, material sent to H. Feis by Charles Dieckman, Chase Manhattan Bank (but formerly at the Berlin Embassy), 29 June 1934.

19. R.J. Overy, 'Hitler's war plans', in Boyce and Robertson, *Paths to War*, pp. 104–5.

20. Overy, *War and Economy*, p. 21.

21. For background to the IIC and Vansittart's private network, see C. Andrew, *Secret Service: The Making of the British Intelligence Community* (Heinemann, 1985), pp. 354–5, 382–5.

22. Malcolm Christie papers, Churchill College Archives, 180/1/24, details of *Wehrwirtschaftberichte* including extracts from situation reports, 1 June and 1 October 1937; see also, report, 1 January 1938, on prospects for the year ahead, and speech by Thomas to Wehrmacht officers, May 1938.

23. Overy, *War and Eonomy*, p. 212.

24. G.C. Peden, 'A matter of timing: The economic background to British foreign policy, 1937–1939', *History*, 69 (February 1984), pp. 23–6.

25. M. Balfour, *Withstanding Hitler in Germany 1933–45* (Routledge, 1988), p. 36.

26. For a recent and incisive treatment of the topic see, B.J.C. McKercher, 'Old diplomacy and new: the Foreign Office and foreign policy, 1919–1939', in M. Dockrill and B.J.C. McKercher (eds), *Diplomacy and World Power: Studies in British Foreign Policy, 1880–1950* (Cambridge: CUP, 1996).

27. Sir Eric Phipps papers, Churchill College Archives, I 3/3, private letter from Hankey to Phipps (in Paris), 11 January 1938.

28. S. Roskill, *Hankey: Man of Secrets, Vol. 3, 1931–1963* (Collins, 1974), pp. 237–8.

29. H.E. Volkmann, 'The National Socialist economy in preparation for war', in W. Deist, *et al.* (eds), *Germany and the Second World War* (Oxford: Clarendon Press, 1990), p. 246.

30. C.H. Wilson, *The History of Unilever: Vol.2* (Cassell, 1954), p. 330.
31. Ibid., p. 335.
32. Marsh, *The Bundesbank* , p. 275, n.86.
33. PREM 1, 335, Tennant's letter to Chamberlain, 4 July 1939, and enclosures.
34. MS. Simon, 78, fol. 94, letter from Tennant to Simon, 20 February 1934.
35. T 160/728/12750/012/2, minute by Leith-Ross,14 September 1934. The information came to the Treasury from the Bank of England.
36. T 160/573/13460/011, Browett (Board of Trade) to Waley, 29 September 1934. The loans would have been taken for five years, repaid in Dutch florins with the marks taken at par, carried interest at 4.5 per cent and guaranteed by one or more of the large German banks.
37. T 160/573/13460/011, report by Edwards (Commercial Secretary); Leith-Ross to Chancellor, 2 October 1934. Leith-Ross suspected that it amounted to a desire to draw on unavailed credit.
38. T 188/147, 4 Oct 1934.
39. PREM 1, 335, Tennant's letter to Chamberlain, 4 July 1939, and enclosures.
40. Wilson, *History of Unilever*, p. 370.
41. The Anglo-German Association had been dissolved in 1933 because it contained so-called non-Aryan elements. For a discussion of the role of the Fellowship as a pressure group, see Schmidt, *The Politics and Economics of Appeasement*, pp. 43–8.
42. FO 371/18878/C2168. See also, PREM 1, 335, Tennant's letter to Chamberlain, 4 July 1939, and enclosures.
43. Runciman papers, 285, letter, 29 May 1937, from the Fellowship to Runciman inviting the latter to become a member.
44. Volkmann, 'The National Socialist economy', p. 267.
45. T 188/147, Walter Fletcher to Leith-Ross, 5 September 1934.
46. T 160/573/13460/011.
47. Ibid., Geddes to Norman, 28 September 1934. The plant was managed by Proctor's German brother-in-law.
48. G. Jones, 'The growth and performance of British multinational firms before 1939: The case of Dunlop', *EcHR*, 2nd Ser., 37, 1 (February 1984), p. 48–9.
49. T 160/573/13460/011, quoted in letter by Vansittart to Fisher, 10 October 1934.
50. Overy, *War and Economy*, p. 7.
51. T 160/573/13460/011, Vansittart to Fisher, 10 October 1934.
52. Ibid., memo by Waley, 1 October 1934. The Governor viewed the Dunlop scheme favourably.
53. CAB 23/79, 33(34)3.
54. T 160/573/13460/011, record of meeting between Geddes, Leith-Ross and Norman. See also letters from Geddes to Fergusson (PPS to Chancellor of the Exchequer), Leith-Ross to Vansittart, and memo by Fergusson, all dated 5 October 1934.
55. T 160/573/13460/011, Edwards to Leith-Ross, 6 October 1934.
56. Ibid., Fergusson to Geddes, 8 October 1934.
57. Ibid., minute by Fergusson, 10 October 1934; Fergusson to Geddes, 29 October 1934.
58. Jones, 'The growth and performance', p. 49.
59. J. McMillan, *The Dunlop Story* (Weidenfeld & Nicolson, 1989), p. 75.
60. Volkmann, 'The National Socialist economy', p. 303.
61. Hayes, *Industry and Ideology*, p. 148.
62. D.J. Payton-Smith, *Oil: A Study of War-Time Policy and Administration*

(HMSO, 1971), pp. 40–4. By 1934 the Petroleum Department comprised three full-time and three part-time officials.

63. Medlicott, *The Economic Blockade*, p. 33.
64. Gillingham, *Industry and Politics*, p. 71. See also, CAB 24/248, CP83, CID Sub-Committee Report, October 1933, 'Economic Pressure on Germany'.
65. D. Yergin, *The Prize: the Epic Quest for Oil, Money, and Power* (Simon & Schuster, 1991), pp. 330–1.
66. Hayes, *Industry and Ideology*, p. 115.
67. For the background on Olex see J.H. Bamberg, *The History of the British Petroleum Company: Vol.2, The Anglo-Iranian Years, 1928–1954* (Cambridge: CUP, 1994), pp. 131–3. For details of barter arrangement see T 160/927/12750/2, Rowe-Dutton (Berlin) to Waley, 1 June 1932. Olex placed an order in the Rhineland as part of a pipeline which they were constructing. The order, worth £200,000, had to be paid for in sterling.The RWM agreed that Olex could either have the sterling resold to them in order to purchase petroleum to import into Germany or they could pay for the pipeline in marks from blocked accounts.
68. BP Archive, University of Warwick (hereafter BP), 72179, Krauss to Morris, 13 July 1934.
69. T 160/534/13460/010/1–2.
70. NA RG59/862.6363/153, report of a meeting, in London on 25 July 1934 of the companies.
71. Wark, *The Ultimate Enemy*, p. 164. See also Young, 'Spokesmen for economic warfare', n.34, for quotation by an annonymous officer which reveals that the IIC knew just how small German stocks of oil were in relation to the vast quantities required in wartime.
72. T 160/602/12750/09, Waley to Leith-Ross, 25 July 1934.
73. Yergin, *The Prize*, p. 369.
74. Smith, *Guilty Germans?*, p. 188.
75. NA RG59/862.6363/155 and 165, reports, 21 August 1934 and 15 February 1935, respectively.
76. T 160/602/12750/09, Leith-Ross to Sir George Barstow (APOC), 26 July and to Waley, 25 July 1934. See also, CAB 24/251, CP252, 9 November 1934, 'Supplies of Pertroleum to Germany'.
77. T 160 602/12750/09, memo, 30 July 1934.
78. Ibid., correspondence between the Treasury and Foreign Office, 1 August 1934 and also Perowne to Leith-Ross,12 September 1934.
79. CAB 24/251, CP 252.
80. T 160/615/13999/07. See minute by Mines Department to Board of Trade, 7 March 1935.
81. BP 72201, Berthoud (APOC's permanent representative at Olex) to Morris, 29 October 1934.
82. Ibid., Krauss to Morris, 7 February 1935.
83. BP 72201, correspondence from Krauss and Berthoud to Morris, 12 February 1935.
84. Ibid., Morris to Berthoud, 14 February 1935. Berthoud had also suggested triangular and barter deals as a way out of the difficulties.
85. Gillingham, *Industry and Politics*, pp. 75,163. The output of hydrogenation-produced petrol rose 300 per cent between 1936 and 1942.
86. Volkmann, 'The National Socialist economy', pp. 263–4, 301.
87. BP 72488, letter from Sir John Cadman (chairman) to Sir Frank Smith (Department of Scientific and Industrial Research), 23 March, and to Sir

Horace Wilson (the government's Chief Industrial Adviser), 27 March 1936, and note for the chairman; see also, record of visit on 17/18 September 1936 by W.H. Cadman and Miles Reid of Powell Duffryn Associated Collieries Ltd, and the former's secret memo (undated), 'On the Present Views of the Anglo-Iranian Oil Company Limited', marked 'property of HMG, committee on synthetic processes'.

88. BP 72201, Berthoud to Morris, 17 May 1935.
89. A. Schweitzer, *Big Business in the Third Reich* (Bloomington, IN: Indianna University Press, 1964), p. 304; T 160/615/13999/07, Petroleum Department to Board of Trade, 1 April 1936.
90. BP 72201, Morris to Coleman (Petroleum Department), 2 September 1936.
91. Ibid., Blackwood (Berlin) to Morris, 29 December 1936. Blackwood refers to Aix-la-Chapelle rather than Aachen.
92. BP 72201, correspondence between Blackwood and Morris, 7/8 October 1936.
93. BP 72177, minute by Morris, 17 March 1939.
94. BP 72201.
95. Bamberg, *History of British Petroleum*, p. 133.
96. For background see, H. Matis and F. Weber, 'Economic Anschluss and German *Grossmachtpolitik*: the take-over of the Austrian Credit-Anstalt in 1938', in P.L. Cottrell, H. Lindgren and A. Teichova (eds), *European Industry and Banking between the Wars* (Leicester: Leicester University Press, 1992).
97. BP 69052, memo by Morris, 25 April 1938.
98. Barkai, *Nazi Economics*, pp. 230–2.
99. Medlicott, *The Economic Blockade*, p. 35.
100. Volkmann, 'The National Socialist economy', pp. 262–7.
101. Hayes, *Industry and Ideology*, p. 145.
102. S. Glynn and J. Oxborrow, *Inter-War Britain: A Social and Economic History* (Allen & Unwin, 1976), p. 73.
103. L.G. Sandberg, *Lancashire in Decline: a Study in Entrepreneurship, Technology, and International Trade* (Columbus, OH: Ohio State University Press, 1974), pp. 159–61.
104. W.R. Garside and J.I. Greaves, 'Rationalisation and Britain's industrial malaise: the interwar years revisited', *JEEH*, 26, 1 (Spring 1997), p. 56.
105. B.W.E. Alford, 'New industries for old? British industry between the wars', in R. Floud and D. McCloskey (eds), *The Economic History of Britain since 1700: Vol.2* (Cambridge: CUP, 1981), p. 325.
106. For a recent analysis of the role of Montagu Norman see W.R. Garside and J.I. Greaves, 'The Bank of England and industrial intervention in interwar Britain', *Financial History Review*, 3, 1 (April 1996).
107. Hannah, *The Corporate Economy*, p. 76.
108. T 160/559/12750/033, Platt to Browett (Board of Trade, Commercial Relations and Treaties Department), 28 January 1935.
109. Ibid., St.Quinton Hill (Board of Trade) to Waley, 29 January 1935 and to Rawlins (Berlin), 31 March 1935.
110. Garside, *British Unemployment*, pp. 228–9.
111. T 160/673/13999/018.
112. Ibid., Waley to Hopkins, 1 October 1936.
113. T 160/673/13999/018, minutes, 3 December 1936 and 22 June 1937.

6

British banks and the
Third Reich:
financing the Nazis or a once smart
business going bad?

Only those initiated in the art of military strategy grasped the significance of how preparedness for war had come to depend upon a secure supply of certain essential commodities such as oil. By way of contrast, the related issue of access to international finance was debated much more widely. The pattern of lending to Germany in the 1920s was well known. While British banks had provided a large volume of finance for German banks and industrial or commercial concerns, many of the credits were originally used for the movement of goods. However, with the contraction of trade after 1929 the credits came to represent general finance for German business. Much of this lending was frozen under the Standstill Agreement of 1931. This then formed the basis for Anglo-German financial relations until 1939.

In agreeing to maintain the Standstill after the collapse of the Weimar Republic, British bankers could be assured of some continuity in relations. Even if the very existence of the Standstill were threatened by the extreme measures to which the Nazis resorted, it was always seen in the Third Reich as an important instrument of policy. Yet, with German industry gearing up for rearmament and the chances of war in Europe looming ever larger, the Standstill was bound to stir up fresh controversy every time it was renewed.

Even greater alarm was caused in Britain by the suspicion that bank lending to the Third Reich also had a private face – hidden from public scrutiny. Rumours circulated throughout the 1930s that the City of London was issuing substantial trade credits that allowed the Nazis to purchase war materials. In one recent study this putative lending is seen as a response to the collapse of the multilateral clearing system and the result of German discrimination in favour of British banks and against underrepresented American bondholders.[1] Nevertheless, it is supporting evidence rather than repetition which confers on an allegation the status of an indisputable fact. If rumours over lending are to be substantiated, the limited amount of material to have emerged from the very private world of merchant banking must be reviewed.

Historically, the City has always sought to operate in the money, goods and capital markets with as little external regulation by the state as possible. Geoffrey Ingham points out that, in spite of the obvious changes brought about by the 1931 crisis, there was no fundamental restructuring of the banking and commercial system. Innovations were introduced cautiously, in order to avoid disturbing orthodox practices, and relations between the City, the Bank of England and the Treasury remained as close as ever.[2] Yet the reluctance on the part of the City and authorities to meddle with the intricacies of international finance had to be reconciled with the changes taking place in international relations. In this regard, the complexity of the structure which connected British banks with German trade served to inhibit changes to financial practices, even after Hitler achieved power.

Although all such banking credits had a bearing on Anglo-German trade, only a small proportion of them were used to finance direct trade between the two countries. The English banking system also provided a large volume of credit for the financing of international transactions in which Germany was concerned, particularly trade with British colonies and the Dominions involving raw materials into, and manufactures out of, Germany.[3] The total volume of credit was very much greater than that for direct Anglo-German trade. Bankers were keen to point out how the continual use of such international credits since the financial crisis had been a vital factor in helping to maintain Germany's export surplus, and consequently her ability to service her long- and medium-term debt. On these grounds the Third Reich, too, had to maintain adequate facilities for buying in the world market.

Yet there were other factors to consider when defining Britain's national interests. Hitler had been in power for less than a year when Vansittart applied one all-important criterion: 'I have always thought that financial stringency in Germany was going to be our principal safeguard against wholesale German rearmament, and that we should do all we can to keep Germany lean, even at a cost to certain people here.'[4] Vansittart hoped that a distinction could be made between short-term lending to Germany, strictly for commercial purposes, and finance for German industry which would provide a direct incentive to the Reichswehr to press on with rearmament.

What remains intriguing today is why Britain, compared with other nations, maintained a much higher proportion of her Standstill credits to Germany, even up to the outbreak of war. As the threat to European peace and stability grew, how could British bankers be sure that the Standstill continued to serve the interests of the nation more than it served the interests of National Socialism? And further, what impact did the growing menace of the Third Reich have on the City's traditional freedom to lend money wheresoever and to whomsoever it chose?

Restraining the urge to do new business

When considering the involvement of Hambros Bank with the Lancashire Cotton Corporation in 1936, the Treasury observed that 'an embargo on commercial credits to Germany, if too strictly applied, does more harm than good politically, besides interfering with legitimate export business.'[5] This intriguing statement of the theoretical position tends to conceal more than it reveals of the reality of British policy concerning new lending to the Third Reich. Surely an embargo that was not strictly applied would have been pointless. Further, officials knew how difficult it was to define 'legitimacy' in the context of the export business to the Third Reich. If an embargo was supposed to be in place, when was the decision taken and under what circumstances?

During the crisis over British bondholders in 1933/34, officials felt that existing loans to Germany were hanging round their necks like millstones. The Treasury confirmed Foreign Office suspicions that quite fresh money was being advanced. Short-term credit had recently been granted in an 'appreciable amount' for the purchase of wool and wheat. This was said to be a healthy development because it was being conducted on a normal commercial basis, or, in other words, the substitution of three months' credit for frozen credit. Although money was thereby released for an alternative purpose, prohibition of the credits carried the risk of damaging Britain's commercial machine.[6] Other schemes to supply raw materials on credit were less healthy and probably formed part of a concerted policy by the Nazi authorities. There was an unsuccessful attempt, in April 1934, to arrange some kind of trade agreement when German interests were negotiating in the City for long-term credits for oil, tin and rubber. The Treasury and the Foreign Office together had already done what they could to discourage the extension of similar credits by the oil companies.[7]

It was in the aftermath of the unfortunate visit by British businessmen to Berlin, in September 1934, that the government first asked the Bank of England to discourage any new arrangements being made for credit in respect of German exports to the UK. The houses thought most likely to be involved were Lazards, Barings and Hambros. Hambros did, indeed, inform the authorities about a £1m credit it had made earlier in the year to IG Farbenindustrie. The objective was to finance IG trading with Britain, the Dominions and other countries with free exchanges. Whenever IG drew on the credit it informed Hambros of where the goods were consigned and the buyers gave an irrevocable undertaking to remit the proceeds in sterling to the bank. The credit was a revolving one: IG could draw at three months' sight on the bank at any time.

The problem was that Hambros wished to continue with the arrangement, believing that it had worked smoothly and resulted in a considerable turnover of trade with Britain and the Dominions. What worried Olaf Hambro was whether the right to terminate the credit, at the end of the year, meant that the credit had to be regarded as a new advance. The likely impact of any clearing had to be considered too. The Treasury did not want credits extended to the point where a large proportion of the income of a clearing system would be absorbed by the claims of the accepting houses. As about 30 per cent of the IG credit was secured on German exports to Britain, nearly all those exports would have come within the scope of a clearing. It was suggested to Hambros that the bank could reduce its credit to the amount covered by IG exports elsewhere.[8]

Although these exports to Britain allowed Germany access to free exchange, they did at least fall within the accepted boundaries of conventional international trade. But Hambros Bank was not always so scrupulous. The London house offered to extend credit to facilitate the purchase by Germany of Egyptian cotton, security being taken on German exports (of machinery rather than finished cotton goods) to Egypt.[9] The transaction would have allowed the Nazis to put pressure on Egypt to buy German goods as a condition of the sale of the cotton. There was an obvious danger that British exports would be displaced and dumping by Germany encouraged. Indeed, German efforts to promote barter transactions were likely to succeed only if her exports could be forced upon foreign markets at the expense of third countries including the UK. This was another scheme which was destined to make no progress: if it sounded attractive in banking terms, the wider commercial audience in Britain would have found it distinctly unappealing.

Many of the activities of Hambros Bank were transparent. The attempt to gain a broader view of the secretive world of merchant banking poses an altogether more exacting challenge. In 1934 the US State Department received information from the General Motors Export Company of New York. The company's finance department in London had asked several of its 'friends' – clearing banks, acceptance and discount houses – whether new German commitments had been taken up by the English banks. The fact that certain export credits outside the Standstill had been granted by English banks to German exporters was definitely confirmed. Hambros Bank was just one of the institutions which told General Motors about its new credit facilities. It was reported that the amounts concerned were quite small and that the credits did not increase commitments in Germany. But, with commission rates of 3 or 4 per cent because of Germany's poor credit standing, such business was very profitable for English banks. As for import credits, General Motors was certain that no new business outside the Standstill had been done in view of the situation with long- and medium-term debts.[10]

So by the end of 1934 a policy of trying to restrain new credit was in operation. But there were several setbacks. In May 1935 there were reports that Schacht had approached the Bank of England for a fresh credit. Siepmann, at the Bank, denied that there was a shred of truth in the story: it was an invention by Einzig, the *Financial News* journalist. Siepmann wondered whether there was anything the Treasury could do to moderate the damage done. The Bank had already made several efforts to 'scrag' Einzig, but he enjoyed a long-term contract with the newspaper. Phillips, in the Treasury, bemoaned the fact that the editor and proprietors could not do much to help, even if they had been on good terms with his department, which they were not. The Bank of England was not without its own friends in the press who could deny, for the purposes of counter-publicity, that a new credit had ever been contemplated. However, Leith-Ross admitted:

> I do not think that we can object to fresh business being done on normal 3/6 month credit: indeed, it was one of the arguments that I addressed to Schacht that if he settled his frozen debts satisfactorily, merchants would resume business on the normal credit terms.[11]

The evidence suggests that an embargo on new credit, official or unofficial, amounted to no more than a vague idea and that the policy of restraint was so insubstantial that it could easily be ignored. There was nothing to impede Hambros Bank and Schroders from becoming involved in other attempts to stimulate Anglo-German business.

In 1936 a plan was developed for the formation of a company called Compensation Brokers Limited which was to be run under the auspices of the two banks.[12] The object was to organize the export, primarily to the Dominions and colonies, of German goods which would not compete with British exports, and to use the proceeds to finance purchases by Germany of raw materials. The facilitation of contacts and agreements between industrialists in Britain and Germany was seen as an added advantage. Compensation Brokers aimed to find foreign buyers for German exports and, in close co-operation with the relevant authorities, arrange payment in sterling for exports of raw materials to Germany. Suppliers prepared to grant subsidies to German exporters would also be contacted. The role of the two banks was to grant acceptable credits to supposedly sound buyers of German goods. To complete the picture, the selling agent acting on behalf of the German principles was to be Tennant and Sons. German exports needed to be stimulated, it was reasoned, in order to allow existing suppliers of raw materials to Germany a chance to receive payment for commodities already sold. The means of escape was said to be at hand for Germany – a country caught in an economic impasse and in semi-isolation with all the attendant political difficulties. The scheme's backers imagined that it would be welcomed in official circles in Britain. Naturally, it had been viewed favourably in Nazi circles.

One of the proposers, Tiarks of Schroders, attempted to enlist the support of Montagu Norman. Tiarks claimed that many agents were carrying on such business without the interests of the Empire at heart; they were unregulated and extracted extortionate premiums. What the Empire required, apparently, were many manufactured articles which could not be supplied just then by Britain but were available in Germany. In an ideological vein likely to appeal to the Governor, Tiarks complained: 'you will readily understand how difficult it is to carry on business when such ordinary commercial transactions have to be explained and submitted for approval.'[13]

It is quite incredible that Tiarks could suppose that it was national policy to promote every practicable way of enabling Germany to obtain access to raw materials. While the idea of bringing the Third Reich back into the sphere of normal international trade relationships commanded universal support, few in government were prepared to apply unreservedly the means suggested to achieve it. Indeed, the meeting of high-ranking officials which considered the scheme, in November 1936, feared that a popular outcry would greet any approval. There were several grounds on which the plan could be opposed: anything which represented a great extension of barter was economic heresy, German trade competition was severe already and British re-exports to Germany had to be protected. Plans for trade expansion between Germany and the Empire were for the Dominions themselves to consider, but a trend of increasing trade was already under way. In terms of national security, however, Britain faced an ever-present danger. While the commodities in question did not represent war *matériel*, making facilities available might have encouraged the development of channels for other, potentially less innocuous, raw materials.

But the economic and strategic arguments seemed to carry less weight when the plan was viewed in the light of diplomatic considerations. The officials vacillated: they assumed that their political masters would want to prevent any new arrangement between British interests and the German government only if, in the opinion of the Treasury, it involved some kind of loan or credit to Germany. It seemed unreasonable to make Compensation Brokers wait for a political settlement between the two countries before commencing operations. Consequently, there was no recommendation that the government should veto the scheme.[14]

The Foreign Office, however, was determined to kill off the

scheme since it was viewed as part of a much bigger structure. Any loan or credit from the City of London would have artificially relieved Germany of the penalty which she was paying for having sacrificed her economy and foreign trade to the intensification of rearmament. Vansittart lambasted the plan as sheer lunacy and suicidal; the sponsors, Tiarks and Piggot, were branded as 'the two arch-German propagandists in this country'. On 26 November Anthony Eden, the Foreign Secretary, wrote in discouraging terms to the Chancellor of the Exchequer.[15]

In the absence of official support the chances that the operation of the plan would be successful were considerably reduced, not just in the event of difficulties with Germany, but because it suggested that the business establishment would treat the scheme with suspicion. Indeed, British industry was not at all happy: the FBI had to write to its members to reassure them that it had been in touch with the new organization to ensure that every effort would be made to safeguard British export interests throughout the world.[16] Unable to overcome the adverse criticism, Compensation Brokers disappeared from sight.

But this did not bring to an end contemporary allegations that a number of banks were continuing to grant new credits to Germany. In a special edition of *The Banker* magazine, devoted to reviewing the effects of four years of Nazism, those who argued that Hitler needed English money to stem the tide of communism were roundly condemned. The magazine regretted that it had to admit that: 'from a small, but rather influential circle, in the City of London there flows a constant stream of propaganda in favour of credits for Germany.'[17] Einzig later claimed that, as a result of persistent criticism in the press and Parliament in the spring of 1937, the Treasury prompted the Bank of England to send out a circular requesting the banks to abstain from granting new credit to Germany. Einzig concluded that not, only did the use of such credits to finance raw material purchases release resources which facilitated German rearmament but that even firms actually engaged in German rearmament, such as IG, received credits from London houses.[18]

It remains difficult to substantiate such claims. Even Nigel Law, the Foreign Office's City informant, admitted that he was passing on 'hardly more than well-authenticated rumours'. Most credits were probably for exports from Germany; they did not create but anticipated the foreign exchange that the Third Reich would eventually obtain. Only those credits capable of being used or misused as working capital could be considered as creating foreign exchange. But Law thought it highly unlikely that any open credits had been granted even by the most pro-German of London firms.[19] Taking this as a basis for calculation, the City did not provide money for German rearmament.

In response to the difficulties surrounding Anglo-German relations, the British Bankers' Association passed the resolution that no new credits should be granted for financing German business which could be financed by means of Standstill lines. There was a particular request to regard the resolution as confidential and to take precautions to ensure that it did not reach the press.[20] Presumably, an inference might have been drawn that the practice of granting credit outside of the Standstill had been widespread up to that point.

But it seems likely that some British short-term credit was still being extended to Germany outside the Standstill. The Bank of England instructed its employees that information on this subject was confidential and was not to be passed to any person inside or outside the Bank without the consent of the Discount Office.[21] A few days after the 1938 Standstill Agreement came into effect – and just before the Anschluss – the British government indicated to the City that in view of the terms of the renewal and the expressed desire to see as many credits as possible put on a sound commercial basis, the granting of credit outside the Standstill was undesirable. The Joint Committee wrote to the Committee of London Clearing Banks regarding a secret letter of 30 November 1937. The subject was the mutual agreement not to grant further credits of any kind to Germany for any purpose which could be achieved by use of Standstill lines – the resolution passed by the British Bankers' Association. The instruction was to remain in force.[22]

But bankers were not immune to the ordinary commercial pressures of international competition just because Europe was tottering on the abyss of war. Towards the end of 1938 Douglas Miller, Commercial Attaché at the American Embassy in Berlin, filed a report entitled *New York Banks Smelling New Business in Germany*. Visiting American bankers were exploring whether they could advance new short-term credits. British bankers, he noted, had already been thinking along these lines.[23]

In Washington the Federal Reserve Board took up with the State Department the question posed by Miller: did the administration share the view of the British government which had discouraged British bankers from extending new German credit because such action was contrary to public policy? The Board felt that it would have no reason to comment adversely; it did not doubt that the banks would find sound credit risks which were unobjectionable from the banking point of view. Winthrop Aldrich, President of Chase Manhattan, was reported as saying that, as much as everyone disliked the things going on in Germany, America had still to do business there.[24]

This was a staunch defence of the time-honoured principle that financiers should devote themselves to the pursuit of profit, however heavy the burden imposed by a troubled conscience. But when the State Department hinted that President Roosevelt was not unsympathetic to the Board's concerns, Chairman Eccles passed word to Governor Harrison to take the matter up informally in New York. In carrying out this delicate task the Federal Reserve Bank of New York criticized the comparison drawn between British and American bankers. British houses had practically liquidated none of their old German commitments and so were hardly likely, in the foreseeable future, to be able to take up new business in Germany. This presented an opportunity for American institutions. They had pushed the liquidation of their old German commitments much further and so might have wanted to reconsider the problem of new business. But as the volume of international trade moving was insufficient for Germany to take up all the credit available under the remaining American Standstill obligations, there was probably next to no new business transacted. The National City Bank, for example, had total commitments under the Standstill of $4.3m, but $1.5m of this sum remained unutilized.[25]

From the cases documented above of actual and proposed business dealings with Nazi Germany, it is possible to draw a tentative conclusion concerning the evolution of government policy on the supply of credit. Whether by instinct or by training, the City clearly found it impossible to stop dealing with Germany altogether. Yet, if Hambros Bank is at all representative of how new business was financed, it would seem that the amounts of money concerned were relatively small and that the transactions were carefully monitored by the Bank of England and the Treasury. Very little business of this kind occurred after the Bank's discreet requests late in 1934. The Treasury retreated, thereafter, from any idea of imposing a hard line. Instead, from 1935 the intention was to bring about a voluntary restriction on new credits for Germany. Ordinary commercial concerns were a factor in determining this policy. Germany had to ensure that frozen debts were liquidated. Of course, the threat to Britain's security posed by Nazi rearmament also weighed heavily. However, if no actual war *matériel* were involved, the government was not going to forbid extensions of new credits.

To some extent, self-policing did work; the City had no wish to be reviled by the British public. Shortly before the outbreak of war, Norman and Sir Otto Niemeyer were criticized in the House of Commons by Hugh Dalton, the Shadow Foreign Secretary. They were accused of attempting to persuade Dr Funk, at a BIS meeting, to devalue the Reichsmark in return for a foreign loan. In a letter to the Chancellor of the Exchequer Norman angrily defended himself by claiming that there was not one atom of truth in the report.[26]

The Americans and French desert the Standstill

Members of London's financial community were among the first foreigners to bear witness to the rise of the Nazi state. The next scheduled round of Standstill discussions began in Berlin in early 1933, just days after Hitler had taken power. The British representatives – Brand of Lazards and Tiarks of Schroders – were given their first taste of negotiating in the new political atmosphere. Information was cabled from London that the clearing banks would object strongly to any reduction in the interest rate for cash advances below 5 per cent – the minimum charged to British nationals. It was estimated that on average Germany already paid rates of below 3.5 per cent for cash advances and acceptances. The Midland Bank, the largest of the contemporary clearers, tried to resist this trend. The bank did not want to see foreign debtors who were unable to fulfil their engagements placed at an advantage compared with many domestic borrowers. Frederick Hyde, the Midland's Managing Director, made it clear that the Bank could see no justification in accepting the revised schedule, and that it was not prepared to do so.[27]

When the negotiations in Berlin finally closed after three weeks, Brand returned to London. It was left to him to explain to the Midland how the representatives had finally unanimously agreed to the new schedule, and to defend them from the charge that they had 'bounced' the London bankers into the revised agreement. Brand exhibited a blend of optimism and realism. He hoped that the creditors might dispense with the Standstill in a year or two; everyone wanted it to end as soon as possible. But the arrangement was not without its advantages. It enabled creditors to present a united front and, enjoying the guarantee of the Golddiskontbank, to avoid being brought under the German Emergency Decrees. The Standstill also provided more exchange for interest and commission on banking debts than would otherwise have been the case. As far as comparative rates were concerned, it could be argued that German industrialists ended up paying higher rates than their British counterparts because of the commission taken by the German banks.

Above all, Brand believed the Standstill to be a set of compromises self-evident to anyone who attended the meetings. The interests of the creditors were dissimilar. The Swiss, the Dutch and the British were not so anxious for a reduction in outstanding credits as they were to avoid any reduction in interest rates. The Americans, on the other hand, regarded a reduction in credit lines as absolutely vital to them and were willing to agree to a reduction in rates, if necessary, to obtain it.

The agreement was, of course, a compromise between the creditors and the debtors. Brand thought that the fact that German credits were not being paid was irrelevant. He recognized the risk associated with Germany and from that point of view considerably higher premiums would have been justified. But the German situation was quite 'abnormal': the transfer problem could not in any way allow rates comparable to the risks involved.

There was a yet more important reason why the Standstill represented a compromise. All the delegates were aware of the political situation and regarded the minimum reduction made as some insurance against the dangers of government interference. Brand noted ominously, 'very powerful interests in the new German Government have opinions about interest rates and foreign debts decidedly different from those of bankers, and there seemed a considerable risk for the future in our adopting a completely uncompromising attitude.' He therefore appealed for unity among banking creditors in the face of all the new political elements in Germany. He regretted that an institution of such importance and world-wide fame as the Midland should dissociate itself from co-operation with all the rest.[28] Of necessity, unity was indeed maintained. For the next six months the rate for cash advances and fixed loans was set at a maximum of just under 4 per cent. In return, unavailed credit lines were cancelled – a substantial amount of credit had not been utilized in 1932.

The American and the French creditors, on the other hand, continued along the road of liquidation. The French, by this time, had become by far the biggest converters of blocked accounts into Register marks which were released to finance additional exports and travel inside Germany. The Americans resorted to a variety of arrangements: some Rm1.5m of US credits affected by the Standstill were used to help to pay for the construction in Hamburg of the largest crude oil refinery in Germany.[29]

Holland-Martin, the Joint Committee's secretary, thought that the greatest amount of 'bad' business had been done by American banks and the 'smartest' by the British banks. Thus, while the Americans wished to liquidate as soon as possible, the British were willing, for genuine short-term finance of trade, to grant credits to Germany free of restrictions, up to an equal or possibly even greater amount than was outstanding.[30] A similar point is made by Sayers: with the London market experiencing a great scarcity of commercial paper at the end of 1934, Standstill bills were traded at almost the best rates; the more questionable names among debtors had been gradually weeded out leaving 'good' bills.[31]

Without doubt, the German Standstill was an issue of the greatest importance for America's domestic banking system. In 1931 American banks had held much of Germany's long-term external debt; they were worried that the banking inspectors would find this position unsatisfactory. At the very least, therefore, American banks wanted to limit their short-term exposure in order to improve their balance sheets; some of the smaller banks had closed out their credits altogether.[32] None the less, the total for German short-term credits in the United States was estimated in late 1932 to be $492m, of which $382m was included in the Standstill. Of the 58 banks which extended credit, 13 had commitments of more than $10m. Bank acceptances represented some $350m of the total short-term credits; the greater part of this was discounted from time to time with the Federal banks and was carried by them. While 30 of the creditor banks were located in New York City, the other 28 were to be found in the major cities across the country.[33]

By 1934 the American creditors had achieved an enormous reduction in both credit lines and availments. Indeed, the reduction was so greatly in excess of the rates provided for in the Standstill Agreement that Cordell Hull, the Secretary of State, asked for information on the methods and sources behind it. Herbert Feis, the administration's economic adviser, shared the sense that there was some unknown element in the situation as currency depreciation could not have been a relevant factor in explaining the apparent flood of dollars in 1934.[34]

But the Federal Reserve Board confirmed the scale of the sales of Register marks by the New York banks, mostly for surplus exports but also for travel. Measuring the amounts against total sales of German goods in America, it seems that a substantial part of American purchases from Germany were financed by means of Register marks. They were sold at varying discounts from par, with one bank reporting an average discount of 34 per cent for 1934. Germany would, then, have received little free exchange for her sales in the United States.[35]

Repayments of American credits were, to a certain extent, counterbalanced by fresh drawings in the case of other creditor countries, and in Britain's case availments actually increased. Nevertheless, the shrinkage in Germany's total foreign trade obviously required a decreasing amount of foreign credit; this was shown in the growing gap between credit lines and availments.[36] Apart from forcing bondholders to go short of interest, Germany was able to cut her foreign debt at a prodigious rate. The first reduction in the Standstill to 1932 was a result of sterling dep-reciation; the second to February 1933 represented actual transfers, and the third reduction to March 1934 was to a large extent due to the devaluation of the dollar. The original Standstill seems to have embraced Rm6.3 billion. In 1935, the German Standstill Committee indicated that indebtedness stood at just under one third of the original total.[37]

Schacht: defender of the last remaining international agreement

By 1935 the distribution of the Standstill credits was quite different from the 1931 pattern. Britain had clearly replaced the United States as the biggest creditor.[38] With other creditors having pulled out on whatever terms they could secure, the Standstill had become mainly an Anglo-German problem. The British creditors were in no hurry to liquidate as their long-standing business connections allowed them to hope that they would benefit, sooner or later, from the revival of Germany's international trade.[39]

But Britain's position was far from secure. It was bad enough that interest rates were being continually forced down. In early 1935 Schacht appeared to jeopardize the chances of renewing the Standstill when, for the first time, he questioned the special position of the arrangement. Creditors had always enjoyed preferential treatment by receiving a full transfer of interest, but Schacht now expressed serious doubts about whether it would be possible to continue with this practice. He continued to encourage the illusion, of course, that he acted as a responsible central banker first and as a Nazi Reichsminister a distant second. It was the only international agreement, he told Tiarks, which had been maintained throughout the whole world economic crisis; it was always renegotiated without political assistance and he hoped it would be possible to maintain it until Germany returned to an economy free from *Devisen* restrictions.[40] Although there was no mention of when this might be, Tiarks believed in Schacht's good faith. Some months before he had told Brand that Schacht was firm in his purpose to look after the Standstill credits.[41]

Other trends which had emerged by the mid 1930s posed new problems. Clearing arrangements, barter and compensation deals all tended to reduce the trade available for cover by Standstill bills. Where British banks had granted new credits, such as those for the South African wool trade, an attempt to bring them into the scope of the Standstill was considered. There was a real danger that the effects of trade diversion, among other things, would cause a progressive deterioration in the quality of Standstill bills. The rigid control of German imports and exports, which interfered with the direct debtor–creditor relationship, tended to make the German authorities arbiters not merely of what foreign exchange would be allocated but also of what bills were to be drawn. With capital repayments suspended and a full transfer of service in doubt, the question arose as to whether the acceptance houses as a whole should split the Standstill by salvaging the good bills while they could.[42]

A basis for renewal of the Standstill, acceptable to both Germans and international creditors, continued to be found. But the arrangements were put under greater scrutiny by Britain's press from 1936. There were comments to the effect that Standstill credits had increased in the preceding year and a question was put down in the House of Commons for 19 May concerning commercial credit to Germany. In response, the Joint Committee released a press statement with the intention that it should be used by the government in the House of Commons. The British bankers explained that the idea that they had increased their credits while every other country had reduced theirs was a misapprehension: no new credit could be granted under the Standstill. However, one of the apparently unwelcome provisions of the agreements obliged creditors to maintain credits, temporarily repaid in the normal course of business, for reuse by the debtors. It was unnecessary, according to the statement, 'to add that the maintenance of these frozen credits is exceedingly unwelcome to the Bankers concerned whose constant efforts have been and are devoted to obtaining repayment of them.' While minor changes were responsible for appearing to show an increase in used credits, total British credits – both used and unused – had decreased in 1935 by £1m. The Joint Committee explained that the larger reductions in the credits of other countries were a result of the willingness of creditors there to accept repayments in marks with the heavy capital losses which they involved. In certain cases, governments assisted their nationals in obtaining repayments by special methods.[43]

The concern to reduce liabilities was a genuine one; it is evident in the attitude of the short-term creditors to the machinery of the Payments Agreement. By 1936, outstanding trade debts had been liquidated through the allocation of 10 per cent of the proceeds of German exports to Britain. Although there was no obligation on the part of the German authorities to allocate the 10 per cent for any other purpose, the Joint Committee, among others, lodged a claim with the Treasury for a portion of the allocation. This move was endorsed by Montagu Norman. He took the view that, while frozen banking credits did not differ in origin from trade debts, they had taken second place on the grounds that traders could not wait for their money but that bankers could. Norman felt every sympathy with the request both on its merits and because every chance had to be taken to reduce the great weight of Standstill debt and to liquefy the frozen positions in the City.[44]

But two leading members of the Joint Committee soon realized that pressing forward with the claim might have put the Standstill in jeopardy. Beaumont Pease and Brand did not want to cause trouble with other Standstill committees nor to provide any opportunity for it to be said that British creditors were now looking to their government rather than to Germany for help. Beaumont Pease informed the chairman of the Acceptance Houses Committee that there did not seem to be any way in which they could accept a share of the 10 per cent allocation without discriminating against short-term creditors in other countries. This would have been a breach of the agreement.[45]

There is more than one way to interpret the role of the City bankers who, by the mid 1930s, had to come to terms with the implications of maintaining the Standstill for the Third Reich. The experiences of 1934 had marked a turning point for the market: despite the pressure applied by the banking lobby, the authorities had been ready to impose a clearing on Germany. For the first time, some bankers now publicly admitted *mea culpa*: the Standstill bill had been a merciful improvisation in the attempt to correct the grave errors committed by the international banking community over a period of years. *The Banker* magazine summarized how the principles of sound banking had been violated. Individual houses had lent, in one foreign country, several times their own capital resources. Moreover, they had granted to particular concerns in that country unsecured lines of credit which frequently represented an undue proportion of such resources.[46]

With the Bank of England giving voice to its wish that there should be a reduction in the volume of bills, the City began tacitly to accept that realization in full would never happen. A pretence was maintained that the claims were 100 per cent, but privately the authorities suggested that the bills were worth a small fraction of their face value. The Governor, Sayers points out, was warning the market by August 1936 that the central European situation would have to be squarely faced: a writing down of the debts was inevitable. In September 1936 the Bank announced that, from October 1937, the amount of Hungarian Standstill paper eligible at the Bank was to be limited to £500,000 for any one acceptor. City institutions were not surprised, therefore, when the Bank notified them on 17 March 1937 that their liabilities on German Standstill bills should be reduced by 30 per cent by the end of September that year.[47]

But Charles Gunston, a Bank of England official, indicated that there were a variety of attitudes in the City. In 1936 the National Provincial Bank decided to accept payments in Register marks where previously, like other London creditors and unlike, for instance, the Americans or Swiss, it had accepted these only to a small extent. The loss to the bank for that year was estimated at £1m. Both Schacht and Tiarks wanted to discourage any tendency which might weaken the banking relationship between Germany and London. They wanted to maintain London's credits to Germany at about their existing level, feeling that Germany would have need of British credits on this scale after the Standstill was wound up.

Gunston noted that however directive the Bank of England wished to be in relation to the dangers associated with Standstill bills, it seemed that some banks could not accept that full realization would be unobtainable. He reasoned that British banks held the largest share of credit lines because they were the least inclined to write off their claims as worthless and they had refused to accept any discount. British banks in general, therefore, maintained their credits in the belief that they would ultimately become good. Moreover, the market had not experienced any particular difficulties – Germany regularly transferred the service in sterling without interruption – which was more than could be said for other debts. So British Standstill claims were regarded as first-class banking credits expressed in sterling.[48]

By 1937, however, the deteriorating political situation in Europe started to put the Standstill arrangement under much greater pressure. The cracks which began to appear from this time, both in the previously united front of British banking creditors and among the international creditors, indicated the build-up in these tensions. At the beginning of the year the clearing bankers contemplated whether, in the absence of a mechanism for the progressive capital reduction of Standstill debt, they should decline to carry their obligations on bills any longer.

Representations to the Governor and the Chancellor of the Exchequer were made independently of the acceptance houses, for the latter were prepared to renew the agreement on existing terms for a further six months. The clearing banks, prompted by Reginald McKenna, the Midland chairman, had become concerned that Standstill creditors had refrained for three years from pressing for any capital repayment and thereby had assisted the financing of

German rearmament. Matters could be brought to a head, it was argued, if bills were no longer accepted. The clearers appreciated that such action would cause great difficulties for the accepting houses, but it was considered better that it should be taken while they were prosperous.

The Treasury responded by advancing a circular argument. The Payments Agreement had worked satisfactorily; anything which imperilled British trade and started a fresh quarrel with Germany had to be avoided. It was admitted, however, that the Nazis had been helped to rearm by the £3m which had been made available since the frozen trade debts had been paid off. Meanwhile, creditors received no interest and holders of non-Reich loans, for example, had to make do with 4 per cent interest not in cash but in funding bonds. The difficult exchange position of the Third Reich made it likely, however, that Britain would need to use threats – scarcely desirable as the will to carry them out seemed to be lacking. As Waley saw it: 'One can only hope that Mr Governor's influence with the Germans on the one hand and with the British creditors on the other will enable some satisfactory agreement to be reached with a minimum of alarms and excursions.'[49]

Nigel Law reported to the Foreign Office, at the beginning of 1937, that the feeling in the City was more anti-German than he had ever known it; the view held, especially in Bank of England circles, was that the Standstill should be brought to an end in the near future. One of the largest private banks in Germany provided the information that, of the £35m in British credits outstanding, £25m were really being used as working capital by German firms. A repercussion of this new City attitude was, Law noted, 'severely to curtail the activities of Mr F. Tiarks ... who is now regarded as having been in the past too easily won over to the German point of view and too fond of presenting his colleagues with a fait accompli.'[50]

Here, then, was a further dimension to the problem. It was reported from Berlin in early February that Tiarks had interpreted the moves of the clearing banks as a kind of revolt against his leadership. Tiarks had good reason to feel rejected: Lidbury of the National Provincial was brought in to lead the negotiations for renewal. In theory, Lidbury's brief from the clearing banks was to demand a 10 per cent repayment or otherwise to consent to a temporary agreement as a warning that Britain intended to break away from the international Standstill.[51]

Even this apparently steadfast edifice was built on shifting sands. The diary of Frederick Hyde, of the Midland Bank, records a conversation with Lidbury about the line the latter was to take at the Berlin negotiations. They hoped that there might be a 5 per cent reduction in the amount of the original Standstill but would have welcomed any move in that direction.[52] So the delegates intended to ask for 10 per cent but were prepared to accept 5 by way of a reduction. When Schacht offered nothing the delegates recommended acceptance. In the middle of the negotiations Lidbury and Brand returned briefly to London. They wanted the opportunity to benefit from any revision of the Payments Agreement in much the same way as the French had been allowed to get their Standstill credits repaid in coal.[53]

Did the British bankers back down in their demands because they were persuaded by arguments over the economic condition of the Third Reich? Germany's export surplus in 1936 was estimated to be Rm550m. But, with 80 per cent of this amount tied up in clearing arrangements, the German authorities claimed that the remaining 20 per cent for free disposal in *Devisen* was insufficient to meet the interest liabilities under the Standstill. Nearly all of the decrease in the volume of credit lines had been repaid in Register marks. In order to bridge the period of time between *Devisen* requirements and *Devisen* influx, the German delegates considered a broad-minded maintenance of the remaining open credit lines to be an absolute necessity.[54] Astonishingly, the international creditors were prepared to be so broad-minded that they did not even try to begin to question why German trade had become structured along such lines.

Political factors, therefore, weighed more heavily than economic arguments. The British Embassy in Berlin took the view that attempts to break down the Standstill would weaken Schacht's position – he was still held to be one of the moderates in the Nazi leadership – and that until Britain was prepared to face the consequence of this any move was inadvisable. The time was not right to make an all-out attack on the German position, not least because the Embassy had doubts about the leadership qualities of the British delegation. Lidbury, for example, was thought to be very unsatisfactory. He made fire-eating remarks about the continuous swindle by the Germans but appeared to work on the assumption that the City would be rescued by the British government. He was ready, in other words, to see the imposition of a clearing rather than to be forced to go without cash.

British officials found it particularly ironic that Standstill creditors once violently opposed to clearings in the interests of others should demand one in their own. No one could be sure whether better terms for creditors would ever be obtained in the future or whether any government support would be forthcoming. Waley, from a Treasury perspective, noted ruefully that there were a great many other and much wider questions about Germany on which the government apparently still had to make up its mind. In any event, Tiarks thought that the demonstration by the creditors in Berlin would satisfy McKenna.[55]

Throughout 1937 the London creditors pondered whether to ask for government help for increased cash payments. At the same time, they did not want to press their claims if Schacht's position appeared to be weakening. Perhaps by way of a distraction, creditors began to refer to the 'recommercialization' of the Standstill. A distinction was drawn between the best type of bill (commercial) on the one hand and other bills and cash advances on the other; each accounted for about half the world total. Creditors believed that recommercialization had one big advantage: if claims on Germany were held in the form of commercial bills, London would be in a good position to retain the financing of Germany's external trade once the Standstill had come to an end.[56]

Any satisfaction felt by McKenna at the renewal of the Standstill in 1937 could not have lasted for very long. When the Joint Committee met in October he at first declared his opposition to any agreement without repayment and his wish to appeal immediately for government support. Brand pointed out that such support would be given very unwillingly. He advised that it would be wiser for the Committee to keep appeals in reserve in case the Standstill broke down and they found themselves in a worse position. McKenna was impressed with the argument that premature action might prejudice requests for help which would be more strongly justified at a later, more crucial stage.[57]

The issue of capital repayment was raised once again when Tiarks met Schacht in Berlin in November 1937. The Golddiskontbank had agreed under the original agreement to guarantee 10 per cent of the bills of each creditor. But the payments had been suspended in 1933; Tiarks wanted the sum involved for that year paid in 1938. Schacht disapproved and simply referred Tiarks to Göring. This timely reminder of the difficulties facing Germany as a whole and Schacht in particular was sufficient to deter British creditors, once again, from pressing their claims.[58] Tiarks, however, told the Acceptance Houses Committee that he thought Schacht's position in Germany was better than it had ever been.[59] Just at that moment, Hitler formally accepted Schacht's resignation as Minister of Economics. But he had already left this post (and that of Plenipotentiary for the War Economy) in abeyance over the summer in protest at Göring's intrigues.[60] Tiarks could not have been more unfortunate in his timing; he clearly suffered from political myopia, if nothing worse.

The talks with Schacht were to prepare for the next round of negotiations between Germany and the Standstill creditors; this took place in London in December 1937. The conference heard how, under the substantial expansion of Germany's international trade, the foreign credits still left to the German economy were all the more urgently required for the future. This increase in the volume of trade also offered, of course, a tempting opportunity to make provision for its financing on an increasing scale in the shape of bills drawn under the Standstill. Again, it seems that international creditors were not prepared to cause embarrassment by asking questions about the composition of this trade expansion. Instead, the ideas advanced by the German committee were seen as an expression of the British plan for the recommercialization of existing credit lines.[61] So a new scheme was introduced under the 1938 agreement. Availment of credit lines was to be restricted to bills drawn for financing international trade and not for the purpose of creating foreign exchange or financing international business. Nevertheless, despite the worsening political climate the agreement was preserved.

A short-term freeze? British bankers left at the 'North Pole'

As Schacht's influence in Nazi circles declined and Hitler started down the path of annexation in Europe, so the Standstill relationship became ever more troubled and confused. Before 1938 the problems had been partially mitigated by the close association between Schacht and Norman, though the latter had to contend with the political charges that the City was lending afresh to Germany.[62]

In the wake of the Anschluss, Britain challenged Hitler's

government over Austrian debt payments. Now a new crisis threatened the Standstill (see Chapter 4). By the end of 1938 the British creditors felt that there was no point in having an international agreement and they looked for ways to come out of the Standstill. Because of the now-delicate relationship between Britain and the Third Reich, the bankers thought it wise to advise the government or the Bank of England of their point of view, before committing themselves to any renewal of the agreement. They knew that they might need to rely on official action through the Payments Agreement to secure the service and amortization of debts.[63] Some improvement in placing credits on a more truly commercial and liquid basis had been achieved in the course of 1938. But with Britain again threatening to impose a clearing on Germany, the creditors realized the difficulty of their position. They were party to an international rather than separate agreements and so were unable to enjoy a free hand to claim the government's protection. However, it suited the Chamberlain government to leave the existing agreement undisturbed. There was no desire to see it denounced in order to obtain better terms for creditors. Although the Treasury could not stop the creditors from taking such action, it was made plain that they could not expect government support.[64]

Throughout 1938 the Bank of England monitored the distribution of Standstill bills in the market to deal with the implications of the continuing lack of liquidity of the bills. The clearing banks had become reluctant to take them as security and had thereby forced up the rates of discount at which they changed hands. The high rates had tempted some of the smaller discount houses which appeared to hold amounts dangerously large in relation to their own capital resources. In February 1939 Norman asked the clearing banks not to refuse to take Standstill bills as security for loans in the market, but only to use the rates to discriminate against them. This helped to keep the market in the bills alive while the agreement was being renegotiated.[65]

But international events were now moving fast and the bankers feared even more for their money. A few days after Hitler annexed the remainder of Czechoslovakia on 15 March the short-term creditors outlined the problems surrounding the Standstill to Montagu Norman. Credits had been generally of a self-liquidating nature. But as Germany's foreign trade had progressively fallen off, so an increasing percentage of the credits had not been employed for financing the movement of goods but had been used as working capital in Germany. The creditors wanted it known that this was contrary to the wishes of the banking institutions who were, in any case, powerless in the matter.

The Governor was reminded that there had been attempts to get the Germans to increase the utilization of credits for financing genuine international trade transactions and to repay credits not so employed. Of the £36m still outstanding, £20m was carried in the form of bills. But Standstill bills, particularly those not drawn against the movement of goods, were becoming increasingly unacceptable to the discount market. The creditors reached the conclusion that an increasing number of bills would have to be taken up for cash, depriving the market of perhaps £10m, and requiring banks and acceptance houses to provide a corresponding amount of cash in a short period.

The bankers wanted, first, an assurance that to negotiate along such lines would not be inconsistent with official British policy and that they were right to assume that they could rely upon the support of the government. And secondly, they wanted the government to confirm that their interests would be protected if negotiations broke down. The Chancellor replied to Basil Catterns, the Deputy Governor, with an affirmative to the first question; but he still would not commit himself on the second.[66]

In June 1939 the Bank told the clearing banks that the Governor had written to the acceptance houses asking them to reduce, in the following six months, the volume of their acceptances of Standstill bills on the market by 40 per cent.[67] In the case of Kleinworts, for example, the Bank of England's Discount Office had first written in April 1937 to request a reduction in their bills by 30 per cent to £3,461,000. A further reduction of £1,485,000 was requested in 1939. In writing off German debts of £3.1m, Kleinworts' partners had to arrange once again an overdraft facility – £1m – secured against their private assets. By the outbreak of war, £4.5m was still owed to Kleinworts – about half the total commitments of the firm frozen under the Standstill agreements with Germany, Austria and Hungary. Kleinworts, like other British banks and finance houses, had preferred not to sever relations with long-established clients in Germany, particularly in view of the need to facilitate the repayment of debts.[68]

Now, therefore, the creditors were in an intractable position. The

Midland Bank felt that, although the Standstill situation was highly unsatisfactory, a determination of the agreement would make matters worse. Creditor nations or groups contemplating leaving the agreement also had to consider the 'official flavour' which from the outset had coloured the Standstill – the original decision to extend credit to Germany in 1931 and the international co-operation to avoid discrimination.[69]

With £36m outstanding to British creditors (two-thirds to the acceptance houses, one-third to the banks), Lidbury visited the Midland to discuss what could be done about the problem. An emphatic McKenna tried to impress on a sceptical Lidbury that the Midland, at least, would not go on with the Standstill unless there was a 10 per cent reduction in the total. Lidbury was asked to pass this message on to Tiarks in very definite terms. As before, little was achieved. In what was to be the last round of negotiations for the renewal of the agreement – from the end of May 1939 – the Germans wanted recommercialized credit lines maintained for three years. Lord Wardington, formerly Beaumont Pease of Lloyds Bank, was not disposed to do this, but the other three clearing banks agreed. The other German proposals were described by the Midland as 'barefaced effrontery' and by Lidbury as 'monstrous'. Even the pretence of mere postponement of the fulfilment of obligations – the sentiment of former agreements – was seemingly abandoned in the new scheme. Instead of a short-term freeze the creditors were offered the 'North Pole', for a period of which the end was nowhere in sight.[70]

The acceptance houses, however, felt inclined to accept the German proposals and, to begin with, disagreed strongly with the banks' insistence that a substantial cash repayment should be made. Finally, all the British creditors agreed that, unless the Germans paid something acceptable within six months, they would put an end to the Standstill. Nevertheless, in return for a cash offer they were also prepared to discuss the possibility of extending to Germany fresh credit from British creditors who had been allowed to contract out of the Standstill.[71] That such a fantastic proposal could emerge at this point is, perhaps, an indication of the desperate circumstances in which creditors found themselves.

As the likelihood of war in Europe became ever greater that summer, the short-term creditors were left to fend for themselves; the British government had set itself against any change in the financial and economic relations with Germany. The force of the argument in favour of renunciation of the Payments Agreement was admitted: it was contrary to Britain's interests to afford Germany the means to buy potential war materials in Britain and free exchange to buy raw materials from the British Empire. But renunciation, it was thought, would not make the Germans any more co-operative.[72]

The British creditors had, therefore, to make plans for a determination of the Standstill Agreement in the event of war. Britain and America were in a position to put this into effect as they held some 75 per cent in face value of the credit lines outstanding. There was already in America, as in London, a reluctance on the part of banks to increase German commitments by the acceptance of fresh bills; the American committee was anxious that, if hostilities broke out in Europe, the agreement should be legally determined with the shortest possible delay. If it were not, and no legislation was passed in America to prohibit the further acceptance of bills for German account, American banks would have been liable to continue acceptances or to run the risk of legal action by the German debtors, as was the case after the First World War. Having resolved to act through the agency of the American creditors, the British Joint Committee cabled the necessary request to the United States on 2 September. The next day the American Bankers Committee determined the Standstill Agreement.[73]

With the declaration of war, Britain made a start on the economic blockade of Germany. Under the Trading with the Enemy Act – which took immediate effect – offending cargoes in the process of being shipped were to be seized.[74] By the middle of September the *Financial Times* described creditors as playing a game of hide-and-seek. The British and the Americans were busy finding the whereabouts of cargoes in respect of which Standstill bills were drawn. American institutions sequestrated about £5m of German gold securities. It was also reported, however, that the termination of the Standstill had not unduly strained the British acceptance houses. The pre-war era of the Standstill was concluded when Lord Wardington, now chairman of the Joint Committee, wrote to the Public Trustee with the information that £34m was owed to Britain at the outbreak of war. The justification offered for this position was that the methods of repayment, such as travel marks which sold at a large discount, had involved creditors in heavy losses.[75]

In the 1930s London's banks were faced with making one of two choices: either to reduce their credit lines at considerable cost, or to trust that the situation in Germany would finally improve. They chose the second course because they believed that a special relationship in financial affairs existed between the two countries. Proof of this condition was to be found in the way in which business relations had become intimate after generations of contact. The friendship between Schacht and Norman also seemed to confirm it. With the political demise of the former, the bankers could no longer retain any illusions about the extent of Hitler's revolution. By then, however, it was too late to change course. In measuring the balance of political and economic factors, they had given insufficient weight all along to the immovable goals of Nazi ideology. But, in this, London bankers were not alone.

TABLE 6: SOME MEMBERS OF THE JOINT COMMITTEE OF BRITISH SHORT-TERM CREDITORS IN 1933

Brand, Hon. RH	Lazard Bros. & Co.Ltd
Caulcutt, Sir J.	Barclays Bank Ltd
Goschen, Sir H.*	National Provincial Bank Ltd
Guinness, A.	Guinness, Mahon & Co.
Hambro, R.O.	Hambros Bank Ltd
Holland-Martin, R.	Martins Bank Ltd
Lever, E.H.	Prudential Assurance Co.
Beaumont Pease, J.W.*	Lloyds Bank Ltd
Rothschild, A.de	New Court
Tiarks, F.C.	J.Henry Schröder & Co.
Tiarks, H.F.	

* Joint Chairman. FC Tiarks was also Chairman of the Joint Committee of Representatives of Foreign Bankers' Committee (of Germany), and Brand was a member.

Source: BoE OV34/133.

TABLE 7: TOTAL RETURNS OF BRITISH BANKS AND ACCEPTANCE
HOUSES UNDER THE GERMAN STANDSTILL AGREEMENTS
(Credit Lines (and availments) in £ million)

Date	German Banks		German Commercial and Industrial		Total	
31 July 1931	46.1		18.6		64.7	
30 Sept.1932	43.1	(36.3)	16.5	(14.0)	59.6	(50.3)
31 Nov.1932	42.4	(35.6)	15.9	(13.4)	58.3	(49.0)
1 March 1933	39.3	(32.9)	14.8	(12.5)	54.1	(45.4)
15 Dec.1933	39.0	(31.6)	15.0	(12.1)	54.0	(43.7)
31 Dec.1934	36.3	(31.0)	13.9	(10.4)	50.2	(41.4)
31 Dec.1935	36.5	(33.6)	12.7	(10.0)	49.2	(43.6)
31 Dec.1936	34.0	(31.7)	11.8	(9.4)	45.8	(41.1)
1 Nov.1937	31.6	(30.4)	10.2	(8.8)	41.8	(39.2)
31 Aug.1938	30.1	(28.9)	8.1	(7.4)	38.2	(36.3)
28 Feb.1939	28.4	(27.3)	7.7	(6.8)	36.1	(34.1)

Source: compiled from BoE OV34/131, OV34/133 and MB 30/190.

TABLE 8: COMPARISON OF TOTAL CREDIT LINES UNDER THE GERMAN
STANDSTILL AGREEMENTS IN RMMILLION

Date	USA	UK	Total for all countries
15 July 1931	1,629	1,051	4,390
31 March 1931	1,698	892	3,841
30 Sept. 1933[1]	1,440	825	
28 Feb.1934[1]	1,196	826	
28 Feb.1934	715	724	2,528
30 Sept.1934	569	660	2,140
28 Feb.1935	511	613	1,961
30 Sept.1935	432	602	1,644
28 Feb.1936	416	611	1,567
30 Sept.1936[2]	343	582	1,330
28 Feb.1937	333	561	1,165
28 Feb.1938	249	518	970
28 Feb.1939	203	463	806

Notes: 1. Rates @ 28 Feb. 1933
2. Rates @ 29 Feb. 1936

Source: compiled from BoE OV34/133, 135, 137, 138, 139, 147, 190.

TABLE 9: PERCENTAGE SHARE BY COUNTRY OF TOTAL CREDIT LINES
UNDER THE GERMAN STANDSTILL AGREEMENTS

Country	8 Oct.1931	30 Sept.1937	28 Feb.1939
USA	36.2	26.7	26.4
UK	28.2	52.3	56.3
Switzerland	16.0	10.1	8.7
Holland	13.0	7.2	6.7
France	4.5	1.1	0.7
Belgium and others	2.1	2.6	1.2

Source: compiled from MB 30/190, German memoranda to the Standstill
Conferences, Dec.1937 and May 1939.

NOTES

1. K.O. Oye, *Economic Discrimination and Political Exchange: World Political Economy in the 1930s and 1980s* (Princeton, NJ: Princeton University Press, 1992), pp. 114–15.
2. Ingham, *Capitalism Divided?*, pp. 79, 190–9.
3. Wool is a good example: in 1933 German imports from the UK were valued at Rm22.5m while imports from the Empire amounted to Rm138.4m. The Australian trade typified such transactions. The German importer arranged a credit with London via his German bank. An Australian agent would buy wool for spot cash, draw a documentary bill for that amount on the London bank and then have it discounted at an Australian bank. After the wool had been shipped (usually in German vessels), the bill was accepted by the London bank when the documents reached the bank's agent at the port of discharge, or the German bank or importer. In the case of a confirmed credit, the London bank, having paid the acceptance at maturity, debited the acceptance credit and in due course was reimbursed by the German bank; otherwise, the German importer undertook to put the London bank in funds before the date of maturity. See T160/534/13460/04, Board of Trade memo. For a contemporary reference work see also R.J. Truptil, *British Banks and the London Money Market* (Jonathan Cape, 1936).
4. FO 371/17675/C76, minute (undated, but December 1933), to Sir Warren Fisher.
5. T 160/818/12681/05/5, Waley to Leith-Ross and Phillips, 3 December 1936.
6. FO 371/17676/C749, minute, 8 February 1934.
7. T 160/573/13460/011, Vansittart to Fisher, 10 October 1934.
8. T 160/573/13460/012, correspodence between (i) Waley and Holland-Martin, 14 October 1934 and 10 January 1935, (ii) Hambro to Norman, 20 December 1934, (iii) Phillips to Norman, 28 December 1934.
9. T 160/573/13460/011, Pinsent to Leith-Ross, 9 October 1934.
10. NA RG59/862.51/4130, letter by James D. Mooney (company president) to William Phillips (Assistant Secretary of State), 20 June 1934.

11. T 160/728/12750/012/3, Phillips to Leith-Ross, 18 May 1935; minute by Leith-Ross, 17 May 1935.
12. See Wendt, *Economic Appeasement*, p. 405.
13. T 177/20.
14. Ibid. The interdepartmental meeting, chaired by Leith-Ross, was held on 17 November 1936.
15. FO 371/19936/C8070 and C8261.
16. Modern Records Centre, University of Warwick Library, FBI Archive (hereafter FBI), Economic Adviser's papers (Glenday files) No.7, 5 January 1937.
17. *The Banker*, February 1937, 41 (February 1937), pp. 106–7.
18. Einzig, *Appeasement*, p. 77.
19. FO 371/19932/C3524, 6 May 1936.
20. MB 301/190, extract from minutes of British Bankers' Association committee meeting, 9 December 1937. An exception was made for the British Overseas Bank; there was no intention to interfere with its longstanding business of financing through credits German imports. See also, Jones, *British Multinational Banking*, pp. 243–4, for details of how an attempt to rescue this bank was just beginning. However, the bank did not survive the war.
21. BoE OV34/139.
22. MB 30/190, internal memo, 4 March 1938, and Joint Committee letter (undated), to Chairman of the Committee of London Clearing Bankers.
23. FRBNY C/261/Germany, copy of report of 28 November 1938.
24. NA RG59/862.51/4702 and 4703, minutes by Livesey (State Department), 7 January and 25 February 1939.
25. FRBNY C/261/Germany, minutes by L.W. Knoke (Vice-President, Head of Foreign Department) to Harrison, 6 and 24 February 1939.
26. T 172/1903, letter, 2 August 1939.
27. MB 30/190, Frederick Hyde (Managing Director, 1929–38) to Holland-Martin (secretary of the Joint Committee), 24 February 1933.
28. Ibid., memo, by Joint Committee. For the Brand qoutation and background on the Midland Bank, see Holmes and Green, *Midland*, pp. 186–7.
29. NA RG59/862.6363/162 and 163, minute by Division of Western European Affairs concerning Hamburg Consular Reports of December 1934/January 1935.
30. BoE OV34/133, note, 10 April 1933.
31. Sayers, *Bank of England*, p. 510.
32. Burk, *Morgan Grenfell*, pp. 146–7.
33. FRBNY 261.12, note for W.W. Aldrich (Chase National Bank) on 'German Short-Term Credits', May 1933.
34. NA RG59/862.51/ 4230A and 4231, telegram, Hull to US Embassy (Berlin), 11 January 1935; minute by Feis, 17 January 1935.
35. NA RG59/862.51/4270, letter by F.E. Crane (Deputy Governor, FRBNY) to Feis, 23 January 1935; minute by Feis for Hull, 25 January 1935.
36. T 160/817/12681/05/1, memo, by Rowe-Dutton, 3 May 1934.
37. For a contemporary estimate of the reduction see, Ellis, *Exchange Control*, p. 193; see also, BoE OV 34/133, memo, by Mendel & Nenk Ltd, 3 February 1934, which suggests that Germany gained Rm500m through dollar depreciation alone. For German Committee memo to the 1935 Standstill

conference see BoE OV34/135.

38. T 160/817/12681/05/2; *Financial Times*, 18 February 1935.
39. Sayers, *Bank of England*, pp. 503, 508.
40. BoE OV34/135, letter to Tiarks, 2 February 1935.
41. Brand papers, File 190, letter, 21 August 1934.
42. BoE OV34/135, note by H.A. Siepmann, 31 January 1935.
43. BoE OV34/137, proposed answer to Parliamentary Question; note by C.F. Cobbold, 15 May 1936; press statement by Joint Committee.
44. T 160/818/12681/05/3; BoE OV34/203, letter, 22 May 1936.
45. BoE OV34/203, minute by Cobbold, 25 May 1936; MB 30/190, letter, 22 June 1936.
46. 'Standstill bills on the discount market', in *The Banker*, 32 (December 1934), pp. 197–204.
47. Sayers, *Bank of England*, p. 510; Clay, *Lord Norman*, p. 449; 'Standstill bills', in *The Banker*, 42 (May 1937), p. 126.
48. BoE OV34/137, notes by Gunston, 29 October and 10 December 1936. See also, FO 371/20724/C2072, letter, 11 March 1937, Law to Sargent.
49. T 160/818/12681/05/4, minute to Phillips and Hopkins, 14 January 1937. See also an anonymous memo, dated 16 January 1937, which may have originated in the City. It made the obvious point that a severe blow would be struck at what remained of Germany's international trade if the services of the London market were withdrawn. But it went on to argue that there was little reason to allow Germany to enjoy the benefits of Britain's liberal exchange policy if Germany responsed negatively to political offers. In other words, the use of the Standstill as an instrument of political policy was advocated.
50. FO 371/20724/C627, letter to Sargent, 22 January 1937.
51. T 160/818/12681/05/4, note by Leith-Ross, 5 February 1937, of conversation with Arthur Guinness.
52. MB 30/99, Hyde's Diary, 2 February 1937.
53. T 160/818/12681/05/4, Pinsent (Berlin Embassy) to Waley, 10 February 1937, and note by Leith-Ross, 15 February 1937.
54. MB 30/190, German Committee memo, to the Standstill Conference, February 1937.
55. T 160/818/12681/05/4, Pinsent to Waley, 18 January and 22 February 1937, Waley to Pinsent, 4 March 1937.
56. BoE OV34/138, note by Gunston, 22 September 1937.
57. Ibid., record of meeting, 20 October 1937.
58. T 160/818/12681/05/5, memo, by Waley, 4 November 1937.
59. Brand papers, File 193, record of meeting on 4 November 1937.
60. Overy, *Goering*, p. 68.
61. MB 30/190, German committee memo, to the Standstill Conference, December 1937.
62. Sayers, *Bank of England*, p. 511.
63. MB 30/190, memo (unsigned), 9 November 1938.
64. T 160/818/12681/05/5, memo, by Waley, 14 November 1938.
65. Sayers, *Bank of England*, p. 511.
66. MB 30/190, memo, and letter of Joint Committee, 31 March 1939.
67. Ibid., extract from minutes of meeting of Committee of London Clearing

Bankers, 1 June 1939.
68. Wake, *Kleinwort Benson*, pp. 254–5.
69. MB 30/190, internal memo, 14 April 1939.
70. Ibid., (i) extract from Herbert A. Astbury's Diary, 19 April 1939, (ii) memo (undated) of Lidbury/McKenna conversation, (iii) note, 27 April 1939. Astbury was Chief General Manager, 1938–43.
71. BoE OV34/140, notes by Gunston, 28 April 1939 and May 1939.
72. T 160/818/12681/05/5, memo, by Waley.
73. MB 30/190, memo, and Joint Committee resolution, 25 August 1939.
74. Medlicott, *The Economic Blockade*, p. 18.
75. MB 30/190, *Financial Times*, 14 September 1939, and letter by Lord Wardington, 26 September 1939.

7

British protectionism and the Third Reich:
a fat or lean Germany?

As Hitler consolidated his power in the months after January 1933, the debate on what role Britain should play in helping to restart the German economic machine began in earnest. Any too rapid increase in German prosperity entailed serious dangers. Believing that Hitler's magic had already transformed Germany's outlook, Vansittart, at the Foreign Office, expressed his anxiety in high rhetoric: 'The most formidable Jericho, standing at the Threshold of the Promised Land, is the economic one. If this fortress were to appear to fall at the first blast of the Nazi trumpet, would not self-confidence inevitably become over-weaning ?'[1] Germany was said to be arriving at the World Economic Conference in the summer of 1933 like a sturdy beggar; the Nazis seemed poised to harness a strength which no preceding German government had ever enjoyed. The great fear in London was that Hitler intended to use any renewed prosperity to rearm and so undermine international security by acting aggressively in foreign affairs. It was clearly desirable to avoid facilitating 'Teutonic' hubris.[2]

Unfortunately, the alternative was no less worrying. There was a danger that the Nazis would be driven to adopt more and more extreme and experimental methods to maintain themselves in power. Continued economic depression might have forced Hitler into a more spectacular foreign policy in order to divert popular attention from domestic difficulties. The Foreign Office assumed that the answers it provided to this critical question would largely determine future government policy. Whether Britain was justified in easing Germany's economic and financial difficulties depended upon how much weight was attached to the several political factors.

Vansittart judged by the militarism and bitterness which he saw and doubted whether Hitler could be trusted. Sir John Simon, the Foreign Secretary, was equally sceptical about Germany's long-run intentions; but he was prepared to strike a bargain, even a bad one, 'before the iron gets too hot'.[3]

In spite of these concerns, Britain's attempt to create a favourable climate through policies which appeared understanding and sympathetic was generally supported. The reaction, for example, to the news in October 1933 that Germany was to leave the League of Nations and the Disarmament Conference was muted. The objective was to secure an agreement with Hitler – perhaps an economic one – while he continued in a supposedly peaceful mood. In this respect, Medlicott's thesis is endorsed by McKercher: Vansittart and others in the Foreign Office were not against making concessions, but only as a means to alter the international status quo peacefully in a way which did not weaken British interests.[4]

The periodic attempts from 1933 onwards to resolve outstanding international trade issues, both bilateral and multilateral, helped to create an impression of concomitant opportunities to make progress on the political front. This was particularly so in the middle of the decade as the long-established trade rivals resumed the struggle over export markets. As the threat of war grew, so the British Cabinet became more inclined to hope that an Anglo-German industrial agreement might provide a basis for achieving an accommodation with Hitler.

This presupposed that a unity of purpose underpinned Britain's economic strategy (never mind political strategy). However, the contradictions which, since 1932 had been implicit in Britain's stance on external economic relations, were to make it virtually impossible to achieve any kind of consensus on the objectives of foreign economic policy. The revolutionary economic changes brought about by the events of 1931/32 had supposedly provided the nation with a way to secure economic salvation. Nevertheless, a deep ambivalence over the effects of protectionism soon began to pervade business and political circles. Some of the advantages Britain had won for herself by turning to protectionism were beginning to disappear by the middle of the decade in the face of industrial competition. And yet here was a paradox. There was an uneasy sense that, by her own actions, Britain had helped to stimulate that competition in the first place. Tariffs were blamed for the way in which they had made it more difficult to achieve stability in international economic and political relations. In spite of that, in the eyes of the National Government and its business supporters tariffs remained a welcome means of defence against what was perceived as the unfair trade practices of industrial competitor nations such as Germany. A reversal of national and imperial policies was inconceivable.

The revival of lagging exports was a fundamental objective of the National Government and remained so throughout the 1930s. Tariffs gave Britain, in theory, the opportunity to protect the home market and to hold a strong position, particularly when negotiating specific trade agreements with countries outside the Empire. A series of 20 bilateral trade agreements were implemented with foreign countries which enjoyed particularly favourable balances of trade with the UK. The effects, however, were strictly local and hardly compensated for the loss of a multilateral trading system.[5] Concessions for British exports were gained by mere promises to refrain from either increasing duties or reducing quotas. A considerable increase in minimum export quotas for coal was one of the most important concessions Britain was able to win. This applied to agreements reached in 1933/34 with France and the Scandinavian and Baltic states.

Coal exports were also at the heart of a treaty Britain concluded with Germany in April 1933. Historically, Britain had enjoyed a large trade with north-west Germany, where imported British coal was used for the bunker trade of the North Sea ports and for domestic consumption because it was cheaper than German coal. The restriction of British shipments was achieved only when coal from the Ruhr began effectively to receive liberal subsidies in the form of preferential freight rates.

The assumption of power by the Nazis made no difference to the coal talks which had been under way since the Lausanne Conference in 1932 (see Chapter 2).[6] The Anglo-German Trade Treaty provided a stimulus to German exports. In return, Britain secured stabilization in the progressive reduction in her coal and coke export quota: Germany promised to take not less than 180,000 tons every month.[7] Exports actually increased because there was a proviso that this figure would rise proportionately for every percentage increase in Germany's total monthly consumption in excess of 7.5 million tons. In spite of this, the value of coal exports (as a proportion of total exports) was to remain below the pre-1931 level.

TABLE 10: BRITISH COAL EXPORTS TO GERMANY

Year	tons	£000
1929	5,520,944	-
1930	-	3,421
1931	-	2,518
1932	2,308,507	1,518
1933	2,360,300	1,552
1934	2,540,929	1,713

Source: Compiled from Political and Economic Planning, British Library of Political and Economic Science, WG 17/2 2503/35/coal, memo, dated 7 June 1935; and League of Nations, *British External Economic Policies*.

The arrangements were criticized in the House of Commons on the grounds that they lowered tariffs to German imports without adequate consultation with British businessmen.[8] In June, Walter Runciman, the President of the Board of Trade, reassured von Neurath, the German Foreign Minister, that the criticism was purely factional and did not indicate any inimical feeling towards Germany. Runciman blamed Austen Chamberlain for instigating the opposition on behalf of his constituents who had interests in the artificial jewellery trade. However, the British minister was also careful to emphasize that he did not feel able to embark on a more comprehensive trade agreement while Germany continued in a 'state of instability'.[9] Runciman regarded the trade treaty as a small one. However, according to Arndt, writing in 1944, it was the only instance before the Anglo-American Trade Agreement of 1938 of 'substantial reductions in duties made by Great Britain'.[10] But the Anglo-German Trade Treaty did not herald an improvement in overall relations: the crisis over Germany's foreign bondholders developed soon afterwards. Rather, the agreement merely reflected the depressed condition of British coal exports and the effect of tariffs on Weimar and Nazi Germany.

None the less, it was evidence of what could be achieved in the mutual interests of both countries. If Britain wished to build on her economic recovery, a plausible case could be advanced in favour of allowing Germany to grow fat, and this was precisely what Professor Henry Clay at the Bank of England advocated. During the negotiations which eventually produced the Payments Agreement the following year, Clay wanted to see Britain recognize Germany's difficulties and co-operate in any plan for restoring the latter's position in the commercial world. To justify this position, Clay did not think it necessary to look further than the distribution of world trade in the 1930s. As an export market for the UK's own products, Germany was merely the eighth largest. But if re-exports were included, Germany became Britain's biggest single market after India – a dramatic illustration of how important this triangular trade was for the British Empire. It was this market which would have been lost with a collapse of German trade or currency. But Clay was more concerned about possible world-wide dislocation: only Britain and America enjoyed a share of world trade greater than that of Germany, and Germany's trade was particularly diversified and widespread.

It was commonplace to believe that the economic stability of the Third Reich could be guaranteed only by Dr Schacht, for all his faults. Clay warned that the alternative to Schacht was something much more extreme and dangerous to the whole world. However, in a familiar refrain, Clay added that while Germany was hit exceptionally hard by British tariffs and bilateral trade agreements, 'The depreciation of our exchange hit them more than any other country because their export industries are mainly competitive with ours, not complementary like the USA's.'[11] There seemed to be just one course to take: Britain had the responsibility, means and self-interest to prevent a collapse and to help to steer Germany back on to the course of economic liberalism. Failure so to do would have the most severe consequences.

It was debatable whether the opportunity for action still existed or whether it had ever existed. What the National Socialists held to be desirable or unavoidable were the ingredients of economic nationalism – rearmament, controlled trade and autarky, even if the régime dithered between 1933 and 1936 over the direction in which this was pushing the economy.[12] It did not take long for Schacht's New Plan to begin to accomplish the tasks for which it had been called into being.[13] Exchange control continued to be the linchpin of the whole system. But the justification for the policy shifted completely from financial or monetary areas. Instead, exchange control was used by Berlin to determine the volume, direction and composition of Germany's international trade – altogether its noneconomic character. With Hitler set against devaluation, the Reichsmark became a kind of fictitious currency; the imposition of multifarious *ad hoc*, but concealed, devaluations became a necessity.[14] In practice, the New Plan involved a great extension of bilateral trading through clearing or payment agreements and barter compensation deals. The Nazi economy also incorporated an extensive system of private compensation agreements which assumed several different forms. 'Aski' marks were frequently employed in such transactions.[15] These were used to pay for certain vital imports, such as copper, but they were blocked: although the imports commanded a premium price, the marks had to be used, in turn, on purchasing German goods. German exports began to receive not only indirect subsidy by such means but direct subsidy as well. A British estimate put the average subsidy on all exports at 20 per cent and up to 40 per cent in particular cases.[16] Between 1936 and 1937 Germany expanded her exports in finished goods by 23 per cent in value.[17]

The implications for the British economy were serious: the advantages gained earlier in the decade for several classes of export stood in danger of being wiped out. Up to 1935 British exports outstripped the growth in world trade.[18] At that point, a new trend seemed to emerge: British export trades faced increasingly stiff competition from German goods, particularly in south-east Europe, Central and South America, China and even India. Indeed, manufacturers began to complain to the British government that they were being completely shut out of continental and Near Eastern markets.[19]

One of the most striking developments in this pattern of foreign trade was the Third Reich's growing politico-economic interest in South-east Europe. With the difficulties in making purchases from strong-currency countries, Germany consistently drifted away from importing from most west European creditor countries and developed with south-east Europe the most extensive barter and bilateral trading system. The effect was to supplant Britain in the trade of the region. Germany's share of Turkey's import trade rocketed from under 18 per cent in 1929 to 44 per cent in 1937; Britain's share dropped from 12 to 7 per cent. In Bulgaria, Germany raised her share from 30 to 58 per cent, while Britain's was halved from 10 to 5 per cent. Germany's share of Greece's import trade increased from 10 to 30 per cent.[20]

The response of the Board of Trade was to produce the extensively researched *Survey of German Competition in World Export Trade*. This offered confirmation of the obvious: Germany was attempting to recapture ground which had been lost because of the world depression and collapse of multilateralism. In 1935 an estimated 60 per cent of world exports, including the bulk of European trade, were paid for through clearings or similar arrangements. But in Germany's case the estimate for foreign trade covered by one kind of agreement or another was put at 80 per cent. Just as Germany imposed clearings on countries with whom she had an import surplus, in those cases where Germany enjoyed an export surplus, the countries concerned imposed the same kind of mechanism. This canalization helped to push world export levels even lower: between 1931 and 1935 trade shrank by 40 per cent in gold values and by 8 per cent in volume. Over the same period, Germany's exports fell by over 55 per cent in value and 14 per cent in volume. Britain did not fare so badly: the value of British exports fell by about 30 per cent but the volume actually increased.[21]

TABLE 11: GEOGRAPHICAL DISTRIBUTION OF BRITISH AND GERMAN EXPORTS IN £000s (AVERAGE EXCHANGE RATE)

Area	UK exports (January to June)		German exports (January to June)	
	1935	1936	1935	1936
Europe	80,828	75,695	120,290	130,150
South and Central America	18,451	18,726	13,360	18,900
Total for all areas	206,475	207,890	162,310	182,040

Source: abstracted from CAB 24/265 CP339, 'The Balance of Payments', by Leith-Ross, 7 Dec. 1936.

The British coal industry was also presented with a serious problem through Germany's determination to challenge Britain's supremacy in world markets. Coal, and dyes based on coal and tar, accounted for some 10 per cent by value of German exports between the wars. Confronted with Britain's devaluation in 1931, Germany drastically reduced her coal export prices. The effect of this, together with exchange restrictions and the severe limitations placed

TABLE 12: COMPARISON OF BRITISH AND GERMAN EXPORT TRADE

(A) *Shares of UK, Germany and USA in World Export Trade*

Year	Gold values (millions gold dollars)	UK (%)	Germany (%)	USA (%)
1913	18,195	14.08	13.21	13.46
1924	25,127	14.01	6.19	17.90
1929	33,021	10.75	9.73	15.62
1931	18,908	9.37	12.09	12.58
1932	12,895	9.92	10.60	12.22
1933	11,740	10.37	9.88	10.90
1934	11,364	10.47	8.62	11.03
1935	11,444	10.83	8.90	11.60

(B) *Value of British and German Import and Export Trade*

Year	Germany (Rmmillion) imports	Germany (Rmmillion) exports	UK (£000) imports	UK (£000) exports	re-exports
1913	10,770	10,097	768,735	525,254	109,567
1924	9,135	6,533	1,277,439	800,967	139,970
1929	13,447	13,483	1,220,765	729,349	109,702
1931	6,728	9,599	861,253	390,622	63,868
1932	4,667	5,739	701,670	365,024	51,021
1933	4,204	4,871	675,016	367,909	49,081
1934	4,451	4,167	731,414	395,986	51,243
1935	4,159	4,270	756,936	425,921	55,265

(C) *Distribution of British and German Exports by Continental Group as a Percentage of Total Exports*

(a) Germany

Continental Group	1913	1926	1931	1934	1935
Europe	75.0	71.0	81.0	76.4	71.6
Asia	6.2	9.4	6.6	9.4	10.9
Africa	1.9	2.5	1.9	2.5	2.9
America	15.0	16.0	10.0	10.8	13.7
Australasia	1.0	0.7	0.4	0.6	0.7

(b) UK

Continental Group	1913	1926	1931	1934	1935
Europe	34.65	26.29	43.29	38.62	37.27
Africa	9.86	12.00	12.85	14.15	15.37
Asia	25.20	25.24	17.91	18.13	17.43
America					
North and Central	11.99	14.18	12.18	11.97	12.81
South	9.59	8.93	7.06	7.49	6.93
Oceania	8.71	13.36	6.71	9.64	10.19

Source: T 160 729/12829/2, 'Survey of German Competition in World Export Trade', Appendix 2, produced by the Board of Trade.

on imported coal by France, Belgium and Germany herself (Britain's major markets), prevented the full advantage of devaluation from being realized. The level of British export prices in the mid 1930s was virtually the same as in 1930, while German and Polish prices were, respectively, more than 50 and 40 per cent lower than at the start of the decade. The German industry was able, therefore, to achieve an export record during the 1930s that was far superior to its British counterpart.[22] In 1929 German coal exports were equivalent to 50 per cent of British exports; by 1937 the figure had risen to 90 per cent.[23]

Some regions of Britain were badly affected by the extent of the competition in foreign coal markets. A drop of more than 2.5m tons in exports from South Wales was reported in 1936. The greater part of this loss was caused because coal from the Third Reich was substituted; the industry there was known to benefit from subsidies.[24] In Spain, Egypt, Palestine and Greece market share was lost to Germany; the last also gained more ground than Britain in France and Scandinavia.

The Anglo-German Trade Treaty had given an indication of how important coal was in Britain's overseas trade. In the mid 1930s coal represented about 8 per cent of British exports.[25] British exports to Germany had increased as a result of the treaty. But towards the end of 1936 there was a 5 per cent shortfall in the allocated monthly quota. This reduction might have reflected a rise in British prices; but a more likely cause was the application of price control measures by Berlin. No approach was made to the Reich authorities: the British coal trade had benefitted more from the increased quota secured under the treaty than had German trade to Britain from the corresponding reduction in tariffs.

The reaction in Britain to this emerging trend was remarkable. Among political and business circles it seemed to confirm the generally held assumption that the Nazi economy, while not on the point of collapse, was certainly in crisis.[26] It was assumed that the concealed devaluation of the mark could not go on endlessly and that a rise in world prices or a collapse of the gold bloc – expected at any time – would then force a formal devaluation. The Third Reich's export drive was taken to be a sign not of strength but of desperation.

But there was also something profoundly disturbing in the good fortune which Britain had enjoyed since 1931 in comparison with

Germany. For if National Socialism were responsible for much of the contraction in Germany's foreign trade it was accepted that Britain too could be blamed for participating in the destruction of multilateralism through 'beggar-my-neighbour' policies. The agreements with the Scandinavian and Baltic states, for example, deprived Germany of markets in those countries. It seemed reasonable to ask, therefore, why the thorny path of central and south-east Europe should not be left to Germany. By bringing forward economic initiatives Britain could help to tackle the distress which, it was assumed, was the cause of Nazism, and perhaps prepare the way for a wider political settlement. Chief among the 'economic appeasers', according to Gustav Schmidt, were Frank Ashton-Gwatkin and Gladwyn Jebb, of the Foreign Office's economic section.[27] The basis of their thesis was that Germany had to be provided with trade outlets which would allow her to expand, in the sense of securing new external markets, and prevent the country from going bankrupt and thus starting a European war.[28]

With the international outlook darkening in the mid 1930s, Britain was forced to contemplate the likely political and economic costs of rearmament. A Cabinet committee was formed in 1936 to consider how to approach the problem of reaching an agreement with Germany. Anthony Eden, the Foreign Secretary, suggested:

> It is only in the economic and financial spheres that Hitler's policy has not proceeded according to plan, and is now having to face extensive and maybe insuperable difficulties ... Perhaps Hitler's economic difficulties may make him less uncompromising than he would otherwise be.[29]

Also before the new committee was Vansittart's memorandum, *Britain, France and Germany*. He had come to accept, in principle at least, that co-operation rather than ostracism was more likely to counter German economic distress and, therefore, military adventurism. He did not think the insistent demand for export markets was in itself unreasonable, given the steady decline in German export totals over the preceding seven years. Britain had already shown her willingness through the trade and payments agreements and Germany's desire for further advances was not in doubt. Vansittart argued that if Britain was to retain the large measure of influence and considerable friendship it still enjoyed in commercial and financial circles in Germany, it was essential that trade was not reduced – by tariffs on Britain's part – except for the pressing needs of industry.[30]

The importance of this point was reinforced by Pinsent, Financial Adviser at the Berlin Embassy. As far as commercial expansion was concerned, Pinsent saw the disadvantages in trying to encourage German trade in particular directions. Instead, to follow a policy of economic understanding with Germany it was necessary to look nearer to home: Britain could make a contribution by moderating its régime on tariffs. He suggested that the time had come when general considerations, more particularly those of foreign policy, should be allowed a far greater weight in determining British tariffs. The theory that Britain had far more to gain in the long run by an increase in the exchange of goods than to lose in the short run by intensified German competition in particular commodities appeared to attract widespread support.[31] Understandably, it seemed less appealing to the manufacturers of the commodities concerned. There were demands for further action to exclude German goods from the British market. The government had to decide whether to resist this pressure.

The notion that the economic question was the prime motive for German action or that a solution was to be found in granting economic concessions did not find support in the Treasury. Sir Frederick Phillips, the Under-Secretary, regarded many of the causes of Germany's plight as irresistible in the sense that they could not be put right in the early future. Britain's adoption of protectionism exemplified the problem: although Germany had been hit very heavily, Britain was not going back to free trade.[32]

Almost immediately, a test case presented itself. Unusually large quantities of calf leather were being imported at prices which appeared to bear little relation to production costs. This was because most dressed leather imports came from Germany and the trade benefited from subsidies of up to 35 per cent of value. With the interest of domestic producers in mind, the IDAC recommended that Britain should increase duties.

Anthony Eden was against any move which might jeopardize the chances of reaching a general European political settlement. But Runciman, President of the Board of Trade, had his eye firmly on the British producers who were being driven out of business. Chamberlain, similarly, saw great difficulty in telling traders that their application had passed all the tests of the IDAC but had failed at the last minute because of political factors. So the Cabinet decided to let commercial, or rather domestic political, considerations prevail: extra duties had to be imposed in order to avoid any danger of provoking a dangerous storm of criticism and resentment.[33]

Just as Runciman was able to prevail over his Cabinet colleagues in this specific case so his department, after consulting the Colonial Office, argued aggressively against all the proposals which emanated from the Foreign Office at the beginning of 1936. None of the options for a policy initiative that were countenanced were thought likely by the Board to alter Germany's political outlook and render her less dangerous. Particular exception was taken to talk of tariff-cutting; Germany had, in any case, increased import duties herself in the previous three years on a number of British exports.[34] The Colonial Office, joining in what had now become a highly charged debate, launched a vitriolic attack on Vansittart and accused him of encroaching on territory that was not his preserve.[35]

Hitler's reoccupation of the Rhineland in March 1936 temporarily set back ideas of an initiative in the economic sphere. Eden made one further attempt to pursue the question of a British tariff reduction, but Runciman quashed it. He decreed, in August 1936, that Eden's proposals were a complete reversal of the government's policy. To abandon Imperial Preference and 'moderate' protection – policies which had been endorsed by the electorate in 1931 and 1935 – would, Runciman argued, only create trouble at home without securing any real advantage abroad.[36]

British companies were also reporting intensified competition from their German rivals in tendering for important contracts overseas. As a result, business was either lost or prices were forced down to uneconomic levels.[37] The Board of Trade survey revealed that the heavy engineering sector was particularly affected: manufacturers of agricultural and textile machinery, locomotives and combustion engines all reported problems. On the basis of figures published by the Reichs Kredit Gesellschaft, the survey tried to show how German export trades were only trying to recapture lost ground. In contrast to the other leading suppliers of engineering products (America and Britain herself), Germany's share of the combined value of exports had fallen from 45 per cent in the second half of 1932 to 28 per cent in the first half of 1935. Resigned to seeing this trend thrown into reverse, the Board could do no more than point to the development of cartels as a way to modify competition. This seemed to be the case in tinplate and chemicals; the only other sector of industry which was effectively organized as a cartel was steel.[38]

But the steel industry was in a unique position in inter-war Britain: the state followed the banks in becoming involved in the affairs of the industry. This was the exception which proved the National Government's rule of non-intervention. The European steel cartel (Germany, Belgium, France and Luxembourg) was revived in February 1933 and then concentrated on undercutting the British tariff by selling cheaply into Britain. In response, the newly formed British Iron and Steel Federation wanted tariffs raised as a bargaining tool to facilitate entry into the cartel.[39] The threat to use tariff power in this way was successful and, in 1935, British steel producers took their place in the Iron and Steel International Agreement (*Entente Internationale de l'Acier*) on favourable terms. Agreements covered the reservation of home markets, allocations of quotas for the world export trade and price fixing.[40]

In October 1936 the decision was made to encourage British industrialists, particularly those who were suffering from competition, to enter into discussions with their opposite numbers in Germany. There would be no direct intervention by the British government in Berlin, even though Germany was believed to be ready to discuss international trade questions.[41] If any economic deals were to be struck with Germany they would be on an industry-to-industry basis rather than at a governmental level.[42] The aim of achieving a rationalization of markets as part of a general political settlement was pushed into the background. The best way to protect British export markets, it was now argued, was by reaching agreements with German industry – the greatest threat to those markets.

The problems over export markets added to the fear that Britain's economic strength was slipping away. Exports to the Dominions in the late 1930s were more than 20 per cent lower than they had been before the depression struck. On the other hand, the trade surplus which the Dominions enjoyed with the UK doubled.[43] Treasury officials warned against the effects of the adverse balance of payments on the country's international purchasing power represented by its gold and foreign exchange reserves, overseas investments and ability to raise international credit.[44] The first stage of an economic review, produced for the Cabinet by Leith-Ross, conveyed the severity of the threat which British rearmament posed to the nation's export trade. The contraction of export markets and the domestic orientation of Britain's recovery from depression were coupled with the effects of rearmament: the country seemed to be in danger of losing, irretrievably, her position in world trade.[45]

The Cabinet paper concentrated on the competition that British exports faced from German and Japanese goods. Because of the close connection between manufacturers and banks, Germany enjoyed a number of structural advantages over Britain. For example, Britain could not suddenly expect the financial establishment to engage in long-term contract financing. Nor was it open to the British state to imitate the expedients the Third Reich had adopted for the development of export markets. The promotion of arrangements between industries in Britain and Germany for a reasonable allocation of markets seemed, therefore, to be one of the few possible ways forward.[46]

As Cain and Hopkins argue, British industrialists did not need to be pushed in the direction of market-sharing agreements; although the outcome of Imperial Preference proved to be a great disappointment, the National Government continued to defend the basic structure of tariffs.[47] This position was broadly supported by the Federation of British Industries: it was committed to exploring the situation in Germany, but believed that it was the power of the IDAC to raise duties to new levels that had induced the German authorities to seek agreements. Indeed, the Federation had already helped industries to make contact with their opposite numbers in Germany. An agreement was reached, for example, between British and German textile machinery makers. This involved fixing a minimum price for each market, quoting a credit term of no more than 12 months and, in markets where Germany had clearing or compensation agreements, quoting prices at parity with Britain.

The FBI regarded Germany as the best industrially organized country with which to negotiate cartel arrangements. Hitler's government had taken an industrial system that was already cartel-minded and imposed centralized controls.[48] There was even a possibility that industry structured along these lines might facilitate a return to prosperity and stability. Gillingham has illustrated how, with liberal economics languishing in a discredited condition, the Reich provided an economic role model for some European states.

The British coal industry was one sector which had an opportunity to benefit from German methods of industrial organization.[49]

The structure of capitalism in Britain was, of course, quite different. Although trade associations were expected to take a lead in organizational matters, any one industry could comprise a number of competing interests and rivals. The FBI also appears to have overestimated the significance of the cordial relationship it thought it had established with its German counterpart, the Reichs-gruppe Industrie (RGI), during previous years.[50] Federation representatives complained about the 'Moscow' atmosphere which prevailed in Berlin when they visited in March 1937: German officials and businessmen were afraid to talk and everywhere political considerations stood in the way.[51] Although the Nazis left the ownership of industry in private hands, this counted for less and less in the Hitler state.

Little progress was made in 1937 in fashioning further industrial agreements, even though there was heightened anxiety over Britain's deteriorating export position in the face of German subsidies. The National Government looked to sponsor private and non-official negotiations. Even the Foreign Office considered this to be sound policy which might act to improve relations between the two countries. Industrial arrangements would serve to meet German complaints about trade restrictions and obviate the bad impression caused by the imposition of duties on German goods.[52] Robert Hudson, appointed Secretary for the Department of Overseas Trade, wanted the government to play a more active role in facilitating negotiations because he was convinced that industrial co-operation would have a favourable effect on political appeasement.[53] In this respect, he was to follow his own advice in 1938 and 1939.[54]

At the end of 1937 the democracies were able to entertain a small degree of optimism over the international political situation. The US State Department announced on 18 November that a trade agreement with Britain was in sight. Walter Runciman, President of the Board of Trade, had visited Washington at the beginning of the year; he agreed in principle to a more liberal trade policy while emphasizing how difficult it would be for Britain to extricate herself from Empire preferences. Indeed, the negotiations were lengthy and bitter.[55] When the Anglo-American Trade Agreement was finally signed, on 17 November 1938, the reduction in tariffs and discrimination, however small, was thought to be very significant:

the two largest trading nations naturally competed on the level of manufactured products and Britain discriminated against American agricultural produce.[56]

For Cordell Hull, the American Secretary of State, the agreement was a triumphal step forward in his plan to preserve world peace by economic appeasement. He believed that the banding together of nations such as Britain and the United States on economic grounds would show recalcitrant nations such as Italy and Germany the undoubted benefits of joining in the same movement. Thus Hull expected the political effect – a reduction in tension – to carry as much weight around the world as the economic.[57] Neville Chamberlain shared this hope; he also calculated that the educative effect of the treaty on American opinion would encourage the country to act more and more in line with Britain.[58]

Dealing with America provided no answer to the competition that British export markets continued to face from Germany. But a connection between the various international trade questions was readily established. The origin of most problems seemed to lie in protectionism and, consequently, Britain's own foreign economic policy. The sense of regret for the impact of that policy on Germany, a constant refrain throughout the decade, was now at its keenest. Self-recrimination was never more evident than in a note composed by Leith-Ross in early 1938 for the Van Zeeland Committee which, on behalf of the League of Nations, was looking at ways to promote international economic co-operation. In it he admitted that protectionism and imperial preference were so successful that German exports to Britain had been reduced by half. The fall in trade between the Dominions and Germany he described as catastrophic. To meet the deficiency, Germany had deliberately turned to European and Near Eastern countries for supplies, the latter having lost their former free entry into Britain. This in turn affected British export opportunities to those countries. While Britain had been successful in passing on part of her difficulties to countries such as Germany, the cost could now be counted: the counterpart to Ottawa, and its concomitant strengthening of political and trade relations, was German buying in Europe. It had become obvious that, in an age of economic nationalism, each country which attempted to take measures to alleviate its own difficulties viewed measures taken by other countries as inspired by deliberate ill will.[59]

There was little that was new or unexpected in this diagnosis. The Foreign Office saw itself as the one department which could be exonerated from all blame. It had recommended, in November 1931, that special reference should be made to the question of security in Europe before tariff policy was definitely decided. Instead, international trade had been killed as a result of the choice made in 1931/32. Ashton-Gwatkin crystallized economic policy in the formula 'Home industries and agriculture first; Dominions second; foreigners last'.[60] There was no scope for Britain to contribute to the economic appeasement of Germany. Some economic departments saw nothing wrong in putting foreigners last. Apart from the continuing crisis over Czechoslovakia, Hudson's plans were undermined by the Board of Trade. Brown, the Permanent Under-Secretary, declared that the main difficulty in negotiations with Germany was that Britain had nothing to give and little to gain.[61] This was not strictly the case. There was a very real economic motive for reaching an agreement with the Third Reich: British industry was trying to resist the threat posed by German export subsidies.

While tariffs did not turn out to be as hard as the emergency duties, and the 1933 trade treaty had provided some relief, it seemed in retrospect that Britain had locked the last door in Germany's face when protection came on top of depreciation. For this reason, Ashton-Gwatkin could only marvel that doors were being opened as wide as they were to the United States. He took this as an indication that the large economic bloc, or *Grossraumwirtschaft,* would soon become dominant. Some consolation was to be drawn from the thought that the richest bloc might comprise Britain and America. Naturally, it was given to few to foresee how the world was about to be turned upside down. Ashton-Gwatkin's prediction that the economic, even political, influence of this group would be the decisive factor in the twentieth century was not so very wide of the mark. Yet, ironically, when Britain did eventually join such a bloc – the European Economic Community – the most powerful member was Germany.

By mid-1938, business circles were becoming alarmed at the state of the export industry; Germany's 'un-economic' trade policies were held to be partially responsible for Britain's balance of payments deficit.[62] In spite of the outcry, the quantity of German exports in 1937 was at 69 per cent of its 1929 level, while the corresponding British figure was 83 per cent. Indeed, Germany's export trade seemed to suffer more than Britain's in the recession of 1937–38. However, while rearmament brought an ever increasing intensity of activity inside the Third Reich, the effect of the recession on Britain caused attention to be paid to the state of export markets.[63] Pressure began to mount on the British government to meet the challenge of German industrial competition around the world and to counter the Nazi penetration of south-east Europe. A scheme was evolved to lessen German penetration of the region by government intervention in the free market: purchases of Romanian wheat, for example, would place sterling at the disposal of the Romanian government. This represented a radical departure and opened up the long-standing political divisions in the Cabinet and in Whitehall.[64]

Chamberlain sought to bring such initiatives into line with his efforts to reach a settlement with Hitler. The Prime Minister was hopeful that a dialogue with the Führer was still possible. The fusion of political with economic diplomacy that took place in the final months of peace has been analysed in many studies.[65] Chamberlain took with him to Munich in September 1938 a proposal for Anglo-German co-operation in the Balkans. Hitler declined to discuss it.[66] This did not deter Halifax, the Foreign Secretary, from pushing for an 'alternative policy' of assisting Germany to develop the countries of the region. He advised that anything which could appear deliberately obstructive, such as direct governmental purchases which diverted trade to Britain, would have to be abandoned and that Germany should be permitted to obtain all she materially required in the region.[67] In meetings between British and German officials, held up to February 1939, schemes were put forward which offered Germany more free exchange in order to pay for increased imports from south-east Europe.[68]

While it was Germany which first mooted, at the World Economic Conference in 1933, the idea of a cartel for coal, it was the British government that had taken the lead thereafter in trying to stimulate interest in some kind of convention. In fact, negotiations between the respective industries did not take place until 1938 and were concluded only when the National Government threatened to subsidize coal exports.[69] Germany's objective was to consolidate the vast economic gains already made with a view to ending subsidies. At the same time, Reich officials did not want to jeopardize foreign exchange earnings.[70] A new agreement was reached on the basis that undercutting was to cease; the ratio of British to German exports would be 65:35 and all prices were to be agreed by a trade association comprising industrialists of both nations.[71] This accord was hailed as a prelude to the formation of a European coal cartel. The British Cabinet, and especially Chamberlain, hoped that the celebrations would be followed by a dialogue with the Nazi leadership.[72] But the agreement was suspended as a result of Hitler's invasion of Czechoslovakia and never put into operation.

Chamberlain believed, however, that all his information went to show that the Germans were in no mood for war and that Hitler was preoccupied with his economic difficulties. It is in this context that the extraordinary and secretive talks took place, in June and July of 1939, between Sir Horace Wilson (Chief Industrial Adviser) and Wohltat, and between the latter and Hudson. This inglorious episode was the final formal attempt to preserve peace by means of working towards some kind of politico-economic agreement with Germany. The negotiations, which had commenced with the FBI-RGI talks and had grown out of a trade drive for British exports against German trading methods, were to end in a blaze of humiliating and damaging publicity over what appeared to be economic appeasement.

Wohltat had already met leading civil servants and City figures when he visited London in June 1938 in connection with the International Whaling Conference.[73] In Berlin, in May 1939, an unofficial British intermediary (Henry Drummond-Wolff) discreetly re-established contact over the economic talks. This was put on to a diplomatic level when Wohltat visited London the next month for discussions on whaling and the refugee problem. On this occasion, Wohltat met Ashton-Gwatkin and Wilson. He proposed to Ashton-Gwatkin an economic settlement in which Britain would recognize the German sphere of influence in south-east Europe.[74]

On his next visit to London Wohltat had further talks with Wilson (18 July) and with Hudson (20 July). Controversy has surrounded these conversations ever since. In particular, the veracity of the records left by the participants remains open to question. Wohltat's memorandum of his talk with Wilson contains proposals put forward by the latter for a far-reaching settlement which included a resolution of Germany's debt problems and loans for the Reichsbank. Wilson's record contains no such proposals.[75] Hudson claimed that he told Wohltat that a readiness by Hitler to disarm, and to accept adequate safeguards against rearming, could open the way to establishing Germany on a strong economic basis. After signing the whaling agreement and meeting Waley over the matter of the Czech gold, Wohltat left London.[76]

On 22 July the British press announced that Britain had proposed a fantastic loan to Germany. The news shocked Europe. Von Dirksen, the German Ambassador, informed Sargent that Wohltat's description of the conversation with Hudson was very different from the press articles. Indeed, in his report to Berlin, von Dirksen put the blame both on Hudson's morbid desire for self-assertion and on his loquacity; this provided an opportunity for 'war-mongering correspondents' and their 'henchmen' such as Churchill and Foreign Office officials.[77] Sir Alexander Cadogan thought even less of Hudson, describing him as 'an eel', and he also believed that the minister had been responsible for recent press leaks.[78]

An angry Chamberlain was left to face a storm of protest in Parliament as he sought to distance the government from the rumours. But the question remained as to how far Hudson had been acting on his own initiative. Chamberlain left a candid record of the affair in his correspondence with his sisters. He wrote that entering into conversations with Germany had been made worse by the rumours over a loan, with different newspapers citing varying amounts. Hudson had made no mention of a loan in his account to Chamberlain, but the latter was not sure that he had been told the whole truth. Hudson was regarded as a clever fellow with a persuasive tongue, but also as someone with a reputation as a disloyal colleague who was always trying to advance his own interests at the expense of his friends. A favourite Hudsonian device, according to Chamberlain, was to take ideas on which other people had been working for years and to put them forward as his own: 'The ideas which he put to Wohltat for instance, as his own personal suggestion, on an economic agreement (not including a loan) are just those which we have been discussing in the Departments for 12 months'. Chamberlain thought that 'Master Hudson' became so pleased with himself when Wohltat did not react unfavourably that he talked to the press, with disastrous results. Much to the Prime Minister's annoyance, Wilson's interview with Wohltat, which covered other matters, had also become public knowledge, 'and so now the loan idea is given a demi-semi-official air and all the busybodies in London, Paris and Burgos have put two and two together and triumphantly made five'.[79]

Chamberlain, still incensed a week later over the extent of the harm caused by Hudson's 'gaffe', did not intend to add to his own troubles by sacking the man just then. But the episode had revealed how completely Hudson lacked a sense of ministerial responsibility. In the meantime, Chamberlain wanted to maintain contact through more discreet channels in order not to discourage those in Germany who were continuing to look for an understanding.[80] Whether the details of a loan were ever discussed must remain, therefore, a matter of speculation. What is clear, however, is that the substance of the scheme advanced by Hudson was not so very far removed from official policy. Certainly, as far as the Prime Minister was concerned, the logic of the policy, with its emphasis on moderates in Hitler's government, still held good.

In the course of the 1930s the process of constructing and revising financial and trade agreements with Germany was never less than tortuous. That said, Britain believed that relations with the Third Reich were better in the economic sphere than in any other. The German authorities largely observed the rules of the agreements and the administrative machinery worked relatively smoothly. Against the odds, the arrangements survived one shock after another and endured until broken by war. The Standstill, established in the last months of the Weimar Republic, continued to operate even after Schacht's political demise. The Payments Agreement withstood the tests of Nazi adventurism and was revised where necessary rather than abandoned. Anglo-German economic and financial relations self-evidently exhibited a quality lacking elsewhere: in a turbulent and increasingly violent age they offered a measure, however small, of stability and continuity.

Ironically, this was taken as evidence of the fragile nature of the economy of the Third Reich. Such reasoning suggested that the agreements survived only because the Nazis depended on them. It seemed highly likely, therefore, that any political understanding with the Third Reich would be preceded by the conclusion of some kind of new trade deal or an offer of economic concessions. But events show that it was never realistic to imagine that the policies established at the beginning of the 1930s could be modified in a substantial way. And, by the end of the decade, only a fantasist could suppose that modifications which tended to increase trade with Europe might also yield political and economic benefits. Finally, with Europe on the brink of war, there never was any question of granting economic concessions to Germany without a return by Hitler to the conference table and a demonstrable and fundamental move towards disarmament.

NOTES

1. FO 371/16696/C5456, 'Political aspects of German economic revival'.
2. Ibid., see also C5931, minute by Ashton-Gwatkin.
3. FO 371/16728/C9489 and C10268.
4. McKercher, 'Old diplomacy and new', p. 114. See Chapter 3 above for reference to Medlicott.
5. M.W. Kirby, *The Decline of British Economic Power since 1870* (Allen & Unwin, 1981), p. 66.
6. For the background see T. Rooth, *British Protectionism and the International Economy: Overseas Commercial Policy in the 1930s* (Cambridge: CUP, 1993), p. 145.
7. See Cmd 4297, Exchange of Notes, 13 April 1933, Anglo-German Commercial Relations.
8. Weinberg, *The Foreign policy of Hitler's Germany: 1933–36*, p. 379.
9. Runciman papers, 265, memo, 16 June 1933, of an informal conversation with von Neurath.
10. Arndt, *Economic Lessons* , p. 113.
11. BoE OV34/6, 3 September 1934.
12. Overy, *War and Economy*, p. 32.
13. The term 'autarky' first came into common usage during the 1930s. Some commentators referred to 'autarchy', or the power to control one's own destiny. Indeed, many understood the basic idea underlying German trade policy to be a combination of these two factors, particularly in regard to south-east Europe where attempts were made to form commercial links so close that the countries of the region would find it impossible to divert exports to alternative markets. See A.G.B. Fisher, *Economic Self-Sufficiency* (Oxford: Clarendon Press, 1939).
14. Ellis, *Exchange Control*, pp. 239–44. It remains difficult, therefore, to establish a reliable index for German prices. In terms of gold, the value of British and German exports declined just about equally from 1929–37; as German prices had not declined so much, she obtained, in theory, more for her exports.
15. 'Aski' was the acronym for *Ausländer-Sonderkonten fur Inlandszahlungen*.
16. CAB 27/599, note by Ashton-Gwatkin, 28 February 1936, 'Present Economic/Financial Situation in Germany'.
17. Guillebaud, *Economic Recovery*, pp. 68,148.
18. D.H. Aldcroft, *The Inter-War Economy: Britain, 1919–1939* (Batsford, 1970), pp. 281–2.
19. T 160/643/8797/04/6, see letter from Textile Machinery Makers to Department of Overseas Trade, 27 February 1936. See also FO 371/19933/C4326, Sir Edward Crowe (Comptroller General, Department of Overseas Trade) to Vansittart, 13 June 1936.
20. Francis, *Britain's Economic Strategy*, p. 278. Germany also made gains at Britain's expense in much of South America, although the trend was reversed in Russia and parts of northern Europe.
21. T 160/729/12829/2.

22. N.K. Buxton and D.H. Aldcroft (eds), *British Industry between the Wars: Instability and Industrial Development 1919–1939* (Scolar Press, 1979), pp. 51–5.
23. Francis, *Britain's Economic Strategy*, p. 251.
24. League of Nations, *British External Economic Policies*.
25. B.W.E. Alford, *Depression and Recovery? British Economic Growth 1918–1939* (Macmillan, 1972), p. 58.
26. CAB 27/599, note by Ashton-Gwatkin, 28 February 1936, 'Present Economic/Financial Situation in Germany'.
27. Schmidt, *The Politics and Economics of Appeasement*, pp. 84–93.
28. FO 371/19884/C807.
29. CAB 27/599, CP13(36), 17 February 1936.
30. Ibid., CP42(36), 11 February 1936.
31. T 160/856/14545/1, note, 7 March 1936.
32. Ibid., minutes, 17 March 1936.
33. CAB 24/260, CP59–60, 24–25 February 1936; CAB 23/83, 11(36), 26 February 1936. On Chamberlain's instructions, improvements in the arrangements for consultation between the Foreign Office and the IDAC were made in order to spare the Cabinet the difficult task of having to resolve such issues.
34. CAB 27/599, G(36)7, 'Possible Development of Existing Commercial Agreements with Germany as Regards the UK and Colonies'.
35. T 160/856/14545/1, 6 March 1936. The author of the attack, Clauson, argued that the English should have had some sympathy with German racial aspirations. He accused Vansittart of exaggerating the German menace but, at the same time, suggested that Britain should book a seat in the German bus before it was too late
36. FO 371/19934/C5567, letter, 23 August 1936.
37. FO 371/19933/C4326, Sir Edward Crowe to Vansittart, 13 June 1936.
38. T 160/729/12829/2.
39. S. Tolliday, *Business, Banking, and Politics: The Case of British Steel, 1918–1939* (Harvard University Press, 1987), p. 309.
40. FO 371/20731, minutes by Laurence Collier and Ashton-Gwatkin, 23–30 December 1936, concerning the instructions by the Board of Trade on industrial co-operation with Germany. These instructions took some in the Foreign Office by surprise and provoked an angry reaction. See also, D.E. Kaiser, *Economic Diplomacy and the Origins of the Second World War* (Princeton, NJ: Princeton University Press, 1980), p. 187.
41. T 160/729/12829/2, record of interdepartmental meeting held at the Board of Trade on 30 October 1936.
42. Wurm, *Business, Politics, and International Relations*, p. 71.
43. Clarke, *Hope and Glory*, p. 176.
44. Peden, *British Rearmament*, pp. 63, 84.
45. Eyers, 'Overseas Trade Policy', p. 204.
46. CAB 24/265, CP339, 'The Balance of Payments', 7 December 1936.
47. Cain and Hopkins, *British Imperialism*, pp. 97–8.
48. FBI 200/1/1/78, Tariffs and Commercial Treaties Committee, minutes of meeting, 15 December 1936, headed 'German Export Subsidies'; see also FO 371/20731/C87.
49. Gillingham, *Industry and Politics*, pp. 90–1.
50. FO 371/20731, memo, by Magowan, and letter to Mullins (Department of Overseas Trade), 15 February 1937.

51. Ibid., Mullins to Browett, 24 March and 5 April 1937; see also, FBI 200/F/1/1/78, Report, 23 March 1937. For a comprehensive treatment of the FBI–RGI talks see, R.F.Holland, 'The Federation of British Industries and the International Economy, 1929–39', *EcHR*, 2nd Ser., 34, 2 (May 1981).
52. T 160/729/12829/4, memo, 9 March 1937.
53. FO 371/20731/C8263, minutes by Ashton-Gwatkin, 2 and 7 December 1937; FO 371/21705/C2239, Hudson to Oliver Stanley (President, Board of Trade), 9 March 1938.
54. FO 371/21647/C7853, Hudson to Halifax, 8 July 1938. Hudson was unfortunate in his timing. His initiatives were delayed by the Anschluss and had to wait until the revised Payments Agreement produced a German request for economic negotiations.
55. D.Cameron Watt, *Succeeding John Bull*, p. 85.
56. Arndt, *Economic Lessons*, p. 82.
57. C. Hull, *The Memoirs of Cordell Hull* (Hodder & Stoughton, 1948), p. 530.
58. NC 18/1/1029, letter to Hilda, 21 November 1937. See also R.N. Kottman, *Reciprocity and the North Atlantic Triangle, 1932–1938* (New York, NY: Cornell University Press, 1968); T.K. McCulloch, 'Anglo-American Economic Diplomacy in the European Crisis 1935–39' (unpublished D.Phil. thesis, Oxford University, 1979).
59. FO 371/21701/C1828, note, 25 February 1938, for the Van Zeeland Committee.
60. Ibid., private note to Leith-Ross, 10 March 1938.
61. BT 11/901, 25 August 1938.
62. The Association of British Chambers of Commerce held a conference in October 1938 to discuss the need for countermeasures. See G.J. Van Kessel, 'The British Reaction to German Economic Penetration in South-Eastern Europe, 1936–1939' (unpublished Ph.D. thesis, University of London, 1982), p. 172; *British Export Gazette*, 31, 371 (November 1938); *British Trade Journal and Export World*, 76, 910 (December 1938); *The Times*, 17–19 November 1938, report on 'German trade aims'.
63. Lewis, *Economic Survey*, p. 92; Guillebaud, *Economic Recovery*, p. 148.
64. CAB 24/277, CP127, 24 May 1938; Einzig, *Appeasement*, p. 91; Middlemas, *Diplomacy of Illusion*, p. 258.
65. See, in particular, D. Cameron Watt, *How War Came: The Immediate Origins of the Second World War, 1938–1939* (Heinemann, 1989), pp. 162–87, 395-403.
66. M.J. Rooke, 'The British Government's Relations with the States of South Eastern Europe, 1934–36' (unpublished Ph.D.thesis, University of London, 1980), p. 201.
67. CAB 24/280, CP257, 10 November 1938.
68. Kaiser, *Economic Diplomacy*, p. 286. The countries of the region would then have been in a position to purchase more from the British Empire.
69. Gillingham, *Industry and Politics*, pp. 96–8.
70. Rooth, *British Protectionism*, p. 280.
71. *The Times*, 2 March 1939. See Gillingham, *Industry and Politics*, p. 91, for the Ruhr's insistence upon applying the *Gruppenschutz* principle which was concerned to prevent competition in established markets; the British industry committed itself to form syndicates.
72. CAB 23/97, 3(39), 1 February 1939; FO 371/22950/C1343, Leith-Ross to Stanley, 31 January 1939. For Chamberlain's reaction to the speech by the Duke of Coburg, at an Anglo-German Fellowship dinner in Berlin, which

welcomed the coal agreement, see NC 18/1/1086, letter to Hilda, 19 February 1939.
73. DGFP, Ser. D, Vol.II, No.279, report by Wohltat, 4 July 1939.
74. Wendt, *Economic Appeasement*, p. 604; S.Aster, *1939: The Making of the Second World War* (Deutsch, 1973), p. 233; DBFP, 3rd Ser., Vol.V, No. 741, minute by Ashton-Gwatkin, 7 June 1939.
75. DGFP, Ser. D, Vol.VI, No.716, Berlin, 24 July 1939; DBFP, 3rd Ser., Vol.VI, No.354, 18 July 1939. See also MacDonald, 'Economic Appeasement', p. 129; MacDonald concludes that while Wohltat probably inflated the contents of the talk and Wilson might have implied more than he subsequently claimed, the approach to the German official was sanctioned by Chamberlain as a last attempt.
76. DBFP, 3rd Ser., Vol.VI, No.370, 20 July 1939; DGFP, Ser. D, Vol.VI, No.698.
77. FO 371/22990/C10371, minute by Sargent, 24 July 1939; DGFP, Ser. D, Vol.VI, No.718, 24 July 1939.
78. D. Dilks (ed.), *The Diaries of Sir Alexander Cadogan O.M. 1938–1945* (Cassell, 1971), pp. 128,150. On the British press and international reaction, see D. Cameron Watt, *How War Came*, pp. 399–401.
79. NC 18/1/1108, letter to Ida, 23 July 1939.
80. NC 18/1/1110, letter to Hilda, 30 July 1939.

Conclusion

From Britain's perspective, the economic dimension to the 'German problem' was present long before the onset of the Great Depression. Under the impact of the financial crisis of 1931 the cancellation of reparations before the end of the Hoover Year became a major objective of policy towards Germany. This position commanded the support of Britain's economic as well as its political élite, although it stimulated a vigorous debate over the significance of reparation payments. Planning to remove an economic handicap from a great trading rival, just when Britain was discovering a new national purpose, was not popular in some business quarters and dissentient voices were raised. But commercial interests in general were poised to derive considerable benefit from the competitive advantage which tariffs and the devaluation of sterling had suddenly given to Britain. In pressing for cancellation of reparations and debts, Britain could afford to discount the commercial risks inherent in a reinvigoration of the German economy. The risks in taking no action seemed, in comparison, infinitely greater – potentially a widespread financial collapse which would severely damage the international position of the City of London. The prevention of such a calamity was an urgent and overriding priority.

On those grounds, the National Government put British banking interests above those of commerce in the struggle to carry on business in late Weimar Germany. Some Whitehall officials demurred; their argument was that relief for commercial interests had to be secured, even if that left the position of banking creditors unprotected.[1] Yet, while everyone in government recognized that it was desirable to liquidate trade debts, official policy before 1933 was shaped by the assumption that the most formidable obstacle to the revival of Britain's export trade was the stoppage of acceptance business.

Distracted by imperial concerns, Britain was slow to identify the political dangers which were inherent in the economic dislocation of Germany. For as long as the Weimar Republic was allowed to continue in a condition of economic distress, fertile ground was provided for Communists and National Socialists to sow their seeds of discontent. Again, there was equivocation over the response which was required from Britain. The Foreign Office was attracted to the idea of using economic concessions as a political weapon. Vansittart desired to see reparations ended, but in exchange for a 'political truce' with Germany; he believed he shared with the public the feeling that getting everything for nothing was not right. Nevertheless, it soon became obvious that a prompt cancellation of reparations stood the best chance of disrupting the dynamic which was leading to the political deterioration of Europe. Conversely, to wait for the most suitable international climate, in order to give the Lausanne Conference the greatest chance of success, was to risk indefinite delay and to court disaster. Although the dire warnings of collapse which issued from Berlin did not go unheeded, Britain was obliged to engineer postponement of the conference.

The concurrent revolution in Britain's external economic policies had a more direct and adverse effect on Germany. The reparations settlement at Lausanne – notwithstanding the effect of the delay – together with Brüning's ruthless deflation policy and the Standstill Agreement, might have succeeded in turning round the Republic's economy. But Germany's effort to attain price and exchange equilibrium was brought to nothing by the depreciation of sterling. The circumstances of the financial crisis did not allow time for consideration of the likely international ramifications of the departure from gold. But the economic and hence the political problems of the Weimar Republic were compounded when Britain brought in protectionism. Just as some of the burdens imposed by Versailles were being lifted, Britain turned to beggar-my-neighbour policies. The triumph of political extremism in Germany – the very danger that co-ordinated diplomatic action was designed to avert – was not long delayed.

Once Hitler had become Chancellor it was difficult to know how, if at all, the damage could be repaired. In an age of nationalism and dictatorship, the democratic powers were aware that little would be achieved by conducting diplomacy along traditional lines. In this respect, economic issues were clearly taking on a new significance. Most pressing of all was the need to revise the criteria for assessing the nature of the risks attached to different policies. As the Nazis tightened their grip on power, opinion in Britain divided over the question of the revitalization of the German economy. Whitehall energetically sought to form a realistic picture of the Third Reich. What was required was an answer to the riddle of whether, by withholding economic concessions, Germany's privation would act to retard rearmament or whether growing prosperity would supply the antidote to political extremism. The problem was one of finding the right circumstances and the right time to offer concessions. When, by the mid 1930s, the threatening scale of Nazi rearmament could no longer be ignored, the spectacle of economic recovery staged by Hitler began to pall. By then, fearful of the hazardous consequences which were likely to follow any radical shift in its position, Britain was paralysed: no move could be made either to promote or stifle German economic recovery.

Nazi attitudes towards the servicing of Germany's medium- and long-term foreign debts ensured that the issue would move from the private and institutional sphere into the realm of international politics. To Britain's surprise and great disappointment, Schacht embarked upon a mission to discriminate between creditor nations in order to split one from another. The Third Reich could then begin the process of withdrawing from its international obligations. These objectives were partially realized. Britain's attempts to co-ordinate diplomatic action with America in protest over the challenge to the Dawes and Young loans could not be sustained.

In addition to the bondholders, conditions for British exporters deteriorated rapidly after 1933. Furthermore, Schacht welcomed the divisions opening up between the different classes of British creditor as a weakness to be exploited. If dealing with the Nazi challenge was to mean something more than a constant stream of defensive reactions, a strategy had to be devised for managing the competing claims arising from the diverse range of Britain's commercial and financial interests. The task was made considerably greater because institutional constraints prevented the formulation of a coherent foreign economic policy. Just when Britain's external role was being reshaped and new international dangers were emerging, the powers and areas of competence of government departments and financial institutions suddenly seemed very poorly defined. Behind a facade of unity, the apparatus of the British state was riven by rivalries. The Board of Trade was highly suspicious of the activities of the Foreign

Office, while the extreme hostility the latter showed to the attitudes of the Bank of England, and to the machinations of Montagu Norman, has been underestimated.

But was the power of finance so over-weening that it influenced policy towards Germany to the detriment of the wider national interest? Demonstrably, the City was in a privileged position in relation to other commercial interests because its representatives enjoyed easy access to the inner counsels of government. The banking community feared that any form of exchange-clearing system – but especially a clearing arrangement – would deprive it of part of its business. Justification for this stance was found in the belief that the Standstill would be put in jeopardy. In vigorously supporting the bankers, the Bank of England was prepared to take extraordinary and clandestine steps to ensure the success of an alternative payments structure – the novel device of the Payments Agreement. The reluctance within the Treasury to implement a policy of clearings was in no small measure attributable to the influence of banking circles. Consequently, calls from exporters and others for a stringent exchange control arrangement were resisted. Traders were made to wait while the problems of the bondholders received attention.

But, beyond that, no preference was shown to finance. Whatever the extent of the pressure applied by the banking lobby, the Treasury remained even-handed in the task of trying to reconcile different interests. As the conflict of opinion between the clearing banks and the acceptance houses shows, there was no unanimity as to the wisdom of maintaining credits in Germany. It is even doubtful whether the bankers themselves should be seen as an homogeneous interest group. They were unable to extract a clear commitment from the government to recognize the special position of the Standstill. Although the bankers represented an important class of creditors, the Treasury did not forget that there were many other interests tied up in doing business with Germany.

Claims that there was a fusion of interests between the City and government cannot be substantiated. There is no evidence of anything which was even remotely conspiratorial about the relationship. The government would certainly have brought in a clearing system in 1934 and 1938 if negotiations with Germany had failed to secure adequate protection for other commercial and financial interests. Complaints from the City that British policy was endangering the Standstill were rejected. While the German short-term debts held by London were a significant factor in helping to determine the structure of policy towards Germany, they remained, after all, just one of several.

At first sight, the special characteristics of the Payments Agreement seemed to favour Germany. The arrangement quickly became the foundation on which business with the Third Reich was constructed or reconstructed. As such, it was also seen as a possible vehicle for making a political approach to Germany. In part, this rested on the mistaken assumption that the Nazi régime comprised moderates and extremists. In seeking to understand the realities of power in the Third Reich, the British political élite were deluded in thinking that Schacht might be a moderating influence, even though he was excoriated for his fraudulent and duplicitous behaviour.

But the Payments Agreement cannot therefore be dismissed as a form of appeasement. Throughout the decade Britain inhabited a world in which there was a constant struggle over Standstill and long-term market debt, and advances to the BIS (which largely formed the cover for BIS long-term debts due to reparations creditors in France and Germany itself). The prospect, as surveyed by Britain's financial authorities, was not altogether pleasing. Although nothing effectively protected the BIS debts, the Payments Agreement – and behind it the threat of a clearing – protected at least the interest of the long-term market and Standstill debts.[2] The amounts involved were not trivial. Total British financial claims on Germany stood at some £135m in late 1937.[3] As the Hitler dictatorship was established, Britain acted to protect, as far as possible, the whole range of her economic and financial interests and vigorously defended the position until the outbreak of war.

Above all else, the Payments Agreement reflected a broad concern to remain as flexible as possible over international trade issues. Britain was highly conscious that, although Germany had been left to suffer the economic and political consequences of the flight from multilateralism, she was, none the less, still expected to uphold a range of international financial obligations. The agreement was felt to be justified, therefore, because it was a comparatively liberal structure which offered, at the same time, some protection for Britain's wider economic interests. It was maintained because it seemed to be the least worst option: Britain could imagine that she had preserved a vestige of the old free trade order and was providing a means to guide Germany away from the extremes of autarky and nationalism. The futility of holding such aspirations was revealed in the course of 1938; attention focused instead on how the agreement affected the strategic defence of the nation. Arguments for and against a fundamental change were finely balanced. But, given the circumstances of the belated rearmament effort it was feared that Britain's security would be impaired rather than enhanced by abrogating the agreement.

In the second half of the 1930s the thrust of British policy was mostly in the direction of seeking to foster agreements between British and German industry and to tackle the growing problem of competition in world export markets. The National Government hoped thereby to achieve a basis for working towards a political understanding. Accommodation rather than confrontation was seen as the way out of the impasse. But little came of the efforts to arrange industrial agreements. The negotiations could not progress within the terms set for them. On the one hand government in Britain was ideologically unsuited to persuade industry to co-operate and, on the other, the political control of industry in the Third Reich extended even further than British industrialists feared.

More importantly, with anxieties over the fragility of Britain's own recovery remaining at a high level, the National Government and its supporters were determined to persevere with the new economic strategy. No evidence can be found to give credence to interpretations of British foreign policy which suggest that vital commercial interests were sacrificed for the sake of political approaches. However persuasive the case for the economic appeasement of Hitler's Germany, domestic conditions simply left no room for manoeuvre. Although the legacy bequeathed to Britain by the depression and the financial crisis was a deeply disturbing one, there could be no retreat from protectionism and a managed currency. The paper schemes of the economic appeasers counted for nothing against the harsh realities of the commercial world. British manufacturers, readily supported by the economic departments of government, easily won the argument for extra protection against imports from Germany.

In all parts of British society there was a concern to protect the commercial livelihood of firms trading with Nazi Germany. In addition, any interruption to Anglo-German trade might have provoked a worsening in Germany's domestic position and, consequently, the international climate – the very thing which

Britain most wanted to avoid. Firms such as IG Farben were always seen to be at the centre of the Nazi rearmament effort; an appreciation that it was unrealistic to draw distinctions between industrial organizations in a command economy – which was itself so powerfully directed towards furthering rearmament – took longer to develop. The deteriorating international situation in the second half of the decade naturally dictated a more prudent approach. It then became appropriate to ask whether Britain should trade with the Third Reich at all. It was assumed that the consequences of stopping trade would be disastrous. The consequences of continuing to trade were, at least, uncertain. The time to engage in economic warfare was at the outbreak of war, not before.

Throughout the 1930s industry resisted the idea that the organization of Britain's armaments production would be best served by the imposition of government controls. Industrial leaders knew full well that, in ideological terms at least, they could count on the sympathies of the National Government. However, Chamberlain's reluctance to intervene was based more on a concern that the resistance of industry would disrupt the rearmament effort and the economy as a whole.[4] Similarly, there was no desire within government to set up controls or even to draw up guidelines on how Britain might continue to trade internationally in strategic raw materials. The commitment to non-intervention was tinged with pragmatism: nothing was to be done to alienate the National Government's business supporters. Some of the raw material transactions were brought to the attention of the government; it seems likely that many more were not. When a British firm ran into difficulties the case was treated individually and on its own merits. As the dilemma over whether to supply vital raw materials to the Third Reich could not be resolved, a clear and consistent policy never emerged.

Just as haphazard were the attempts to formulate policy over the related matter of providing new credits to the Third Reich, and to communicate this policy to the financial and commercial world. A partial Treasury embargo on long-term foreign issues was imposed in 1930 and intensified in 1931. But no law was ever passed against anybody giving a commercial credit to Nazi Germany and it was unnecessary, of course, to obtain permission from the Foreign Transactions Advisory Committee.[5] Nevertheless, the operation of the City's credit machinery was effectively constrained by political factors. Montagu Norman certainly resented such interference, but he did not want to see the Bank of England exposed to criticism in Parliament over the question of new lending to Germany.[6]

It is frequently asserted that Britain was extremely reluctant to relinquish the idea of empire in the twentieth century. This is supposed to have impeded the development of an alternative vision – the nation as an important member of a family of European nations. The uncertainty in Britain over the rejection of economic internationalism did not dissipate after the traumatic upheavals of 1931/32 but rather grew in intensity in the years before the Second World War. Sterling's devaluation and the imposition of tariffs opened up a breach with Europe. In the face of economic nationalism at home and abroad, leading figures in British commercial and political life struggled to prevent a complete breakdown in economic relations with Germany – by far the most important trading partner in Europe. Many feared that their problems were partially self-inflicted: the new economic burdens which Britain, in abandoning multilateralism, had imposed on Germany had helped to bring on the collapse of the Weimar Republic. Such guilt-ridden anxieties over the effects of British strategy became more pronounced in the course of the 1930s.

The consequences were severely destabilizing; a consensus on how the national interest should be redefined was never achieved. Ultimately, in trying to confront the growing menace of the Third Reich, Britain failed to devise mechanisms which could reconcile a panoply of political, financial, economic and strategic considerations. A self-confident and powerful nation would have found this a difficult task to accomplish. For Britain, with resources stretched to the limit, it was quite impossible.

NOTES

1. FO 371/15954/C8042, memo, by Rowe-Dutton, 14 October 1932.
2. BoE OV9/100, minute by Sir Otto Niemeyer, 17 January 1938.
3. T 160/759/14466/1, estimate (undated) by Waley, based on a memo, by Lever (of the Prudential). The total comprised: Standstill – £44m., Dawes and Young loans – £26m, non-Reich loans – £21m, states and rents – £37m, and Funding Bonds – £7m.
4. R.P. Shay, *British Rearmament in the Thirties* (Princeton, NJ: Princeton University Press, 1977), pp. 291–3.
5. RIIA, *The Essential Interests of the United Kingdom: Vol.I* (1938), p. 71. The committee was set up in 1936 to examine all foreign borrowing proposals.
6. Per Jacobsen papers (British Library of Political and Economic Science), Diary, Vol.3, conversation with Norman, 6 April 1936. Per Jacobsen was Head of the Monetary and Economic Department, BIS.

Bibliography

Unpublished Sources

Private papers (individuals and organizations)
Bank of England Archive, Bank of England, London
Lord Brand papers, Bodleian Library, University of Oxford
BP Amoco Archive, University of Warwick
Neville Chamberlain papers, University of Birmingham Library
Malcolm Grahame Christie papers, Churchill Archives Centre, Churchill
  College, Cambridge
Paul Einzig papers, Churchill Archives Centre, Churchill College,
  Cambridge
Federal Reserve Bank of New York Archive, New York
Federation of British Industries Archive, Modern Records Centre,
  University of Warwick
Group Archives, HSBC Holdings plc, Midland Bank Archives
Sir Maurice Hankey papers, Churchill Archives Centre, Churchill College,
  Cambridge
Per Jacobsen papers, Archives Division, British Library of Political and
  Economic Science
National Archives, Washington, DC
Sir Eric Phipps papers, Churchill Archives Centre, Churchill College,
  Cambridge
Political and Economic Planning, Archives Division, British Library of
  Political and Economic Science
Viscount Runciman of Doxford papers (Walter Runciman), Robinson
  Library, University of Newcastle upon Tyne
Sir John Simon papers, Bodleian Library, University of Oxford
Sir Robert Vansittart papers, Churchill Archives Centre, Churchill College,
  Cambridge
Vickers Archive, Cambridge University Library

Public Record Office
Cabinet: CAB 23   Minutes and Conclusions of Cabinet Meetings
                  CAB 24   Cabinet Papers (Memoranda)
                  CAB 27   Cabinet Committees
PREM I: Prime Minister's Office
Board of Trade: BT 11   Commercial Relations and Treaties
                            Department
                  BT 59   Overseas Trade Development Council
                  BT 64   List of Industries involved in FBI–RGI
                            discussions
Foreign Office: FO 371   Country Series (Political/Central
                            Department/Germany)
                  FO 800   285-91: private papers of Sir Alexander
                            Cadogan, Lord Halifax, Sir Orme Sargent, Sir
                            John Simon
Treasury   T 160   Overseas Finance Division (the 'F' preceding
                            the piece number is omitted from this class)
                  T172   Chancellor of the Exchequer's Office
                  T177   Sir Frederick Phillips papers
                  T188   Sir Frederick Leith-Ross papers

Theses

Diaper, S.J., 'The History of Kleinwort, Sons & Co., in Merchant Banking,
    1855–1961' (Ph.D., University of Nottingham, 1983).
Eyers, J.S., 'Government Direction of Overseas Trade Policy in Britain,
    1932–37' (D.Phil., Oxford University, 1977).
McCulloch, T.K., 'Anglo-American Economic Diplomacy in the European
    Crisis 1935–39' (D.Phil., Oxford University, 1979).
Rooke, M.J., 'The British Government's Relations with the States of South-
    Eastern Europe, 1934–36' (Ph.D., University of London, 1980).
Van Kessel, G.J., 'The British Reaction to German Economic Penetration in
    South-Eastern Europe, 1936–1939' (Ph.D., University of London,
    1972).

Published Sources

Official publications

Documents on British Foreign Policy, 1919–1945, 2nd and 3rd Series
    (HMSO, 1946 on).
Documents on German Foreign Policy, 1918–1945, Series C and D
    (HMSO, 1948 on).
Parliamentary Debates (House of Commons).

Parliamentary Papers (Command Papers).
UK Customs and Excise Department, *Annual Statement of the Trade of the United Kingdom* (1931–1939).
UK Department of Overseas Trade, *Economic Conditions in Germany: Annual Reports* (1931–1934, 1936).

Publications by organizations

League of Nations, *Monetary and Economic Conference* (Geneva, 1933).
—— *Commercial Banks 1925–1933* (Geneva, 1934).
—— *Present Phase of International Economic Relations* (Geneva, 1937).
—— *British External Economic Policies* (Paris, 1939).
—— *Commercial Policy in the Interwar Period: International Proposals and National Policies* (Geneva, 1942).
—— (Nurske, R.) *International Currency Experience: Lessons of the Interwar Period* (Geneva, 1944).
Royal Institute of International Affairs, *The Problem of International Investment* (1937).
—— *Germany's Claim to Colonies* (1938).
—— *Anglo-American Trade Relations* (1938).
—— *The Essential Interests of the United Kingdom: Vol.I* (1938).
—— *South-Eastern Europe* (1939).

Newspapers and periodicals

British Export Gazette.
British Trade Journal and Export World.
Daily Telegraph.
Economist.
Financial News.
Financial Times.
Manchester Guardian.
New Statesman.
The Banker.
The Times.

Books and articles

Adamthwaite, A. P., *The Making of the Second World War* (Allen & Unwin, 1979).
Aldcroft, D.H., *The Inter-War Economy: Britain, 1919–1939* (Batsford, 1970).
—— *From Versailles to Wall Street, 1919–1929* (Allen Lane, 1977).
—— *The European Economy 1914–1970* (Croom Helm, 1978).
Alford, B.W.E. *Depression and Recovery? British Economic Growth 1918–1939* (Macmillan, 1972).
—— 'New industries for old? British industry between the wars', in R. Floud and D. McCloskey (eds), *The Economic History of Britain since 1700: Vol.2* (Cambridge: Cambridge University Press, 1981).

Anderson, D.G., 'British rearmament and the "merchants of death": The 1935–36 Royal Commission on the Manufacture of and Trade in Armaments', *JCH*, 29 (1994).

Andrews, C., *Secret Service: The Making of the British Intelligence Community* (Heinemann, 1985).

Arndt, H.W., *The Economic Lessons of the Nineteen Thirties* (Oxford University Press, 1944).

Ashton-Gwatkin, F.T., *The British Foreign Service* (New York: Syracuse University Press, 1950).

Aster, S., *1939: the Making of the Second World War* (André Deutsch, 1973).

Balderston, T., *The Origins and Course of the German Economic Crisis 1923–1932* (Berlin: Haude & Spener, 1993).

Balfour, M., *Withstanding Hitler in Germany 1933–45* (Routledge, 1988).

Bamberg, J.H., *The History of the British Petroleum Company: Vol.2, The Anglo-Iranian Years, 1928–1954* (Cambridge: Cambridge University Press, 1994).

Barkai, A., *Nazi Economics: Ideology,Theory, and Policy* (Oxford: Berg, 1990).

Barnes, J. and Nicholson, D. (eds), *The Empire at Bay: The Leo Amery Diaries, 1929–1945* (Hutchinson, 1988).

Barnett, C., *The Collapse of British Power* (Stroud: Sutton, 1984).

Bassett, R., *Nineteen Thirty-One: Political Crisis* (Macmillan, 1958).

Beloff, M., 'The Whitehall Factor: the role of the higher civil servant 1919–39', in G. Peele and C. Cook (eds), *The Politics of Reappraisal, 1918–1939* (Macmillan, 1975).

Benham, F., 'the muddle of the thirties', *Economica*, 12 (1945).

Bennett, E.W., *Germany and the Diplomacy of the Financial Crisis, 1931* (Cambridge, MA: Havard University Press, 1962).

—— *German Rearmament and the West, 1932–1933* (Princeton, NJ: Princeton University Press, 1979).

Bidwell, P., 'Prospects of a Trade Agreement with England', *Foreign Affairs*, 16 (1937/38).

Blum, J.M., *From the Morgenthau Diaries: Years of Crisis, 1928–1938* (Boston, MA: Houghton Mifflin, 1959).

Boelcke, W.A., *Die Kosten von Hitlers Krieg: Kriegsfinanzierung und Kriegserbe in Deutschland 1933–1948* (Paderborn: Schöningh, 1985).

—— *Deutschland als Welthandelsmacht 1930–1945* (Stuttgart: W. Kohlhammer, 1994).

Borchardt, K., 'Could and Should Germany have followed Great Britain in leaving the Gold Standard?', *JEEH*, 13, 3, Winter (1984).

Booth, A., *British Economic Policy, 1931–49* (Hemel Hempstead: Harvester Wheatsheaf, 1989).

—— 'The British reaction to the economic crisis', in W.R.Garside (ed.),

Capitalism in Crisis: International responses to the Great Depression (Pinter, 1993).

Born, K.E., *Die deutsche Bankenkrise 1931* (München: Piper, 1967).

—— *International Banking in the 19th and 20th Centuries* (Leamington Spa: Berg, 1983).

Boyce, R.W.D., *British Capitalism at the Crossroads, 1919–1932* (Cambridge: Cambridge University Press, 1987).

—— 'World depression, world war: some economic origins of the Second World War', in R.W.D. Boyce and E.M. Robertson (eds), *Paths to War: New Essays on the Origins of the Second World War* (Basingstoke: Macmillan, 1989).

Boyle, A., *Montagu Norman: A Biography* (Cassell, 1967).

Bracher, K.D., *Die Auflösung der Weimarer Republik* (Stuttgart: Ring-Verlag, 1955).

—— *Deutschland zwischen Demokratie und Diktatur* (Bern: Scherz, 1964).

Brand, Lord, 'A banker's reflections on some economic trends', *Economic Journal*, 63, 252 (December 1953).

Branson, N. and Heinemann, N., *Britain in the Nineteen Thirties* (St. Albans: Panther, 1973).

Bruck, W.F., *Social and Economic History of Germany from Wilhelm II to Hitler* (New York, NY: Russell & Russell, 1962).

Brüning, H., *Memoiren 1918–34* (Stuttgart: Deutsche Verlags-Anstalt, 1970).

Bullock, A., *Hitler and Stalin: Parallel Lives* (BCA/HarperCollins, 1991).

Burk, K., *Morgan Grenfell 1838–1988: The Biography of a Merchant Bank* (Oxford: Oxford University Press, 1989).

Buxton, N.K., 'The role of "new" industries in Britain during the 1930s: A reinterpretation', *Business History Review*, 44, 2 (1975).

Buxton, N.K. and Aldcroft, D.H. (eds) *British Industry between the Wars: Instability and Industrial Development 1919–1939* (Scolar Press, 1979).

Cain, P.J. and Hopkins, A.G., *British Imperialism: Crisis and Deconstruction 1914–1990* (Longman, 1993).

Cairncross, A. and Eichengreen, B., *Sterling in Decline* (Oxford: Basil Blackwell, 1983).

Capie, F., *Depression and Protectionism: Britain between the Wars* (Allen & Unwin, 1983).

Caplan, J., *Government without Administration: State and Civil Service in Weimar and Nazi Germany* (Oxford: Clarendon Press, 1988).

Carroll, B.A., *Design for Total War: Arms and Economics in the Third Reich* (The Hague: Mouton, 1968).

Chapman, S.D., *The Rise of Merchant Banking* (Allen & Unwin, 1984).

Child, F.C., *The Theory and Practice of Exchange Control in Germany: A Study of Monopolistic Exploitation in International Markets* (The Hague: Martinus Nijhoff, 1958).

Clarke, P., 'The Treasury's analytical model of the British economy between the wars', in M.O. Furner and B. Supple (eds), *The State and Economic Knowledge* (Cambridge: Cambridge University Press, 1990).

—— *Hope and Glory: Britain 1900–1990* (Penguin, 1996).

Clarke, S.V.O., *Central Bank Co-operation, 1924–31* (New York, NY: Federal Reserve Bank, 1967).

—— *Exchange-Rate Stabilisation in the Mid-1930s: Negotiating the Tripartite Agreement* (Princeton, NJ: Princeton University Press, 1977).

Clavin, P., 'The World Economic Conference 1933: The failure of British internationalism', *JEEH*, 20, 3 (Winter 1991).

Clay, Sir H., *Lord Norman* (Macmillan, 1957).

Coghlan, F., 'Armaments, economic policy and appeasement. Background to British foreign policy, 1937–39', *History*, 57 (1972).

Colvin, I., *Vansittart in Office* (Victor Gollancz, 1965).

Conze, W. and Raupach, H., *Die Staats – und Wirtschaftskrise des deutschen Reichs 1929/33* (Stuttgart: Klett, 1967).

Cottrell, P.L., 'The Bank of England in its international setting, 1918–1972', in R. Roberts and D. Kynaston (eds), *The Bank of England: Money, Power and Influence 1694–1994* (Oxford: Clarendon Press, 1995).

Cowling, M., *The Impact of Hitler: British Politics and British Policy 1933–1940* (Cambridge: Cambridge University Press, 1975).

Dayer, R.A., *Finance and Empire: Sir Charles Addis, 1861–1945* (Basingstoke: Macmillan, 1988).

Deist, W. et al. (eds), *Germany and the Second World War* (Oxford: Clarendon Press, 1990).

Deist, W. (ed.), *The German Military in the Age of Total War* (Leamington Spa: Berg, 1985).

Dilks, D. (ed.), *The Diaries of Sir Alexander Cadogan OM 1938–1945* (Cassell, 1971).

—— 'Appeasement and "intelligence"', in D. Dilks (ed.), *Retreat from Power: Studies in Britain's Foreign Policy of the Twentieth Century. Vol.1, 1906–1939* (Macmillan, 1981).

Drummond, I.M., *British Economic Policy and the Empire, 1919–1939* (Allen & Unwin, 1972).

—— *Imperial Economic Policy, 1917–1939: Studies in Expansion and Protection* (Allen & Unwin, 1974).

—— *The Floating Pound and the Sterling Area, 1931–1939* (Cambridge: Cambridge University Press, 1981).

Dutton, D., *Simon: A Political Biography of Sir John Simon* (Aurum Press, 1992).

Eichengreen, B., *Golden Fetters: the Gold Standard and the Great Depression, 1919–1939* (Oxford: Oxford University Press, 1992).

Einzig, P., *Germany's Default: The Economics of Hitlerism* (Macmillan, 1934).

—— *World Finance: Vol.1, 1914–35* (New York, NY: Arno Press, 1978).

—— *Appeasement Before, During and After the War* (Macmillan, 1942).

—— *In the Centre of Things* (Hutchinson, 1960).

Ellis, H.S., *Exchange Control in Central Europe* (Cambridge, MA: Harvard University Press, 1941).

Erbe, R., *Die nationalsozialistische Wirtschaftspolitik 1933–1939 im Lichte der modernen Theorie* (Zurich: Polygraphischer Verlag, 1958).

Eucken, W., 'On the theory of the centrally administered economy: An analysis of the German experiment', *Economica*, 15, Pt I, 58 and Pt II, 59 (1948).

Eyck, E., *A History of the Weimar Republic: Vol.2* (Cambridge, MA: Harvard University Press, 1964).

Feiling, K., *The Life of Neville Chamberlain* (Macmillan, 1946).

Feinstein, C.H., *National Income, Expenditure and Output of the United Kingdom, 1885–1965* (Cambridge: Cambridge University Press, 1972).

Feis, H., *1933: Characters in Crisis* (Boston, MA: Little, Brown, 1966).

Ferris, J.R., 'The Air Force brats' view of history: Recent writing and the Royal Air Force, 1918–1960', *International History Review*, 20, 1 (March 1998).

—— '"The greatest power on earth": Great Britain in the 1920s', *International History Review*, 13, 4 (November 1991).

Fischer, A.G.B., 'Economic appeasement as a means to political understanding and peace', *Survey of International Affairs: I* (Royal Institute of International Affairs, 1937).

—— *Economic Self-Sufficiency* (Oxford: Clarendon Press, 1939).

Forbes, N., 'London banks, the German Standstill Agreements, and "economic appeasement" in the 1930s', *EcHR*, 2nd ser., 40, 4 (November 1987).

Forster, F., *Geschichte der Deutschen BP 1904–1979* (Hamburg: Deutsche BP/Reuter & Klöckner, 1979).

Francis, E.V., *Britain's Economic Strategy* (Jonathan Cape, 1939).

Fry, G.K., *Statesmen in Disguise: The Changing Role of the Administrative Class of the British Home Civil Service 1853–1939* (Macmillan, 1969).

Fry, R., 'The work of a financial journalist', *Manchester Statistical Society paper* (Manchester, 1945).

Gannon, F.R., *The British Press and Germany 1936–1939* (Oxford: Clarendon Press, 1971).

Garside, W.R., *British Unemployment, 1919–1939* (Cambridge: Cambridge University Press, 1990).

Garside W.R. and Greaves, J.I., 'The Bank of England and industrial intervention in interwar Britain', *Financial History Review*, 3, 1 (April 1996).

—— 'Rationalisation and Britain's industrial malaise: the interwar years revisited', *JEEH*, 26, 1 (Spring 1997).

Geyer, M., 'Military revisionism in the interwar years', in W. Deist (ed.),

The German Military in the Age of Total War (Leamington Spa: Berg, 1985).

Gilbert, M., *The Roots of Appeasement* (Weidenfeld & Nicolson, 1967).

Gillingham, J., *Industry and Politics in the Third Reich: Ruhr coal, Hitler and Europe* (Methuen, 1985). .

Gladwyn, Lord, *The Memoirs of Lord Gladwyn* (Weidenfeld & Nicolson, 1972).

Glynn, S. and Oxborrow, J., *Inter-war Britain: A Social and Economic History* (Allen & Unwin, 1976).

Graves, R. and Hodge, A., *The Long Weekend: A Social History of Great Britain 1918–1939* (Hutchinson, 1985).

Green, E.H.H., 'The influence of the City over British economic policy, c.1880 – 1960', in Y. Cassis (ed.), *Finance and Financiers in European History, 1880 –1960* (Cambridge: Cambridge University Press, 1992).

Gregory, T.E., *The Gold Standard and its Future* (Methuen, 1934).

—— 'Lord Norman: A new interpretation', *Lloyds Bank Review*, 88 (1968).

Griffiths, R., *Fellow Travellers of the Right* (Constable, 1980).

Guillebaud, C.W., *The Economic Recovery of Germany from 1933 to the Incorporation of Austria in March 1938* (Macmillan, 1939).

Hannah, L., *The Rise of the Corporate Economy* (Methuen, 1983).

Hardach, K., *The Political Economy of Germany in the Twentieth Century* (Berkeley, CA: University of California Press, 1980).

Harris, C.R.S., *Germany's Foreign Indebtedness* (Oxford: Oxford University Press, 1935).

Harvey, J. (ed.), *The Diplomatic Diaries of Oliver Harvey, 1937–40* (Collins,1970).

Hawtrey, R.G., *The Art of Central Banking* (Longman, 1932).

Hayes, P., *Industry and Ideology: IG Farben in the Nazi Era* (Cambridge: Cambridge University Press, 1987).

Heineman, J.L., 'Constantin von Neurath and German policy at the London Economic Conference of 1933: Backgrounds to the resignation of Alfred Hugenberg', *JMH*, 41 (1969).

Helbich, W.J., *Die Reparationen in der Ära Brüning* (Berlin: Colloquium Verlag, 1962).

Henderson, H.D., *The Inter-war Years and Other Papers* (Oxford: Clarendon Press, 1955).

Hillman, H., 'The comparative strengths of the great powers', *Survey of International Affairs: the World in March 1939* (Royal Institute of International Affairs, 1939).

Hodson, H.V,. *Slump and Recovery 1929–1937* (Oxford: Oxford University Press, 1938).

Holland, R.F., 'The Federation of British Industries and the international economy, 1929–39', *EcHR*, 2nd series, 34, 2 (May 1981).

Holmes, A.R. and Green, E., *Midland: 150 Years of Banking Business* (Batsford, 1986).

Howson, S., *Domestic Monetary Management in Britain 1919–38* (Cambridge: Cambridge University Press, 1975).

Howson, S. and Winch, D., *The Economic Advisory Council 1930–1939* (Cambridge: Cambridge University Press, 1977).

Hull, C., *The Memoirs of Cordell Hull* (Hodder & Stoughton, 1948).

Ingham, G., *Capitalism Divided? The City and Industry in British Social Development* (Macmillan, 1984).

Jacobsen, H.A., *Nationalsozialistische Aussenpolitik 1933–38* (Frankfurt-am-Main: Metzner, 1968).

Jaitner, K., 'Aspekete britischer Deutschlandpolitik 1930–32', in J. Becker and K. Hildebrand (eds), *Internationale Beziehungen in der Weltwirtschaftskrise 1929–1933* (München: Vögel, 1980).

James, H., *The Reichsbank and Public Finance in Germany 1924–1933* (Frankfurt-am-Main: F.Knapp, 1985).

—— *The German Slump: Politics and Economics, 1924–1936* (Oxford: Clarendon Press, 1986).

—— 'Innovation and conservatism in economic recovery: The alleged "Nazi recovery" of the 1930s', in T. Childers and J. Caplan (eds), *Reevaluating the Third Reich* (New York, NY: Holmes & Meier, 1993).

James, H., Lindgren, H., Teichova, A. (eds), *The Role of Banks in the Interwar Economy* (Cambridge: Cambridge University Press, 1991).

Jones, G., 'The growth and performance of British multinational firms before 1939: The case of Dunlop', *EcHR*, 2nd Series, 37, 1 (February 1984).

—— *British Multinational Banking, 1830 –1990* (Oxford: Clarendon Press, 1993).

Kaiser, D.E., *Economic Diplomacy and the Origins of the Second World War* (Princeton, NY: Princeton University Press, 1980).

Kennedy, P., *The Rise of the Anglo-German Antagonism, 1860–1914* (Allen & Unwin, 1980).

—— *The Realities behind Diplomacy* (Allen & Unwin, 1981).

—— *Strategy and Diplomacy, 1870–1945* (Allen & Unwin, 1983).

—— *The Rise and Fall of the Great Powers: Economic Change and Military Conflict from 1500 to 2000* (New York, NY: Random House, 1987).

Kent, B., *The Spoils of War: the Politics, Economics and Diplomacy of Reparations, 1918–1932* (Oxford: Clarendon Press, 1989).

Kenwood, A.G. and Lougheed, A.L., *The Growth of the International Economy, 1820–1960* (Allen & Unwin, 1971).

Kershaw, I., *The 'Hitler Myth': Image and Reality in the Third Reich* (Oxford: Clarendon Press, 1987).

—— *The Nazi Dictatorship: Problems and Perspectives of Interpretation* (Edward Arnold, 1993).

—— *Hitler. 1889–1936: Hubris* (Allen Lane, 1998).

Keynes, J.M., *The Economic Consequences of the Peace* (Macmillan, 1920).

—— 'Essays in persuasion' (1931), in D. Moggridge (ed.), *The Collected Writings of John Maynard Keynes*, Vol.9 (Macmillan/Cambridge University Press, 1972).

Kindleberger, C.P., *The World in Depression, 1929–1939* (Allen Lane, 1973).

Kirby, M.W., *The Decline of British Economic Power since 1870* (Allen & Unwin, 1981).

Kitson, M. and Solomou, S., *Protectionism and Economic Revival: The British Inter-war Economy* (Cambridge: Cambridge University Press, 1990).

Klein, B.H., *Germany's Economic Preparations for War* (Cambridge, MA: Harvard University Press, 1959).

Kolko, G., 'American business and Germany, 1930–41', *Western Political Quarterly*, 15, 4 (1962).

Kottman, R.N., *Reciprocity and the North Atlantic Triangle, 1932–1938* (New York, NY: Cornell University Press, 1968).

Kreider, C.J., *The Anglo-American Trade Agreement* (Princeton, NJ: Princeton University Press, 1943).

Kunz, D.B., *The Battle for Britain's Gold Standard in 1931* (Croom Helm, 1987).

Leith-Ross, F., *Money Talks: Fifty Years of International Finance* (Hutchinson, 1968).

Leitz, C.M., 'Arms exports from the Third Reich, 1933–39: the example of Krupp', *EcHR*, 51, 1 (February 1998).

Lewis, W.A., *Economic Survey 1919–1939* (Allen & Unwin, 1949).

Ludlow, P., 'Britain and the Third Reich', in H. Bull (ed.), *The Challenge of the Third Reich* (Oxford: Clarendon Press, 1986).

Luther, H., *Vor dem Abgrund 1930–1933: Reichsbank-präsident in Krisenzeiten* (Berlin: Propyläen Verlag, 1964).

MacDonald, C.A., 'Economic appeasement and the German "moderates" 1937– 1939. An introductory essay', *Past and Present*, 56 (1972).

Macmillan, H., *Winds of Change 1914 –1939* (Macmillan, 1966).

Marks, S., *The Illusion of Peace: International Relations in Europe 1918–1933* (Macmillan, 1976).

Marrison, A., *British Business and Protection 1903–1932* (Oxford: Clarendon Press, 1996).

Marsh, D., *The Bundesbank: The Bank that Rules Europe* (William Heinemann, 1992).

Mason, T., 'Some origins of the Second World War', *Past and Present*, 29 (1964).

—— *Social Policy in the Third Reich: The Working Class and the 'National Community'* (Oxford: Berg, 1993).

Matis, H. and Weber, F., 'Economic Anschluss and German *Grossmachtpolitik:* the take-over of the Austrian Credit-Anstalt in 1938', in P.L. Cottrell, H. Lindgren and A. Teichova (eds), *European Industry and Banking Between the Wars* (Leicester: Leicester University Press, 1992).

McKercher, B.J.C., 'Old diplomacy and new: the Foreign Office and foreign policy, 1919–1939', in M. Dockrill and B.J.C. McKercher (eds), *Diplomacy and World Power: Studies in British Foreign Policy, 1880–1950* (Cambridge: Cambridge University Press, 1996).

—— *Transition of Power: Britain's Loss of Global Pre-eminence to the United States, 1930–1945* (Cambridge: Cambridge University Press, 1999).

McMillan, J., *The Dunlop Story* (Weidenfeld & Nicolson, 1989).

Medlicott, W.N., *The History of the Second World War: The Economic Blockade. Vol.1* (HMSO, 1952).

—— *Contemporary England 1914–1964* (Longman, 1967).

—— *Britain and Germany: The Search for Agreement 1930–37* (Athlone Press, 1969).

Meredith, D., 'British trade diversion policy and the "colonial issue" in the 1930s', *JEEH*, 25, 1 (Spring 1996).

Merlin, S., 'Trends in German economic control since 1933', *Quarterly Journal of Economics*, 57 (February 1943).

Middlemas, K. and Barnes, J., *Baldwin: A Biography* (Macmillan, 1969).

Middlemas, K., *Diplomacy of Illusion: The British Government and Germany, 1937–39* (Weidenfeld & Nicolson, 1972).

—— *Politics in Industrial Society* (Andre Deutsch, 1979).

Middleton, R., *Towards the Managed Economy: Keynes, the Treasury and the Fiscal Policy Debate of the 1930s* (Methuen, 1985).

Mommsen, W.J. and Kettenacker, L. (eds), *The Fascist Challenge and the Policy of Appeasement* (Allen & Unwin, 1983).

Morton, W.A., *British Finance, 1930–1940* (Madison, WI: University of Wisconsin Press, 1943).

Moulton, H.G. and Pasvolsky, L., *War Debts and World Prosperity* (Washington, DC: Brookings Institution, 1932).

Nathan, O., *The Nazi Economic System* (Durham, NC: Duke University Press, 1944).

Neal, L., 'The economics and finance of bilateral clearing agreements: Germany 1934–8', *EcHR*, 32, 3 (August 1979).

Newman, S., *March 1939: The British guarantee to Poland* (Oxford: Clarendon Press, 1976).

Newton, S., *Profits of Peace: The Political Economy of Anglo-German Appeasement* (Oxford: Oxford University Press, 1996).

Noel-Baker, P., *The Private Manufacture of Armaments* (Victor Gollancz, 1936).

Orde, A., *British Policy and European Reconstruction after the First World War* (Cambridge: Cambridge University Press, 1990).

Ovendale, R., *'Appeasement' and the English-Speaking World* (Cardiff: University of Wales Press, 1975).

Overy, R.J., *The Nazi Economic Recovery 1932–1938* (Macmillan, 1982).

—— *Goering: The 'Iron Man'* (Routledge & Kegan Paul, 1984).

—— 'Hitler's war plans', in R.W.D. Boyce and E.M. Robertson (eds), *Paths to War: New Essays on the Origins of the Second World War* (Basingstoke: Macmillan, 1989).

—— *War and Economy in the Third Reich* (Oxford: Oxford University Press, 1994).

Oye, K.A., *Economic Discrimination and Political Exchange: World Political Economy in the 1930s and 1980s* (Princeton, NJ: Princeton University Press, 1992).

Parker, R.A.C., 'Economics, rearmament, and foreign policy: The United Kingdom before 1939 – A preliminary study', *JCH*, 10 (1975).

—— 'The pound sterling, the American Treasury and British preparations for war, 1938–1939', *EHR*, 98, 387 (April 1983).

—— *Chamberlain and Appeasement: British Policy and the Coming of the Second World War* (Macmillan, 1993).

Payton-Smith, D.J., *Oil: A Study of Wartime Policy and Administration* (HMSO, 1971).

Peden, G.C., *British Rearmament and the Treasury: 1932–1939* (Edinburgh: Scottish Academic Press, 1979).

—— 'Sir Warren Fisher and British rearmament against Germany', *EHR*, 94, No. 370 (January 1979).

—— 'Sir Richard Hopkins and the "Keynesian revolution" in employment policy, 1929–1945', *EcHR*, 2nd Ser., 36, 2 (May 1983).

—— 'A matter of timing: The economic background to British foreign policy, 1937–1939', *History*, 69 (February 1984).

Pentzlin, H., *Hjalmar Schacht: Leben und Wirken einer unstrittenen Persönlichkeit* (Berlin: Ullstein, 1980).

Petzina, D., *Autarkiepolitik im Dritten Reich* (Stuttgart: Verlags-Anstalt, 1968).

—— 'Germany and the Great Depression', *JCH*, 4 (1969).

—— *Die deutsche Wirtschaft in der Zwischenkriegzeit* (Wiesbaden: Steiner, 1977).

Plummer, A., *International Combines in Modern History* (Pitman, 1934).

Pollard, S., *The Development of the British Economy, 1914–1980* (Edward Arnold, 1983).

Porter, B., *Britain, Europe and the World 1850–1986: Delusions of Grandeur* (Routledge, Chapman & Hall, 1987).

Pratt, J.W., *Cordell Hull, 1933–44* (New York, NY: Cooper Square, 1964).

Pugh, M., *The Making of British Politics 1867–1939* (Oxford: Basil Blackwell, 1982).

Reader, W.J., *Imperial Chemical Industries: A History, Vol. 2* (Oxford University Press, 1975).

Reynolds, D., *Britannia Overruled: British Policy and World Power in the Twentieth Century* (Longman, 1991).

Richardson, H.W., 'The economic significance of the depression in Britain', *JCH*, 4 (1969).

Richardson, J.H., *British Economic Foreign Policy* (Allen & Unwin, 1936).

Robbins, K.G., *Munich 1938* (Cassell, 1968).

Roberts, R., *Schroders: Merchants and Bankers* (Basingstoke: Macmillan, 1992).

Rooth, T., *British Protectionism and the International Economy: Overseas Commercial Policy in the 1930s* (Cambridge: Cambridge University Press, 1993).

Roseveare, H., *The Treasury: The Evolution of A British Institution* (Allen Lane, 1969).

Roskill, S., *Hankey: Man of Secrets, Vol. 3, 1931–1963* (Collins, 1974).

Sandberg, L.G., *Lancashire in Decline: a Study in Entrepreneurship, Technology, and International Trade* (Columbus, OH: Ohio State University Press, 1974).

Sayers, R.S., *Modern Banking* (Oxford University Press, 1938).

—— *The Bank of England, 1891–1944: Vol.2* (Cambridge: Cambridge University Press, 1976).

Schacht, H., *End of Reparations* (Jonathan Cape, 1931).

—— *Account Settled* (Weidenfeld & Nicolson, 1949).

—— *My First Seventy-Six Years* (Wingate, 1955).

Schapiro, L., *Totalitarianism* (Macmillan, 1972).

Scharf, A., *The British Press and Jews under Nazi Rule* (Oxford University Press, 1964).

Schmidt, G., 'The domestic background to British appeasement policy', in W.J. Mommsen and L. Kettenacker (eds), *The Fascist Challenge and the Policy of Appeasement* (Allen & Unwin, 1983).

—— *The Politics and Economics of Appeasement: British Foreign Policy in the 1930s* (Leamington Spa: Berg, 1986).

Schoenbaum, D., *Hitler's Social Revolution: Class and Status in Nazi Germany 1933–1939* (Weidenfeld & Nicolson, 1967).

Schweitzer, A., *Big Business in the Third Reich* (Bloomington, IN: Indiana University Press, 1964).

Scott, J.D., *Vickers: A History* (Weidenfeld & Nicolson, 1962).

Shay, R.P., *British Rearmament in the Thirties* (Princeton, NJ: Princeton University Press, 1977).

Siegfried, A., *England's Crisis* (Jonathan Cape, 1933).

Simpson, A.E., 'The struggle for control of the German economy, 1936–37', *JMH*, 31 (1959).

—— *Hjalmar Schacht in Perspective* (The Hague: Mouton, 1969).

Skidelsky, R., *John Maynard Keynes: Vol.2, The Economist as Saviour 1920–1937* (Macmillan, 1992).

Smart, N., *The National Government, 1931–40* (Basingstoke: Macmillan, 1999).

Smith, A.D., *Guilty Germans?* (Victor Gollancz, 1942).

Smith, A.L., *Hitler's Gold* (Oxford: Berg, 1996).

Snyder, R.C., 'Commercial policy as reflected in treaties from 1931–1939', *American Economic Review*, 30a (1940).

Stachura, P.D., 'National Socialism and the German proletariat,1925–1935: Old myths and new perspectives', *Historical Journal*, 36, 3 (1993).

Stewart, R.B., 'Great Britain's foreign loan policy', *Economica*, 5 (1938).

Stiefel, D., *Finanzdiplomatie und Weltwirtschaftskrise: Der Krise der Credit-Anstalt für Handel und Gewerbe 1931* (Frankfurt-am-Main: F.Knapp, 1989).

Stolper, G., *The German Economy 1870 to the Present* (New York, NY: Harcourt, Brace & World, 1967).

Taylor, A.J.P., *English History 1914–1945* (Harmondsworth: Penguin, 1975).

Teichert, E., *Autarkie und Grossraumwirtschaft in Deutschland 1930–1939* (München: Oldenbourg, 1984).

Teichova, A., *An Economic Background to Munich: International Business and Czechoslovakia 1918–1938* (Cambridge: Cambridge University Press, 1974).

Temin, P., *Lessons from the Great Depression* (Cambridge, MA: MIT Press, 1989).

Tennant, E.W.D., *True Account* (Max Parish, 1957).

Thorpe, A., *The British General Election of 1931* (Oxford: Clarendon Press, 1991).

Tolliday, S., *Business, Banking, and Politics. The Case of British Steel, 1918–1939* (Harvard University Press, 1987).

Tomlinson, J., *Problems of British Economic Policy 1870–1945* (Methuen, 1981).

Treviranus, G., *Das Ende von Weimar: Heinrich Brüning und seine Zeit* (Düsseldorf: Econ-Verlag, 1968).

Truptil, R.J., *British Banks and the London Money Market* (Jonathan Cape, 1936).

Vansittart, Lord, *The Mist Procession* (Hutchinson, 1958).

Volkmann, H.E., 'The National Socialist economy in preparation for war', in W. Deist, *et al.* (eds), *Germany and the Second World War* (Oxford: Clarendon Press, 1990).

Wake, J., *Kleinwort Benson: The History of Two Families in Banking* (Oxford: Oxford University Press, 1997).

Wark, W.K., *The Ultimate Enemy: British Intelligence and Nazi Germany, 1933–1939* (Oxford: Oxford University Press, 1986).

Watt, D. C(ameron), *Personalities and Policies: Studies in the Formulation of British Foreign Policy in the Twentieth Century* (Longman, 1965).

—— 'The European civil war', in W.J. Mommsen and L. Kettenacker (eds), *The Fascist Challenge and the Policy of Appeasement* (Allen & Unwin, 1983).

—— *Succeeding John Bull: America in Britain's Place 1900–1975* (Cambridge: Cambridge University Press, 1984).

—— *How War Came: The Immediate Origins of the Second World War, 1938–1939* (William Heinemann, 1989).

Weinberg, G.L., *The Foreign Policy of Hitler's Germany: Diplomatic Revolution in Europe 1933–36* (Chicago, IL: University of Chicago Press, 1970).

—— *The Foreign Policy of Hitler's Germany: Starting World War II* (Chicago, IL: University of Chicago Press, 1980).

Welch, D., *The Third Reich: Politics and Propaganda* (Routledge, 1993).

Wendt, B.J., *Economic Appeasement: Handel und Finanz in der britischen Deutschlandpolitik 1933–1939* (Düsseldorf: Bertelsmann Universitätverlag, 1971).

—— 'Economic appeasement – a crisis strategy', in W.J. Mommsen and L. Kettenacker (eds), *The Fascist Challenge and the Policy of Appeasement* (Allen & Unwin, 1983).

Williamson, P., *National Crisis and National Government, 1926–32* (Cambridge: Cambridge University Press, 1992).

—— *Stanley Baldwin* (Cambridge: Cambridge University Press, 1999).

Wilson, C.H., *The History of Unilever: Vol.2* (Cassell, 1954).

Wiskemann, E., *The Europe I Saw* (Collins, 1968).

Wurm, C.A., *Business, Politics, and International Relations* (Cambridge: Cambridge University Press, 1993).

Yeager, L.B. *International Monetary Relations: Theory, History and Policy* (New York, NY: Harper & Row, 1966).

Yergin, D., *The Prize: The Epic Quest for Oil, Money, and Power* (Simon & Schuster, 1991).

Young, R.J., 'Spokesmen for economic warfare: The industrial intelligence centre in the 1930s', *European Studies Review*, 6 (1976).

Index